AL-SHABAAB IN SOMALIA

STIG JARLE HANSEN

Al-Shabaab in Somalia

*The History and Ideology of a
Militant Islamist Group, 2005–2012*

OXFORD
UNIVERSITY PRESS

OXFORD
UNIVERSITY PRESS

Oxford University Press, Inc., publishes works that further
Oxford University's objective of excellence
in research, scholarship, and education.

Oxford   New York
Auckland   Cape Town   Dar es Salaam   Hong Kong   Karachi
Kuala Lumpur   Madrid   Melbourne   Mexico City   Nairobi
New Delhi   Shanghai   Taipei   Toronto

With offices in
Argentina   Austria   Brazil   Chile   Czech Republic   France   Greece
Guatemala   Hungary   Italy   Japan   Poland   Portugal   Singapore
South Korea   Switzerland   Thailand   Turkey   Ukraine   Vietnam

Published by Oxford University Press, Inc
198 Madison Avenue, New York, New York 10016

www.oup.com

Library of Congress Cataloging-in-Publication Data
Hansen, Stig Jarle.
Al-Shabaab in Somalia : the history and ideology of a militant Islamist group,
2005/2012 / Stig Jarle Hansen.
p.   cm.
Includes bibliographical references and index.
ISBN 978-0-19-932787-4 (alk. paper)
1. Shabaab (Organization) 2. Insurgency—Somalia—History—21st century. 3. Terrorism—
Somalia—History—21st century. 4. Somalia—Politics and government—1991– 5. Islam
and politics—Somalia—History. 6. Islamic fundamentalism—Somalia—History. I. Title.
DT407.4.H36 2013
320.557096773—dc23
2012049898

1 3 5 7 9 8 6 4 2

Printed in the United States of America
on acid-free paper

CONTENTS

FOREWORD

I have been working with Somalia now for over fourteen years, and have observed the radical change in dynamics—how the warlords of the 1990s lost power, and how political Islam gained attraction as a mobilizing force. This book is an attempt to explore how international ideology and local dynamics fused to produce one of Somalia's most efficient political organizations over the last twenty years, which is, at the time of writing, the only Al-Qaeda affiliate to control a considerable amount of territory. The collapse and downfall of this organization have continually been predicted, but it has survived, and remains important today.

I would like to dedicate this book to Ahmed Dei, a friend who started out as a child soldier in Mogadishu and ended up as an airline manager, before he was abruptly killed by the local police because he failed to give them his mobile phone. I have to thank Yahya Ibrahim, Muhamed Gaas, Brynjar Lia and Thomas Hegghammer for valuable comments, Michele Cesari for his support, and my family for their patience. This book is based on a report written for the Norwegian Defence Research Establishment (FFI), and a report for the Swedish Life and Peace institute, and previous versions of chapters 1, 3, 4, 5, 6 and 7 have appeared therein. Al-Shabaab today, after the defeat in Kismayo, is weaker than it has been since 2007, but its influence in the wider East Africa, its previous resilience, and its experience in radical Islamic governance makes its history important for the wider phenomena of radical Islamism as well future developments in the Horn of Africa.

Stig Jarle Hansen   Oslo, February 2013

CHRONOLOGY

1998	Al-Qaeda attacks the American embassies in Dar es-Salaam and Nairobi
2002	Al-Qaeda attacks Paradise Hotel in Mombasa and an aircraft of the Arkia airline
2003	Killing of a British teacher couple in Somaliland, several future leaders of Harakat Al-Shabaab are later convicted for the attack, as well as an attack on a GTZ car in Hargeisa
2002–2005	The shadow wars in Mogadishu
2005	Founding of Harakat Al-Shabaab
2006	The rise and subsequent fall of the Sharia Courts; Ethiopian intervention/invasion in December
2007	Al-Shabaab praises Osama Bin Laden in public for the first time, declares independence from the Sharia Courts; first AMISOM contingent deployed in Mogadishu
2008	Killing of Aden Hasi Ayro by an American missile attack
2009	Ethiopian withdrawal and subsequent Harakat Al-Shabaab expansion; Al-Shabaab in control of most of southern Somalia
2010	Defeat in the Ramadan offensive; leadership crisis
2011	Famine and Kenyan intervention; Fazul Abdullah Mohamed killed in Mogadishu

ABBREVIATIONS

AIAI	Al-Itihaad al-Islamiya
AMISOM	African Union Mission in Somalia
AMYC	Ansar Muslim Youth Centre (Tanzania)
APRCT	Alliance for Peace Restoration and Counter Terrorism
AQAP	Al-Qaeda in the Arabian Peninsula
AQIM	Al-Qaeda in the Islamic Maghreb
ARS	Alliance for the Re-liberation of Somalia
ARS-A	Alliance for the Re-liberation of Somalia—the Asmara wing
ASWJ	Aluh Sunna Wah Jamaa
CTC	Combating Terrorism Center (USA)
ICG	International Crisis Group
ICU	Islamic Courts Union
IED	Improvised Explosive Device
JIC	Joint Islamic Councils
KATJ	Katiibatu Ansaru Tawheed Wal Jihad
NGO	Non Governmental Organization
NTV	Nation TV (Kenya)
PRMC	Pumwani Riyadha Mosque Committee (Kenya)
RCIED	Remote Controlled Improvised Explosive Device
SSDF	Somali Salvation Democratic Front
TFG	Transitional Federal Government
UNDP	United Nations Development Programme
UNICEF	United Nations Children's Fund
UNOSOM	United Nations Operations in Somalia
USC	United Somali Congress

GLOSSARY

Amir	ruler
Amniyat	can be translated into 'Securities'; Al-Shabaab's secret police
bidah	innovation
dawah	missionary work
dhimmi	non-Muslim
fatwa	legal opinion
fedayeen	those who sacrifice themselves
fiqh	Islamic jurisprudence
hadith	tradition
ijtihad	independent reasoning
jahiliyyah	ignorance, barbarism
jihad	holy war/struggle
jihad-e-akbar	the greater *jihad*
jihad-e-ashgar	the smaller *jihad*
jizya	tax
kafir	unbeliever
Khalifah	historical head of Muslim state
kuffar	unbelievers
kufr	unbelief
madrasah	Islamic school
Mu'askar Mahkamat	'Camps of the Islamic Courts' the rapid deployment
Mukulal Maddow	'The black cat,' referring to practices in Mogadishu for blackmailing members of minority clans
muhajiroun	emigrants
qital	fighting

riddah	return to apostasy
Salafi	A Muslim who emphasises the Salaf ('predecessors' or 'ancestors'), the earliest Muslims, as models of Islamic practice
salah	righteousness
salam	peace
salat	prayer
Sharia	Islamic law
Shia	minority faith group within Islam
shirk	polytheism
Sufi	follower of a mystic Islamic tradition; in Somalia based around the Ahmadiya, Salihiyah, and the Qadriya
takfir	refers to the practice of one Muslim declaring another Muslim an unbeliever
tawhid	monotheism
ulama	scholars
waqf	endowment
zakat	charity/the giving of alms

1

INTRODUCTION

I still remember the first time I encountered the name Al-Shabaab (Harakat Al-Shabaab), talking with friends in Mogadishu under the rule of the Sharia Courts, in the heat of September 2006. In one sense my first experience with Al-Shabaab was positive. The organization was part of the Sharia Courts at the time, whose rule had revitalized Mogadishu as the city awoke from years of torment and war. I was happy witnessing the unusual sights and sounds of that autumn: Somali girls walked past us at night laughing and gossiping; we drove across the entire city without passing a single checkpoint, with only one guard from the Sharia Courts to take care of us.

However, I also remember how I was warned against a specific subgroup of the Courts—the 'Youth'—which had fielded commanders with names like '*Gaal dille*', translated as 'Christian-killer'. Several friends also expressed joy over the various campaigns in the south, claiming that since Al-Shabaab was there, I was safer in Mogadishu. According to my Mogadishu friends at the time, of whom too many have passed away today, my visa to Mogadishu was processed by the future Amir of Al-Shabaab, Ahmed Abdi Godane, and so some in the group were aware that I was 'in town', but my stay was peaceful and without any events save sightseeing. In one sense this initial experience first presented me with the two faces of Al-Shabaab: how it can contribute to stability through justice, but at the same time be feared and promote a sense of cosmic war between Islam and the West; a 'Clash of Civilizations', so to speak. The two faces should not be forgotten, and Al-Shabaab today still has both.

Harakat Al-Shabaab has since 2006 attracted increasing attention. The use of suicide bombings, the presence of foreign fighters, various declarations of loyalty towards the international Al-Qaeda network, and the Kampala attacks on the 11 July in 2010 are factors that have contributed to this development, as have reports that the Al-Shabaab has trained Islamists from other African countries, such as Kenya and Nigeria.[1] Indeed, Al-Shabaab is Al-Qaeda's only self-proclaimed ally that wields substantial territorial control, and it has been used as an example of an Islamist form of governance by prominent ideologues such as Anwar Awlaki.[2] The organization is also global, in the sense that it has reached out to the Somali diaspora, a fact that has made Western countries more concerned over Al-Shabaab's activities. These factors might have contributed to the United States declaring it a terrorist organization in 2008, Australia doing the same in 2009, and the United Kingdom and Canada following suit in 2010; it has also been targeted by the United Nations Resolution 1844, as well as the EU's EC 356/2010 directive, supporting the definition of Al-Shabaab as a terrorist organization.[3] The group also has training camps indoctrinating Somali youths in the teachings of Al-Qaeda, and it functions as a practising ground for recruits inspired by the global worldview of Al-Qaeda, drawn to Somalia by a quest for *jihad* but potentially able to take the struggle back home.

Nevertheless, as will be shown in this book, Al-Shabaab's *modus operandi* suggests an organization with a local focus, and its attacks since 2007 have been directly connected to local warfare, even when attacking outside Somalia. The group cannot be understood without grasping Somali clan politics and the local historical background. However, it cannot be understood only in a local context—it is rather an organization formed by global Jihadist philosophies, local needs to provide some form of rudimentary justice and tactical considerations on behalf of its various members. As will be shown, there is tension within the organization between local and global agendas, in which local dynamics still dominate but ideological convictions are often blurred, self-contradicting and unclear.

This book explores Al-Shabaab's background; it will look at the drastic changes the organization has experienced—developing from a small network of Afghanistan alumni to a large organization recruiting among poor youths of Mogadishu, undergoing collapse and rebirth, again as a small organization, and subsequently successfully conquering most of southern Somalia in the face of superior enemies, but then again facing defeats. It is today a large and heterogeneous organization, in which recruits are motivated by a variety of factors such as financial gain, fear (forced recruitment), siding with the winner, anti-Ethiopian feelings, clan grievances, a quest for justice through Sharia legislation, or an idea of defensive or offensive jihad. In light of these variations, it becomes surprising that Al-Shabaab, over a period of five years since its creation, despite internal disagreements, has maintained its relative unity, with political sub-groups opting to stay in the organization. There have been differences within the ranks of Al-Shabaab, but these tensions have so far been controlled, and the frequent rumors of emerging splits, starting in 2008, have all been confounded. The key to Al-Shabaab's success in the years 2008–10 was simply unity based on having a rudimentary common ideological platform and a world view. This book will explore mechanisms of coordination and training. In the pressured situation in 2010–11, this unity was challenged and several Al-Shabaab leaders attempted to leave the organization, but again centralization mechanisms kept it together, albeit in a weakened state.

Social mechanisms explaining Al-Shabaab

In his inspiring book about the Iranian revolution, *Class, Politics and the Iranian Revolution*, Mansoor Moaddel explores how religion created a discourse in which class issues and economic issues could unfold.[4] In one sense this resembles Somalia, in which the strengthening of religion as a political discourse created a field for Al-Shabaab to grow. Religious rhetoric was always a part of its vocabulary. A religious discursive game defined Al-Shabaab's repertoire of symbols, gave impetus to its speeches and also ensured it a certain level of support in a society where religious symbols had become more common since the collapse of the Somali state.

Researchers like Tom Rees indicate that poverty and personal insecurity in themselves are correlated with religious attitudes.[5] In Somalia insecurity had been on the increase since the outbreak of the civil war, and religion became a beacon of hope, a thing to turn to. Islam has certain commandments that deal with social justice and promote solidarity with the weak and poor in society, and religious leaders understandably became more popular because of this. The use of religious symbols increased drastically. Al-Shabaab benefited from the 'Somali' resurgence of religion; it was able, at least initially, to project an image of pious and law abiding individuals, and legal justice based on Islam was a major element in its propaganda, while religious institutions aided the Somalis when no aid was forthcoming from other sources.

Al-Shabaab was allowed to grow in an ideological vacuum. Hansen, Mesøy and Karadas suggest that the situation in the Middle East allowed for the expansion of Islamism, as Moaddel argues was the case in Iran with regard to Marxism and liberalism.[6] In one sense Somali society followed a pattern similar to that of the Middle East and Iran, where rival ideologies to Islamism, such as Marxism, Nasserism and Liberal Democracy, became discredited by the fall of the Soviet Union, Nasser's defeat in the 1967 war, and Western support for local dictators respectively. A confusing and anarchic democracy (1960–1969) had been tried, discredited, and abolished by an initially very popular military coup. The replacement regime was a military dictatorship inspired by Marxist/Fascist nationalism (1969–91), which proved to be predatory and corrupt and dissolved into clanism. The clan-based warlords that followed, and gained power from 1991 onwards, were at the start seen by many as genuine representatives, but in the end the warlords' failure to protect their own clans delegitimized them. So democracy, nationalism, Marxism and clanism had been tried out and had yielded little for the Somalis. In the end religion, employed as a political ideology, had only weak rivals to contend with, although clanism in different forms remained important.

The popularity of religious leaders and the growth of self-proclaimed religious political factions also opened the way for the misuse of religion for instrumental gains, an example being the warlord turned Islamist Yusuf Mohamed Siad 'Indaadde', but it should not be forgotten that even instrumentalism can be caught up by its own hypocrisy. Religion can in itself be viewed as a game, where actors, including instrumentalists who are not genuine believers have to adhere to a certain set of rules in order to participate. A religion has 'core beliefs' that you have to adhere to in order to be defined as a member of that religion. If these core beliefs are challenged, you define yourself as outside of the religion you are not believed to be a person adhering to that religion. In general religions, as suggested by Scott Thomas, are dynamic standards for acceptance of certain actions do change over time.[7] Religious quarrels might result in an actor challenging 'fringe assumptions' of a religion within a religious system; if this is done successfully, it could change some of the values of a religion itself—though only rarely the core assumptions. If a mode of practising a religion is relatively unsuccessful it might bring a new sub-group into existence, as when the Jehovah's Witnesses, amongst others, challenged the Christian doctrine of the Trinity, or Ayatollah Khomeini successfully challenged the assumption that Shiism should be apolitical in the case of Iran.[8] In Somalia Al-Shabaab redefined some of the assumptions of traditional Islam, for example defining the resurrection of the Caliphate as a target for religious activism, as well as depicting its struggle in 'Clash of Civilizations' rhetoric, while also keeping a focus on the Sharia and on charity and justice.

These games are influenced by the material context surrounding them, as well as theological interpretations, and both aspects should be studied if one wishes to understand religion. Instrumentalism, the use of religion to achieve personal or political gain—and personal religious belief have similar effects, in that one has to appear to play by the rules of the game. Religion matters even for hypocrites. Al-Shabaab probably had both hypocrites and 'real believers', and not all of these 'real believers' believed in the global assumptions of the group.

Al-Shabaab was also a child of the War on Terror. Many people, Robert Pape amongst them, see the presence of armies of occupation as a major cause of terrorism, at least in its suicide attack form, and such views find an echo in Somalia.[9] It has been argued that the invasion by Ethiopia, from 2006 to 2009, created fertile breeding grounds for terrorism in Somalia. Notable researchers such as Roland Marchal and indeed Robert Pape himself claim that the invasion of Ethiopia was crucial for Al-Shabaab recruitment from 2007 to 2009, and indeed for the creation of the organization.[10] The renowned Somalia scholar Ken Menkhaus follows a somewhat similar line of thought in illustrating how aggressive Western policies and Ethiopian occupation pushed Al-Shabaab into organizing, aiding its recruitment.[11] The argument can easily be oversimplified—it should be noted that large clans and sub-clans, such as the Rahanwhein and the Majerteen, supported the Ethiopian invasion/intervention. One should remember that Al-Shabaab became organized before the Ethiopian intervention, and that Ethiopian military doctrine, with its emphasis on intensive use of artillery, hurt the Ethiopians' own efforts to win 'hearts and minds.' Some of the events that helped build up Al-Shabaab were actually not a product of a Ethiopian occupation, but of large-scale corruption and misuse of funds by the Western-backed governments of Somalia, and a sad tendency of the United Nations Development Programme (UNDP) to train Somali police without ensuring that they would receive pay when entering government service; in this way the UNDP and the government of Somalia in one sense became the best allies Al-Shabaab could wish. They generated a climate of corruption that enabled Al-Shabaab to appear as a more credible alternative through its implementation of the Sharia and through its less exploitative police forces.[12]

Al-Shabaab is more than a product of insecurity; it is also a product of the export of Al-Qaeda's ideology into Somalia. The importance of international informal networks in this process should not be forgotten. Mark Sageman, for example, argues that social bonds often predate ideological commitment, and are used to recruit jihadists.[13] It was a network of former Afghanistan veterans that established Al-Shabaab, and the diffusion of ideas has gone through individuals with Al-Qaeda connections.

Al-Shabaab's strategies changed over time, but it took a while before analysts understood the group to be special in a Somali setting. Reuven Paz was in many ways a pioneer in describing the new methods adopted by the group, including the use of Improvized Explosive Devices (IEDs) and suicide missions.[14] He analyzes the Al-Shabaab newspaper *Milat Ibrahim*, the group's confused early manifestations on the internet and the variety of Islamist groups that emerged and disappeared online in 2007. Paz also looks at the anti-nationalist rhetoric of the top leadership. He sees Somalia as a success for the wider Al-Qaeda strategies. Evan F. Kohlman bases his research on court reports and Al-Shabaab's own internet material, correctly highlighting the drastic differences between it and other Somali organizations: the Al-Shabaab's critique of nationalism, its use of suicide bombers, and its online interaction with Al-Qaeda.[15] Andrew McGregor also presents various analyses that are not based on field studies, and again draws upon internet sources. He examines important analytical points, such as the differences in tactics between Al-Shabaab and other organizations, as well as its previously staunch rejection of negotiations. He also explores the Jaysh al-Hisbah, Al-Shabaab's police, and analyzes the group's aims, such as creating an Islamic state in Somalia, evicting peacekeepers, rejecting democracy and striving for the Caliphate. In a further report of 2010 McGregor goes back to the organization's own statement of its aims in propaganda videos to argue that it has anti-nationalist goals, for example criticizing borders and national symbols for creating separation between Muslims.

These reports highlight important issues, such as the surprising amount of anti-nationalist rhetoric in Al-Shabaab's statements targeting an international audience, the clear similarities between its tactics in the 2007–09 period and the tactics deployed by jihadist groups in countries such as Iraq and Afghanistan, and the factors that—together with manifestations of jihadi ideology in their publications—separated Al-Shabaab from other Somali based political organizations, at least until 2010. However, similarities between Al-Shabaab and other Somali organizations are treated lightly. One such example is the clan factor. The Somali clan system is fundamentally patrilinear; each Somali traces his clan through his forefathers. For most Somalis a common ancestor on the father's side will create some loyalty, and the closer this ancestor is to yourself, the stronger the bounds of loyalty will grow. A clan will be divided into sub-clans, often claimed to be originating in various brothers of the common clan father. In Somali society, clan commands more than mere loyalty, it becomes a constructed filter for social reality, as clans often have common meeting places, even in the diaspora. A common discourse is often constructed, created by members of a clan meeting in the same place, discussing the same issues, constructing a common reality.[16] Younger members of the Somali community might dislike the clan system, and Al-Shabaab to a certain extent challenged clan loyalties, but no organization in Somalia can escape the clan trap. A report by Taarnby and Haellundbaek put some emphasis on clan issues, in contrast to previous work, but without analyzing these issues in much depth.[17] While several of these reports state that Al-Shabaab is fragmented, little is written on the dynamics between various political sub-groups within the organization; the argument seems to be left outside the scope of analysis.

The second group consists of area experts with in-depth knowledge of Somalia. Some of the scholars who have worked on Somalia have extensive knowledge of the country and an excellent contact network there. My 2008 article was a first effort to explore the clan mechanisms within Al-Shabaab, combining clan study with ideological analysis. Roland Marchal's 2010 article is perhaps the best academic work on the subject so far, except perhaps for his 2011 report.[18] It provides a thorough background brief, presenting Al-Shabaab's roots in the confused Al-Itihaad al-Islamiya (AIAI), the first militant Islamist organization in Somalia after 1991, created between 1982 and 1984 and becoming militant after the downfall of Siad Barre in 1991. His article explores the actions of the first generation of Somali jihadists, with their clan differences and complex loyalties before looking at the rise of the strongest of the Sharia

Courts, the Ifka Halane, which was to emerge as one of the founding courts of the Sharia Court alliance in 2006. The article also analyzes how Al-Shabaab managed to transcend clan better than its rivals, and maintain an impressive unity by comparison with other Somali actors. David Shinn's 2011 article is an important addition to Marchal's article, stressing what Al-Shabaab has learned from Al-Qaeda and pointing to all the techniques that former has adopted for the first time in Somalia.[19]

The reports of the International Crisis Group (ICG) are also based on researchers conducting in-depth field research on Al-Shabaab. Since the Crisis Group has followed Somalia over time, its work provides a unique opportunity to follow Al-Shabaab's growth. Indeed, it was the ICG, in 2006, which first used the label 'Al-Shabaab' in an English text. Its reports 'Counter-Terrorism in Somalia: Losing Hearts and Minds' and 'Somalia's Islamists' provide the background in which the organization crystallized: a shadow war between the United States and Al-Qaeda in East Africa, in which the United States attempted to use warlords to kill members of the network.[20] It was in this setting, as the reports examine, that a new group of more radical Somalis, the nucleus of Al-Shabaab, is said to have emerged in 2003. The reports also explore how the group drew upon the Ayr clan for protection in the early phase. The 2010 report 'Somalia's Divided Islamists' contained an in-depth analysis of the organization and suggested that its popularity was in decline partly because of Ethiopian withdrawal in 2009, and partly because of its drastic use of suicide attacks, especially the 2009 attack on a graduation ceremony.

In its more recent reports the ICG sees Al-Shabaab's core ideology as Salafi jihadism, with a small fringe within the organization focusing on Takfirism, the denouncing of other Muslims. One report on 'Somalia's Divided Islamists' sketches how a small circle around Godane has grown to dominate the organization, which increasingly has grown more centralized.[21] However, the ICG sees a conflict between more clan minded elements, such as Muktar Robow and Ali Dheere, and others. The report suggests that the former elements should be targeted for reconciliation efforts. It should be noted that the term 'Salafism' in a Somali context, indeed everywhere, has to be treated with caution. Despite a widespread tendency within Somalia to brand most adherents of Salafism or Wahhabism as 'Al-Shabaab', the Salafi movement of Somalia has a variety of components, and the 'Salafiya Jadida' network, a loose constellation of scholars and activists arguing for the peaceful spread of Salafism, also has followers within Al-Shabaab. There are other attempts to explore analytically ideological and practical divisions within Al-Shabaab. Weinstein analyzes the rifts using a comparative model taken from the study of Marxist and communist movements and internationalist/transnationalist revolutionary movements. He highlights the dilemma of two competing doctrines of Marxism, the 'world revolution' version (Trotskyism) and the 'socialism in one country' version (Stalinism), claiming that most transnationalist movements will face this dilemma. According to Weinstein, Al-Shabaab consists of a nationalist as well as a transnationalist faction, and these are competing for power.[22]

My 2011 article stresses the center-periphery tension within Al-Shabaab and the fact that the gropup has grown more centralized administratively. I view the organization as detached, with a top leadership consisting of an 'old boys network' of the Al-Shabaab *shura*. The creation of this top leadership originated in 2003–04; its members have relatively similar world views, and three of them travelled to Afghanistan before. However, as the rank and file organization rapidly expanded in 2007–2008, there were new recruits consisting of clan fighters, unemployed youth, nationalists and fortune seekers, even coopting new leaders. Considerable variation exists between areas such as Mudug and Galguduud and the southernmost regions.[23] Nevertheless, I have stressed that there are centralizing mechanisms, and a tradition of problem solving amongst the leadership, and that these mechanisms grew in importance until the Ramadan offensive of the autumn of 2010.

There is a conflict among analysts regarding Al-Shabaab's unity. While the 2010 ICG report 'Somalia's Divided Islamists' actually stresses that the organization was becoming more unitary, having been more fragmented, later ICG analysts suggested a deeply divided organization on the verge of collapse.[24] Some analyses, such as the *Jane's* article 'Al-Shabaab's Mixed Messages', suggest a very fragmented organization, and there where frequent predictions of Al-Shabaab's collapse from 2008 onwards.[25] However, Roland Marchal, and the early works of the ICG under the auspices of Matt Bryden, also highlight Al-Shabaab's relative unity in a Somali setting. These views, although not commonly held, were proved right, and the frequently predicted fracture of the organization did not take place. This does not mean that Al-Shabaab is without internal sub-groups, but rather that it has been much more successful in uniting these sub groups than most other Somali political factions, which tend to collapse relatively quickly, usually divided along clan lines and over clan issues. Such area experts, stressing the surprising unity that Al-Shabaab has shown in the period 2008–10, point to the way the organization successfully handled internal strains and how income became more centralized.

Al-Shabaab's ideology is most usually analyzed using the expressions Salafism, Wahahbism and Takfirism—Salafism and Wahhabism being left poorly defined. Insufficient attention is given to the differences between a defensive international jihad, in which individuals are committed to defend any country attacked by a non-Muslim power; a defensive revisionist jihad in which individuals are committed to defending Muslims all over the world, removing the borders separating Muslims, and favoring reform; and a nationalist-Islamism stance in which Islam is seen as one identity marker of Somaliness. This might be due to what Patrick Desplat refers to as 'blurred ideological lines'—the fact that various ideological stands might overlap and change from setting to setting, and clear ideological distinctions are hard to identify on the ground.[26]

Previous analyses have treated Al-Shabaab as a static organization, or at best as an organization with a teleological development. It is not contextualized sufficiently to make clear that it changed between 2006 and 2011. The needs, and thus often also the inner dynamics of an organization that was a part of a Sharia Court alliance (2005–06) were quite different from those of an organization facing an Ethiopian occupation (2007–09). Similarly, the challenges facing an organization wielding large territorial control (post-2009) are different from the needs of a guerrilla organization (2007–09). Tactical choices influence both internal conflicts and discussion over ideological issues. There are other issues neglected by the above analysis, such as Al-Shabaab's financial and governance structures. In general, the group is stated to have little popular support in Somalia, but the interviews conducted for this report, with respondents coming from the Kismayo area, seem to indicate that Al-Shabaab's law and order agenda creates some local support. This book will attempt to address the above mentioned shortcomings.

Diaspora, international network and radicalization

Al-Shabaab was perhaps the first Somali organization that drew non-Somali fighters into its ranks, often attracted by its global rhetoric and also, at times, by money. At the same time Somalis in the diaspora returned to fight for Al-Shabaab, creating the possibility for what Western intelligence called 'blow back'—a trained or indoctrinated fighter returning to a Western country and staging a terror attack.[27] Radicalization theory identifies several issues that can radicalize individuals. Tedd Robert Gurr, for example, stresses relative deprivation, the feeling of not getting what you believe you are entitled to.[28] Issues of foreign occupation and general humiliation have also been touched upon by several researchers.[29] Identity issues are discussed in depth by Olivier Roy and Turfyal Choudhury, and Jeff Victoroff presents a good overview of psychological issues.[30] Poor political and socioeconomic integration is also an issue.[31] The Somali diaspora is in itself vulnerable in many of these accounts; in general Somalis abroad are poorer and less educated than other diaspora groups, creating a sense of humiliation. However, it should be noted that examples of radicalization often come from rather well-off strata inside the diaspora; in fact jihadists seem to be well educated young men with families.[32] Humiliation and occupation are nevertheless important, but rather indirect.

Farhad Khosrokhavar refers to the phenomenon of 'humiliation by proxy' propaganda, material usually focusing on the humiliation of the Muslim *ummah* in events taking place in the Middle East.[33] Places like Afghanistan and Pakistan become important, although the individuals radicalized have weak connections to those places. In this sense, the radicalization of Somalis can be connected with events inside Somalia, although the individuals could be well-off and with little knowledge about the local conflicts. In fact, limited knowledge about Somalia could be a push factor, as clan dynamics could be overlooked, and the conflict could be viewed through a Muslim vs Christian lens, rather than a clan conflict lens. Importantly, the motivation of a Somali returning to fight in Somalia might be connected with both issues inside Somalia—such as the humiliation due to the Ethiopian intervention, or the misuse of power by the Al-Shabaab's police—and more general humiliation of the *ummah* (even a wish for Muslim unity). A non-Somali fighter will probably have more *ummah*-related motivation. Radicalization is also seen in general as a staged process, and one where some group dynamics are involved; for some models a radicalizer, a person doing the indoctrination, is involved, while other theories rather focus on an individual trying to find like-minded fellows.[34]

In a 2010 article Lorenzo Vidino, Raffaello Pantucci and Evan Kohleman suggest that the pattern of Al-Shabaab recruitment in the West responds to the low income of Somalis, psychological problems and identity issues, but stressed that there are many paths to radicalization, which leaves an opening for the 'humiliation by proxy' factor.[35] The article also places emphasis on social networks.[36] Steven Weine et al. make more in-depth research into the patterns of recruitment in Minnesota, focusing on push as well as pull factors. The main pull factor is claimed to be the Ethiopian invasion in 2006, the main push factor being the troubled situation of the Minnesota Somalis. The article highlights important points in relation to, for example, the suspected difference between the recruitment of foreign fighters before and after the Ethiopian withdrawal in 2009, and the possibility that religion and nationalism might be mutually reinforcing.[37] However, there are problems with the article, such as the lack of clan analysis—as previously mentioned, some clan groups have defined Al-Shabaab as being the foreign invaders (because of its alleged Al-Qaeda connections)—and failure to mention Al-Shabaab's international links before the Ethiopian intervention. As will be shown later, foreign, non-Somali fighters were always present in Al-Shabaab.

All the above writers neglect the clear presence of Al-Qaeda and foreign fighters before 2007, and clear manifestations of ideas about global jihad before that year are also rather neglected.[38] This book will argue that Al-Shabaab's international connections were strong from the start of the organization, and illustrate that it was much easier to maintain ideological unity in the small early network than in the large organization we see today.

Some methodological considerations

Some of the controversies described above, as well as some of the inadequacies in exploration of some issues so far, could be due to the methodological obstacles encountered when studying Al-Shabaab. First, access to Al-Shabaab-controlled areas is restricted. The group has been known to frequently execute suspected spies, and its secret police, the Amniyat, is feared even in the ranks of Al-Shabaab itself.[39] Foreign researchers are in general not allowed to enter Al-Shabaab-controlled areas. The lack of access to those areas makes all research on the organization rather vulnerable to the so-called 'Nairobi Reality' problem: dependence on sources in Nairobi. Often sources within the diplomatic community and the staff of Non Governmental Organizations (NGOs) tend to be self-referential, based on rumors circulating in the capital of Kenya, owing to limited access to primary sources in Somalia. The only part of Southern Somalia accessible to Western researchers is that controlled by the African Union Mission in Somalia (AMISOM), with the African Union peace keeping forces in a part of Mogadishu, where Al-Shabaab sympathizers are afraid to visit and the presence of Transitional Federal Government (TFG) troops as well AMISOM forces, and their intelligence services, can prevent individuals from speaking freely.

Public statements by Al-Shabaab can be used as sources. It has itself produced a variety of leaflets, videos, speeches and press commentaries. Several webpages, such as Hegaan (spring 2007 only), then Kataaib, Al Hesba and Al Qimmah, the two first now closed, claimed to be affiliated with Al-Shabaab, or have published its statements in English, Arabic and Somali. Radio Koran, as well as Al-Shabaab's various Andalus radio stations, also contain information and propaganda from the organization, as does its newspaper, *Milat Ibrahim*. Leaders such as Muktar Robow (alias Abu Mansoor), Godane, Shongola and even some foreign fighters like the late Saleh Ali Saleh Naban and Omar Hammami (alias 'Abu Mansoor Al-Amriki'), have all presented their thoughts and philosophies in various media outlets.[40] Al-Shabaab interviews have also appeared frequently in Al-Qaeda affiliated publications.[41] A considerable number of videos have been deposited on YouTube and remain there, and some of the interviews contain in-depth analysis of the Somali situation. Al-Shabaab leaders, especially their formal spokespersons—first Muktar Robow 'Abu Mansoor', then from 2009 onwards Ali Mohamed Rage (alias Ali Dheere)—have given speeches and interviews; some mid-level leaders such as Abdullah Muhalam Mohamed, the deputy Wali (governor) of Bakool, have also given interviews to the press.[42]

There are several reasons to treat Al-Shabaab's own statements with caution. First, its statements might be influenced by issues other than ideology, such as a need to harness funds from the Middle East and a need for recognition and belonging within a larger in-group, namely a global jihadist movement. Secondly, some of the webpages might be hosted by more radical individuals on the fringes of Al-Shabaab; the Al Qimmah site was, for example, hosted by the Swedish convert Ralf Wadman 'Abu Osama El Swede', and some of the materials on the page, including a variety of Al-Qaeda texts, might have been inspired by his global views rather than beliefs genuinely held by Al-Shabaab.[43] However, it should be noted that Al-Shabaab's information efforts and press releases seem to have been highly centralized in 2008–09, and that there is consistency in their statements. It should also be noted that several press statements are intended for local consumption, mainly published in Somali. Press statements might thus be given with thought to the Middle Eastern audience and the Western audience as well as the Somali audience, and it should always be kept in mind which audience Al-Shabaab is targeting in its videos.

This study uses source triangulation plus the principle of the proximity of sources (closeness to the event described) as a rule of thumb. It also practices 'clan triangulation': sources from different clans are asked about specific events, to control for clan bias. The information presented here is drawn from Al-Shabaab's own publications, as well as interviews with Al-Shabaab leaders, conducted both by others and by the writer. Locals frequently travelling in Al-Shabaab-controlled areas have been interviewed, as have defectors and serving members. These approaches have their dangers, and I have seen how individuals have claimed to be defectors in order to get payment for interviews, and how journalists have been fooled by fake leaders lining up for phone interviews from Somalia. This work bases itself on so-called 'proof of life' techniques, namely asking respondents questions that demand intimate knowledge of the organization, in order to confirm that they are close to the organization. The book is based on the findings from my field studies in Mogadishu (2006–2010), where interviews were conducted in more neutral settings, in the government-controlled part of Mogadishu, but as far as possible from both AMISOM and government bases. Lastly, it is based on secondary source material such as reports from a variety of actors on the ground within Somalia.

2

SETTING THE STAGE

THE RESURGENCE OF RELIGION IN SOMALIA

Somalis have been following Islam for over a thousand years, yet the expression of Islam has changed over the last twenty years. Old Somali culture has been reinterpreted and expressions of it are being replaced by religious assumptions often transferred from the Arabian peninsula. Traditional nomad dress for Somali women, for example, is seldom worn in an urban setting, being replaced by the *niqab* and the *hijab*. One might talk about a resurgence of religion, as religious symbols have grown in importance. This resurgence can be said to have two different parallel developments, the resurfacing of new Islamist organizations and a general increase in the use of religious symbols and titles inside Somalia.

As for the first process, it can be traced back to the 1960s, with the formation of three groups, the Waxda Al-Shabaab al Islaami and the Jama'at al Ahl al-Islaami (known as the al-Ahli group) and, most important, the Munadamat al-Nahdah al Islāmiyah (the Organization of the Islamic Renaissance), all of which worked to promote Islam's influence on politics.[1] One of these, the Waxda, was ironically to have indirect organizational ties to Harakat Al-Shabaab. The Waxda was a founding partner of the Al-Itihaad al-Islamiya (AIAI), created in 1983. As will be explored later, AIAI in turn was to have many future Harakat Al-Shabaab activists as members. The Waxda Al-Shabaab al Islaami, however, was initially a more Sufi inclined movement, and then swung towards a more brotherhood-oriented approach to Islam. It had some contacts with a southern group, the Jamaaca Islaamiyah, created in 1979, which also had a fluid ideological foundation initially. It first adhered to brotherhood ideology, but changed when Somali students from Saudi Arabia joined it, to become more Wahhabi.[2] It was Islamism in its Wahhabi form that was to inspire Al-Shabaab. However, Wahhabism had many shapes in Somalia. Wahhabism could be apolitical, it could be Islamist with a focus on peaceful change, but it could also be violent. Several Somali Wahhabi politicians, such as the present-day veteran Somaliland politician Dr Mohamed Abdi Gabose argue for peaceful and slow societal change while condemning Al-Shabaab.[3] Other Somalia Wahhabis are simply not politicized and stay out of politics.

Wahhabism was nevertheless to leave its mark on the trajectory of militant Islamist organizations inside Somalia. The developments have to be seen in the light of Saudi Arabia's increased power in the Middle East. By 1973 the oil crisis had created a drastic increase in the funds available for missionary work, as well as for scholarship, and this influenced Somalia. Ironically this created divisions among Islamists within Somalia, by opening the way to relatively new interpretations of the Koran following a more Saudi-style Wahhabi ideology, which condemned more traditional forms of Islam such as the Sufi traditions so popular inside Somalia. However, this was a fluid and complex process, and it was the push for Islamic unity that drove the formation of AIAI, the organization that was later to enlist many Al-Shabaab leaders before they joined the latter. Many Somali religious leaders pushed for compromises on ideology, and there were attempts to create umbrella organizations. Some of these attempts were aided by Sudan's Hassan Turabi, who attempted to create African pan-Islamic unity and challenge his rivals in the Egyptian Muslim Brotherhood. In the end this resulted in the merger of Waxda and Jamaac into AIAI.

AIAI is often said to have been a Wahhabi organization, and was in the end listed as a terrorist organization by the United States. However, the philosophy of AIAI was far from clear, and reasons for joining varied. Protests against Siad Barre's secular family laws were one important reason to join the organization. The so-called Wahhabi credentials varied from member to member. Several of AIAI's early leaders including one of the most famous, Sheikh Ali Warsame, had been member of Al Islah, the Somali Muslim Brotherhood, which illustrates how pragmatism is an important factor in determining which organization you join in Somalia.

It seems safe to say that the early AIAI was strongly focused on a local Somali agenda. Nevertheless, many scholars in the organization adhered to Takfirism, the practice of one Muslim declaring another Muslim an unbeliever. In this sense AIAI contained a trait that was quite unusual in Somalia.[4] Over the years, Takfirism and Wahhabism were to become more important as adherents of other ideologies left the organization.

In 1991 the Siad Barre regime collapsed, but AIAI was divided on the issue of violent jihad in Somalia. Parts of the organization engaged in the battle for Arrare in April 1991, defending the interests of the Darod clan; this illustrated the centrifugal forces of clanism influencing AIAI. The group at Arrare later withdrew to the Puntland region, where a large AIAI conference was convened. However, Puntland was already dominated by a military group, the oldest in Somalia, the Somali Salvation Democratic Front (SSDF). The SSDF and AIAI turned into rivals. There were several clashes, and AIAI was also hostile to Western aid, to the great irritation of the SSDF.[5] In the summer of 1992 the differences between the SSDF and AIAI grew into a conflict which the latter lost. Several AIAI activists quit the group, while others fled south.

One of these groups later established itself in the province of Gedo. This group gained territorial control, and was supported by Al-Qaeda fighters, as will be described in more detail later.[6] Importantly, Al-Qaeda was at that stage based largely in Sudan, and to a certain extent functioned as a long arm of Sudanese foreign policy, acting to support several African Islamist-based insurgency movements.[7] Some analysts, such as the Combating Terrorism Center (CTC), estimated that Al-Qaeda withdrew because of its operational problems inside stateless Somalia, but as these conditions were also faced in both Afghanistan and the frontier areas of Pakistan without problems, it is rather likely that the scaling down of operations was due to Osama bin Laden leaving the region for Afghanistan; Al-Qaeda support for other organizations in the region also dwindled.[8] Crucially, several future Al-Shabaab leaders ended up in Afghanistan, most likely drawing upon networks established when Al-Qaeda had a Somali presence.

In this sense global networks were very important in preparing the ground for Al-Shabaab. However, there were other factors that were to prove equally important. The increase in the use of religious symbols and titles in Somalia after the outbreak of the civil war was to create an atmosphere favorable to Islamist-inspired movements. Religion gave comfort in a tough situation. Reputation for religious piety and respect for the Qur'ān, perhaps because of the strong condemnation of theft and rape within Islam, was one factor that made Somalis trust fellow countrymen to handle security and justice issues.[9] The activities of religious charities in Somalia contributed to this, creating a positive perception of religious scholars.[10] Religious leaders gained a reputation for trustworthiness, and many of them also acted directly to prevent the injustices they saw around them. As claimed by Ali Mahdi, former—contested—President of Somalia, religious leaders enjoyed 'much trust and respect'.[11] Somalis tended to expect that religious clerics would be 'well behaved', that they believed in justice, and that the belief system of Islam created an ideational focal point, a solution that felt natural because of the dominating role Islam had in society.[12] Religious symbols also gained new meanings, as the *niqab* was seen as making women less tempting for rapists: according to Virginia Luling, a practical tool to lessen insecurity.[13]

In one sense, Islamic charities, the trust put in religious leaders, the use of religious symbols, all contributed to open up a discourse that was friendly to Islamist organizations, and in this sense the stage was set for Al-Shabaab; local conditions favored it. However, the group cannot be properly understood by focusing on local currents alone, it was very much a product of global currents interacting with local conditions.

3

ORIGINS

There are many claims about how Harakat Al-Shabaab began. Roland Marchal points to the formation of the Mu'askar Mahkamat (Camps of the Islamic Courts).[1] According to him the Mahkamat was later renamed Jamaa'a Al-Shabaab (Youth Group), and this was the origin of Al-Shabaab. The latter thus originated in the form of a rapid reaction corps of various Sharia Courts in Mogadishu, created to transcend clan and the power of the business community, to give independence to various courts from the support of the Mogadishu business community.[2]

The Somali journalist Abdirahman 'Aynte' Ali claims that Al-Shabaab originated in a 2003 meeting in Hargeisa.[3] The old Al-Shabaab-affiliated webpage Kataaib claimed that it was established in the Al Huda camp in Bay in 1996.[4] A later version, aired in Somali broadcasts, can be interpreted as claiming that it emerged as an organization after the Sharia Courts' attack on Kismayo in September 2006, having existed for several years as a loose network.[5] Interestingly, the field research conducted in Mogadishu for the present work seems to indicate that all of these claims have some truth in them, but that they are also misleading. Part of the confusion comes from the existence of a loose network of like-minded individuals, long before the formal founding of the Harakat Al-Shabaab, which often has been mistaken for a fully-fledged organization. This network, originating in Afghanistan veterans returning from the jihad against the Soviet Union, was nevertheless highly important for the future Al-Shabaab.

A proper exploration of the history of Al-Shabaab should start with the origins of this network, which are amongst the Somalis travelling to

Afghanistan in the wake of the Soviet intervention, during the Afghan war of 1979–89. Somali jihadists were drawn to Afghanistan by belief in a form of defensive jihad, a form of defense of Muslim brothers in another country attacked by 'infidels,' a loose form of solidarity not unlike the liberal Risorgimento nationalism that swept Europe in the 1840s, where nationalist activists went to fight in support of fellow nationalists in other countries.[6] However, solidarity cutting across borders comes in different forms; one type wants to remove the borders that separate countries with similar political beliefs, and such views influenced the Somali Afghanistan fighters.[7] For several of the first generation Somali Afghanistan veterans, for example the future Al-Shabaab leader Ibrahim Haji Jama Mee'aad 'Al-Afghani,' Adan Ahmed Arale 'Adan Jihad' and Mohamed Abdi Farah, the borders separating Muslims from each other must be removed, and a common Muslim state, the Caliphate, must be established. This group actively circulated propaganda videos from Afghanistan in closed circles inside Somalia. In these videos, the voice and thoughts of Abdallah Yusuf Azzam (killed in 1989 in Peshawar in Pakistan) were central; in one sense the group transferred a new type of ideology to Somalia. The influence of the group should not be overestimated, however; it was a loose collection of veterans keeping contact and sharing their ideas about the international sphere and religion, and a notion of loyalty towards a wider entity than simply the Somali nation: towards the wider *ummah*. This pan-Islamism was new in modern Somalia.[8]

By coincidence, and quite unrelated to events in Afghanistan, the previously described Al-Ittihad Al-Islamiya (AIAI) emerged. Sources within the family of the current Al-Shabaab leader Ahmed Abdi Godane studied at an AIAI school in the early 1990s, an illustration of how AIAI was to influence Al-Shabaab leaders of the future.[9] There were other clear connections between AIAI and Al-Shabaab. According to respondents in Mogadishu, as well as the obituary of Aden Hashi Ayro, the latter fought for AIAI in the early nineties.[10] Other current Al-Shabaab leaders, Muktar Robow 'Abu Mansoor' and Khalif Mohamud Warsame 'Khalif Adale', did the same.[11] However, Al-Shabaab emerged from a small sub-group of AIAI, a sub-group dominated by the group of Afghanistan veterans described earlier, originating in the war against Soviet intervention in Afghanistan.

Veterans returning from Afghanistan promoted a more violent jihad in Somalia. During the United Nations' expanded military intervention in 1993–95 (UNISOM II), several Afghanistan veterans—Hassaim Fargab, Mallim Kassim, Hassan Dheere, and the jihadist nicknamed Ashariaf, together with Sheikh Abdulahi Ahmed Sahal—fought the Americans on the streets of Mogadishu. They claimed to be fighting a 'defensive jihad,' protecting the Muslim *ummah*, against Western intrusion. UNISOM convoys were attacked, and mines were laid on UNISOM-patrolled roads.[12] Their radical views, and their will to action, attracted several youngsters such as Aden Hashi Ayro, a youth from the Absiye Ayr clan of Haber Gedir, and a member of AIAI. Muktar Robow, later nicknamed 'Abu Mansoor,' from the Leysan clan of the Rahanwhein, was also attracted to the radical views of the sub-group within AIAI.[13] The two were to become central for the future Harakat Al-Shabaab.

After UNISOM II's withdrawal, Moalin Adan Ayrow went to the Gedo region. Muktar Robow was sent to command the Bar Huda camp, which according to the Al-Shabaab affiliated Kataaib website (now closed) was to be where Al-Shabaab was formed.[14] However, the training created networks rather than a new organization; it increased Robow's contacts around Somalia. By 1996, Ethiopia had grown tired of attacks by AIAI, which included an assassination attempt on an Ethiopian minister, as well as several bomb blasts at Ethiopian hotels. The attempt on the life of Egypt's President Hosni Mubarak in Addis Ababa in 1995 also made the Ethiopians wary of Somali Islamists, who were suspected of providing aid to the attackers. Ethiopia intervened in Somalia, marching against AIAI bases in Luuq and Bulo Hawa; the result was the large battle of the *Hilac wayne* (the big lightening), also known as the Battle of Dolow city, in August 1996, in which both Ayro and Robow probably played a role.[15] The Ethiopians claimed to have captured more than eighty foreign fighters. Al-Qaeda on the other hand maintained that twelve foreign fighters were killed or captured, which also indicated an international presence in the battle.[16] Since Robow and Ayro fought in those battles as sub-commanders, it is highly likely that international jihadists fought side by side with them, and this might have been the occasion when the two first established contacts with Al-Qaeda. The two certainly established contacts with the radical AIAI leader Hassan Turki, who at the time had Al-Qaeda contacts.[17]

The defeats of AIAI in Gedo, as well as ideological differences over how Wahhabism should be promoted and clan differences, led to serious fragmentation within AIAI. One section was renamed the Jama'at al-

I'tisaam Bil-Kitaab Wa Sunna, while the most aggressive part of the organization, the Ethiopian part, retained the name Al-Ittihad al-Islamiya. Because of internal troubles, AIAI was by 1998 a spent force, fragmented and weak. However, the old personal networks within the organization continued to exist; the fringes of the Al-Shabaab movement are not always clearly demarcated and networks between old friends sharing loose ideological convictions remain important. Amongst the former young radical AIAI members who had been fascinated by the Afghanistan veterans, the idea of a pan-Islamist form of solidarity, as well as respect for the training that could be received in the camps of Afghanistan, prompted a new generation of Somalis to go to Afghanistan. Aden Hashi Ayro visited Afghanistan for the first time during 1998, according to Muktar Robow on his own initiative. He is said to have met Osama Bin Laden in Afghanistan as early as 1998, and even to have been present during the American Tomahawk missile attacks the same year. He became highly admired amongst the older Somali Afghanistan veterans.[18]

In this period new political actors, the so-called Sharia Courts, emerged inside Mogadishu, consisting of clan-based, independently-established ad hoc courts implementing justice in the anarchic city, and growing highly popular, as they were seen as standing up for the 'common man.' The growth of the Sharia Courts became very important for the development of Al-Shabaab, and many of the early leaders had joined courts even in the late 1990s. The Afghanistan veterans had several reasons to join other Islamists to form the Sharia Courts of Mogadishu, and the leaders of the courts, often relatively skeptical towards the ideological viewpoints of the Afghanistan veterans, had several reasons to accept them. The clan-based Sharia Courts offered the first and second generation Afghanistan veterans access to clan protection, since most of the courts were created and protected by specific clans. Islamists like Ayro also had a comparative advantage in the eyes of the court leaderships: his Islamist credentials and military training made him an ideal choice for a court leadership who saw an Islamist as a good choice since believers were perceived as just, and because of his foreign military training. The Islamists' access to a wider network transcending clan structures also made them ideally suited to coordinate between courts with different clan affiliates, having loyal contacts that transcended clan fissures.

The Sharia Courts and the future Al-Shabaab leaders were to ride on a wave of popularity that would prove essential in bringing about the

Harakat Al-Shabaab. But this popularity had little to do with radical ideology. First, as will be described in more depth later in this chapter, the Sharia Courts presented an alternative to the unpopular warlords.[19] From 1998 onwards the factions of the warlords had fragmented, and clan support had declined, as warlords failed to provide protection against crime for the clans they drew their support from.[20] The fragmented warlord factions wielded little control, and warlords could offer little opportunities to businessmen, who actually had to be able to cross the borders between the warlords' territories to survive. The warlords' fiefdoms simply had become too small to sustain larger business activities; the business community in Mogadishu needed other solutions such as the Sharia Courts. In the end the Mogadishu business community became a major backer of the Courts, also benefiting radical members of the courts like Ayro. Secondly, the so-called Transitional Federal Government (TFG) of Somalia, created over the period from 2002 to 2004 in Kenya, led to a counter-mobilization in Mogadishu attempting to prevent the TFG from entering the city. The clan dominating in Mogadishu, the Hawiye, and especially the Haber Gedir sub-clan felt alienated by the process, as they lost the presidency they had held in the TFG's predecessor, the Transitional National Government (TNG). The president of the TFG was seen as from an alien clan, and as an ally of Ethiopia, and while the prime minister in the end was a Hawiye (not from the Haber Gedir), there was a general feeling of having lost the leadership of that government. Somalis in Mogadishu were also highly skeptical of Ethiopia's role in the negotiation process leading to the TFG. As the warlords weakened, the Islamists in the Courts were seen as champions of the cause of the Hawiye (Haber Gedir) clan, as well as the struggle against Ethiopia. Thirdly, but perhaps most important, the citizens of Mogadishu were tired of the anarchy, rape, robbery, theft and murder that had been the order of the day, and the various ideologies that had influenced Somali history, nationalism, fascism, Marxism and clanism, were all discredited. By the late 2000s, Islam was the only belief system in Somalia that had not been discredited, and citizens went to religious leaders with their needs for protection. They were simply seen as the best alternatives. The pre-Al-Shabaab network were seen as upholders of justice and fairness, since they were ostensibly dedicated to Islam. Their resistance to the negotiations in Nairobi made them valuable allies for clanist politicians struggling against the loss of power of the Haber Gedir clan.

Simultaneously, the 9/11 attacks and the subsequent American intervention in Afghanistan drew a new generation of Somalis into international jihad and reinvigorated the radical sub-group in Mogadishu. According to a former Al-Shabaab member interviewed in Mogadishu, 'The Americans attacked Afghanistan, more than 100 Somalis went for jihad, eighty-nine entered Afghanistan. Abdullah Salad, Ayro, Robow, they all participated.' According to Muktar Robow, 'Moalin (Ayro) had managed again to travel to Afghanistan with his friend Abujabbal who passed away in Afghanistan.'[21] In this way members of the network that was to become Harakat Al-Shabaab came closer to global jihad, but global jihad came closer to Somalia as well. .

Al-Qaeda in East Africa was regionalized, as the big East African operations dwindled, and post-9/11 surveillance made it harder for Al-Qaeda to operate on a global scale. In one sense Al-Qaeda in East Africa 'went native', and grew much more dependent on its local sympathizers. Al-Qaeda had been involved in Somalia in 1991–96, sending instructors as well as training forces in Sudan; few Somalis seem to have been involved as instructors. By 1996, perhaps owing to Osama Bin Laden's return to Afghanistan, perhaps because of an increasingly tense relationship between Al-Qaeda and Sudan (where several of the training sessions were organized), perhaps as a result of trouble with their local allies, the focus on training local allies in East Africa was abandoned.[22] In the second half of the 1990s, the new focus was on attacks against 'the far enemy', the United States, and later, Israel. Nevertheless, even for this task Al-Qaeda preferred non-local agents. In 1998 Al-Qaeda struck against the American embassies in Nairobi and Dar es-Salaam, in perhaps the most successful attack in its pre-9/11 history. The attacks were well planned, well coordinated, and drew upon Al-Qaeda's global network. Finance was handled by a Sudanese, Tariq Abdullah (alias Abu Talha al-Sudani).[23]

Al-Qaeda's East Africa branch was able to draw upon Al-Qaeda assets in Pakistan, the UK, and Afghanistan.[24] The strike teams (originally planned as suicide teams), one targeting the American embassy in Nairobi, one the embassy in Dar es-Salaam, were selected in Pakistan; they flew into East Africa in June 1998.[25] The bombs were prepared by specially trained 'engineers', all of them with training from Al-Qaeda camps in Afghanistan; indeed one of them, Muhsin Musa Matwalli Atwah 'Abdulrahman', was one of Al-Qaeda's chief instructors in bomb making.[26] All of the bomb makers, with the notable exception of Ahmed Khalfan 'Ghai-lani', who was a Tanzanian, were from the Middle East, and had also been flown into the region in support of the operation. The explosives had been acquired from Luanda in Angola.[27] The technical staff of Al-Qaeda had prepared the bombs several days in advance, and used special cars to carry them, but left the target cities days before the attacks themselves, most of them going to Pakistan.[28]

With some exceptions, such as Fazul who handled logistics, the local Al-Qaeda operatives had only minor tasks, such as buying the cars used for the attacks, renting safe houses, creating charitable organizations that gave the international operatives access to visas, intelligence gathering, and dealing with the aftermath of the attacks.[29] The locals also followed the attackers physically to the vicinity of the targets on the attack day to ensure that the attackers did not lose their way or change their minds. In tasking and responsibility, the attacks were a global operation rather being based on local resources. Somalia was not needed for basing or resources: Al-Qaeda could evacuate to other places, and it could draw on resources in other countries.[30]

This was to change, perhaps because of 9/11 and new police measures that made it harder to transport resources and manpower; anyway, Al-Qaeda's branch in East Africa grew more local. The second, and so far last, round of large-scale attacks by Al-Qaeda in East Africa drew more upon local resources and, importantly, it drew more on Somali resources. On 28 November 2002, Al-Qaeda suicide bombers targeted the Paradise Hotel in Mombasa, while an Israeli airliner of the Arakia airline was hit in a parallel attack. Safe houses in Mogadishu had been used to organize a part of the attacks; other safe houses, in Kismayo (Somalia) and Lamu (Kenya), had been used as bases to smuggle arms and Al-Qaeda personnel. Somalis and Kenyans played the major roles in the attack.[31] While the 1998 attackers had been flown in from around the world, the 2002 attackers were brought in from Somalia by a small boat, as were the hand-held air to air missiles used in the attack.[32] According to reports on Somalia by the International Crisis Group (ICG) and the Kenyan authorities, the major part of the planning was done in Somalia and Kenya by local Al-Qaeda members, led by participants in the 1998 attacks who had stayed behind in the region.[33] The teams did not evacuate to far-away countries in the aftermath, but dispersed into Somalia and into Kenyan cities such as Lamu, often using these cities as transit points to Somalia.

Thus Somalia had become more important as Al-Qaeda decentralized its East African efforts. It was used as a place to hide, and a place to plan and re-supply. The East African Al-Qaeda of 2002 was locally recruited; it was led by remaining participants in the 1998 operations, Abu Talha al-Sudani, Fadil Harun aka Fazul Abdullah Mohammed and Saleh Ali Saleh Naban, of whom the last two had only held very low rank in the network in 1998. The three were all to become essential for the early Al-Shabaab, and would command sizeable contingents. It was the somewhat isolated remains of Al-Qaeda in east Africa that were so essential in the early Al-Shabaab, not the leadership around Osama bin Laden in Afghanistan/Pakistan. It even seems as though this group had little contact with the central leadership. Fazul, for example, lost contact with Al-Qaeda central from 2003 to 2006, while Al Sudani was suspended from the organization.[34]

Nevertheless, the involvement of this local group in Mogadishu was more than enough to draw the attention of the United States and its allies. The remains of Al-Qaeda in East Africa was targeted by the United States and its allies in covert operations, and Al-Qaeda struck back at the latter's agents. This was the so-called 'Shadow War' of Mogadishu.[35] This 'war' (2002 to 2006) was in reality several parallel conflicts. The most eye-catching was perhaps the War on Terror between Western intelligence and Al-Qaeda. However, the situation was confused by the Western allies, the warlords, and their hunger for profit, and several parallel struggles interacting with the War on Terror but external to it; one example being that between Ethiopia and Somali nationalists. Warlords also had an ongoing conflict with civil society and the business community, making the West's support for them more controversial. There was an element of opportunism as warlords tried to convince the Americans to support them financially, 'since they were in the frontline against Al-Qaeda', and Somali militias attempted to sell innocent Arabs living in Mogadishu to Western intelligence services in return for money.[36] Somali Afghanistan veterans were targeted. According to Al-Shabaab itself this was one of the reasons why it came into being and defectors support this view.[37] As claimed by Muktar Robow, the need for better and more united organizations than had previously existed also seems to have been a reason for the initiators of Al-Shabaab to come together:

Some officials of the Islamic movements who were in the country at the time held a meeting having felt that their groups were not that active as far as jihad was concerned. There were various Somali Islamic movements that have in the past tried to carry out jihad but they were faced with many obstacles and dropped their operations altogether. The men who were previously in these groups held a meeting and decided to form a movement and take part in the jihad and spread the religion. They decided to spread the religion alongside the jihad.[38]

The early Al-Shabaab initially included a variety of Afghanistan veterans, some with offensive and global aims, some joining because of fear, and some driven by both considerations. According to my interviews in Mogadishu, in 2005 a small group consisting of Afghanistan veterans and sympathizers, some with friends amongst the East African Al-Qaeda members, was formed, and retaliated against warlords targeting them.[39] The front lines were not clear, and the conflict was multipolar. A variety of factions, including criminal groups, were fighting for a variety of targets. Officers of the Transitional Federal Government (TFG), the internationally recognized Somali government, were killed if suspected to be in league with the Americans, and some Afghanistan veterans were engaged in protecting the few Al-Qaeda operatives, as well as former operatives, who themselves participated in the 'shadow wars'. There were losses on all sides; an alleged Al-Qaeda member, Salim Hemed-Issa 'Tanzania', was for example snatched on 18 March 2003 at the Global Hotel in Northern Mogadishu, and escorted out of Somalia.[40]

The network that later was to become Harakat Al-Shabaab struck back and started targeted assassinations even of their verbal critics. Early in 2005, an AU/IGAD fact-finding mission was targeted by the first IED in Somalia since 1995; according to the Global Islamic Media Front, this was the work of Nabhan of Al-Qaeda. The killing of Abdulkadir Yahya Ali, a peace activist, also shocked Somalis. Local sources claimed that Nabhan had organized the attack; this was confirmed by respondents close to the event in Mogadishu as well as by a blog writer under the name of Abu Zubeyr on a Jihadist-affiliated webpage.[41] Local sources in Mogadishu told the writer that this had been revenge for an attack on a house owned by Ayro leading to the abduction of Mohamed Abdi 'Isse', during the summer of 2004. This attack, and the following events, illustrate the interaction between Islamism and clanism, as the conflict turned into a conflict between the Ayr clan of Ayro and the warlords who were allegedly behind the attack, Muhamed Qanyare Afrah and Abdi Waal, and their Murosade clan. Ayro sought protection from his own clan.

The exact boundaries of the group were not clear, there were sympathizers who never became members, and the organization had allies amongst clan fighters as well as clanists and nationalists. However, the ideology, at the time a mix of international offensive and defensive jihad and a campaign for reform of Somali society, was special, as was the network's closeness to the remnants of Al-Qaeda in East Africa.

Ayro was often mentioned as the first leader of Al-Shabaab, but former fighters in Mogadishu point to him as the first Amir of training only, with Robow acting as a highly potent military leader, the political leader being 'Arrale', also known as Ismael Mahmoud Muhammad, hailing from the northern part of Somalia, from the Isaq clan but resident in Mogadishu at the time.[42] Other legendary figures were a part of the team, for example Khalif Mohamud Warsame, alias Khalif Cadale, later in charge of the Al-Shabaab NGO office, but at the time involved in planning the so-called Italian cemetery incident, which put Shabaab on the international map. This incident was in many ways Al-Shabaab's founding moment, since it acquired its first training centre then. In February 2005, the old Italian cemetery in Mogadishu was seized by an ad hoc group (not by Al-Shabaab, it was not formed as an organization yet), using two 'technicals'—the common term in Somalia for improvised fighting vehicles based on ordinary pick-ups—from the Ifka Halane militia and some other Islamist militias. A new mosque was built and a new training center, the Abu Ayub, was constructed. The whole area was renamed the Salaaxudiin camp (named after the famous anti-Crusade commander, 'Saladin' to Westerners). Extensive training under the Al-Shabaab network took place, including training of infiltrators. The infiltrators were people who were students or had work, and could only come during battles. They were also given security training to help them to blend into their neighborhoods and know what to say to curious people about their disappearances, especially when called to battle; hence the now infamous uniforms of the Al-Shabaab soldiers, which hide the face. The training was a first step in transforming Al-Shabaab from a network into an organization.

Al-Shabaab could now start to recruit independently and expand, targeting youngsters who were far from their families and living as orphans. Al-Qaeda in East Africa was almost integral to the group, and Nabhan and Abu Taha Al Sudani were highly respected by Al-Shabaab. According to some defectors they functioned as informal leaders.[43] The new group started shutting down cinemas in parts of Mogadishu by force. It managed to take over the village of Cel Garas near Celbur in Central Somalia and defeat the Duduble warlord Botan Isse's troops there.[44] This was Al-Shabaab's first ever territorial gain, and it would never lose control over that area afterwards. By the start of 2005 Al-Shabaab, now more organized but yet not an organization, including its resident Al-Qaeda members, was a small but successful network of only thirty-three core members, but it was to drastically expand.[45]

4

THE FIRST EXPANSIVE PHASE, 2005–06

IN THE SHADOW OF THE COURTS

Several aspects of Somali politics in the mid-2000s provided the Harakat Al-Shabaab with major advantages during the early part of its history. First, it was perceived as being on the side of the Hawiye clan, because of its hostility to the Western-backed Transitional Federal Government (TFG) created in Nairobi in 2002–04. The TFG was considered by many Hawiyes, especially within the Haber Gedir sub-clan, to be dominated by the Darod and Rahanwhein clans, and to have been a tool for Ethiopian dominance over Somalia.[1] The young Al-Shabaab was seen as a counterweight to the influence of the perceived Ethiopian-supported Majeerteen-Rahanwhein alliance. Of course, this view neglected the multi-clan nature of Al-Shabaab at the time, but it nevertheless provided the group with sympathy amongst the Hawiye.

Secondly, the high crime level in Mogadishu also aided Al-Shabaab's cause, which was perceived as an organization of pious Muslims, as just and transparent compared with warlords and political leaders. This was indeed true; Al-Shabaab did react against and criticize what it considered to be unfair practices, and this also gave it considerable local support and goodwill.

Lastly, perhaps an underestimated aspect, international issues mattered. Pictures of Palestine, Iraq and Afghanistan created feelings of pan-Islamic solidarity. Indeed Palestine, Iraq and Afghanistan aided a feeling that Islam itself was under attack, and that it needed defense and defen-

31

sive jihad. The lack of knowledge of the core ideology of the small group at the time, a focus on Takfirism, a clear hostility towards important traits of Somali culture, and the will to implement extreme physical punishments (*hudud*) were also advantages for the young group. These ideological traits were not popular in Mogadishu, but the small Al-Shabaab group had few opportunities to indicate its ideology; it controlled just a few mosques and had to compromise when participating in the Sharia Court structure.

In addition, Al-Shabaab's rise to power was aided by several deeper structural changes; their enemies were on the decline while potential allies were on the rise militarily. The first change was the waning of the warlord system. By 2005, this system had been in decline for a long time in Mogadishu, and the large factions fighting the Americans in the early 1990s were a thing of the past. The various blocs had broken down according to clan lines, partly because the warlords refused to pay their militias regularly (only paying them when they were going on the offensive), which created little loyalty towards their leaders.[2] Warlord militias plundered and 'taxed' the population through checkpoints in order to survive, but this made them highly unpopular, both with the average Somali and with the Somali business community. Moreover, the limited protection warlords could provide to ordinary Somalis dwindled as each warlord became weaker and weaker while the system disintegrated more and more.

The warlords' random attempts to provide justice were also a failure, as they had little legal competence and seldom managed to fully control their own forces.[3] This too was partly due to the fact that warlords seldom attempted to pay their own militias. Warlord militias had to plunder/'tax' in order to sustain themselves, and people knew that there were few economic rewards for staying loyal to a particular warlord. In this sense local commanders would face strong incentives to start factions on their own, rather than remain in a relationship with a warlord who failed to pay them but only demanded loyalty.[4] By 2005 the warlord cliques in Mogadishu were weak; the fourteen factions varied from Muhamed Qanyare Afra's 1,000 men to Hussein Aideed's fifty—a huge drop in power since the golden days of Somali warlordism, when Muhamed Farah Aideed could command perhaps 6,000 men alone.[5]

Moreover, alternative sources of power had emerged. The Somali business community had grown in strength. Many Somali investors returned from Dubai and re-established themselves from 1998 onwards, in a period when front lines in Mogadishu had become more stable and predictable and it had become easier to do business in Mogadishu. The businessmen were becoming less dependent on the warlords. At the same time, the business community faced big problems with criminals, which led the businessmen to assemble a considerable amount of arms and soldiers. By the end of 2005, the cartel around Abkour Umar Adane had a militia of 2,000 men, while the telecommunications company Hortel had 1,000 men-at-arms, and Coca Cola's local franchise employed 200 militia fighters.[6] Business companies in Mogadishu were thus more than ordinary business firms, they were military actors. Increasingly, the business militias worked to provide safety for the business community, in the process developing alliances with Islamists, and with Islamic Courts, that were seen as tools that could enable the business community to escape plunder by the various warlord militias.

The second structural change was the increase in the power of the Sharia Courts, partly connected with the growth of the business community, as the latter to a large extent supported the former. In the beginning the Sharia Courts had been weak and defined according to clan. There were several attempts to transcend the clan divisions, to unify the courts, even as early as in 1993.[7] However, the attempts were troubled by political problems, with division at first between the Haber Gedir and the Abgal sub-clans of the Hawie clan, a split that divided Mogadishu into two. In February 1999 several courts managed to appoint a common spokesperson, Sheikh Hassan Adde, and deploy around 1,000 militiamen for the negotiations surrounding the creation of a regional administration.[8] The Ifka Halan Court, the court of the Ayr clan, and also the court of Al-Shabaab's very own Aden Hashi Ayro, was central in the process. In April 1999, the Joint Islamic Councils (JIC) were formed, consisting of a few courts in Mogadishu only and mainly intended to handle justice in the Bakara Market.[9] The JIC were accused of being based on one clan only, and were not successful. Another attempt to organize the courts, the Sharia Implementation Council (SIC) also known as the Islamic Courts (IC), was launched in 2000. There was a decline in the number of courts when the transitional government created at Arta in 2000 sought to include them in its governance structures, and the governing council of the courts was disbanded. All of the pre-2004 unions of courts were partly created to facilitate jurisdiction outside of the clan base of each separate court. From 2004 onwards four courts, the Ifka Halane, the Shircole, the Towfiq and the Sii Sii, drove a new process of unification forward. It should be noted that Al-Shabaab members were highly active in two of them, the Shircole and the mightiest court of them all, the Ifka Halane.

Al-Shabaab was an ideal partner in the push for Sharia Court unification; it was the political group in Mogadishu that had most success in transcending clan—in fact it was one of the most multiclan factions inside Mogadishu, perhaps because of its ideology which claimed to transcend clan and ethnicity, seeing Islam as transcending such differences.[10] Al-Shabaab driven by its own jihadist ideology, also emphasized the Sharia in its many lectures. Law and order were very important to it, and this brought the group considerable sympathy.[11] Its members were also well trained compared with the average Somali militiaman.

It is important to note that, contrary to many newspaper articles, Al-Shabaab was not the armed wing of the Courts.[12] In fact there were other groups under the Court umbrella that were more militarily important than Al-Shabaab. Abokour Omar Adane's business militia was, for example, very prominent, perhaps the most important of all the armed factions within the Sharia court system.[13] On 12 January 2006 Adane clashed with the warlord Bashir Raghe Shirar, his former business partner whom he had previously backed financially.[14] It was this clash that initiated the Sharia Courts takeover of Mogadishu, and fighting continued afterwards.[15] From February onward the Sharia Courts Union supported Adane; strategically it could not afford to see him lose, it would most likely have ended his financial support for the Union.

The creation, in February 2006, of a new alliance of warlords, the so-called Alliance for Peace Restoration and Counter Terrorism (APRCT), was a move by the declining warlords to ally and get foreign support, partly to face Adane's militias. This support came; the United States was at the time aware of various members of the Al-Shabaab network, their presence in the court militias, and the role of the local Al-Qaeda veterans with them, and the Pentagon saw the APRCT as a valuable local ally, though there was strong resistance to this view from the State Department.[16] However, such a view ignored the previously described structural weakness of the warlord militias, their lack of regular payment and their lack of loyalty to their leaders. The American strategy also neglected the general unpopularity of the warlords compared with the

Sharia Courts. The differences between the Courts and the warlords when it came to successfully delivering local safety and security meant that the Courts could draw upon popular support, as well as the support of important elements of the business community.

In February and March 2006 Adane's militia, backed by an ever larger number of militias of the larger courts, managed to gain control over El Maan and El Adde, Mogadishu's major ports. They also managed to gain control over the Eisley airport, and with it the most important sources of revenue in and around Mogadishu. This in turn meant that the Sharia Courts alliance had access to new sources of revenue that could be used to hire militias, as well as to bribe the warlords who remained as sub-lieutenants to encourage them to change sides or abstain from fighting.[17]

The Sharia Courts contained many factions—businessmen, Islamists, clanists, former warlord militias, all under one umbrella. This did not mean that Al-Shabaab lacked importance. Its members were fierce believers and highly efficient fighters, their level of ideological motivation was also higher than that of any other group of fighters in Somalia. Al-Shabaab also lost prominent members during the initial fighting, such as its famous sub-commander 'Gaal-Dile' (a name meaning 'Christan-killer') in the fighting in Sii Sii in May 2006. Its reputation for fierceness still allowed it to command larger forces; it was admired by other parts of the courts, which at times allowed it to hold command over their forces, including even Adane's militias. Moreover, Al-Shabaab's close cooperation with the court structures allowed it access to new funds.[18] Lastly, the mystery around Al-Shabaab's leaders probably also contributed to its popularity—it became 'trendy', something 'secret and efficient, fighting for law and order', and was admired by many local youths.

Empowered by the courts

Over time the Sharia Courts alliance became more structured. The loose alliance turned into the Islamic Courts Union (ICU). By June 2006, Al-Shabaab commanded a far larger force than it ever had before, including non-Al-Shabaab court militias. The leaders now had tactical responsibilities influencing all Court forces. Muktar Robow, by now a rising star in the hierarchy of the Courts, was put in charge of bringing together defectors from the TFG. The appointment was partly because of his clan background—he hailed from the Rahanwhein clan, underrepresented in the ICU, but supplying many fighters to the TFG—and it was hoped to create defections amongst the latter's forces. Robow also became commander of the battles against the warlord Abdi Qaibdeed's forces on 9 and 10 July 2006.[19] He had built up a considerable power base around the Bur Hakaba area. In the end Robow was promoted to be second in command of the Sharia Courts' security forces. Aden Hashi Ayro also commanded substantial forces, and achieved a notable propaganda victory when conquering the Baledoogle airport and Walaweyne on 16 July the same year, commanding 300 men in the operation.[20] Perhaps because of their battlefield successes, Al-Shabaab also gained power within the formal structures of the Court system, the earlier mentioned appointment of Muktar Robow as second in command of the security forces being one fact indicating this. The new *shura* council of the Courts, an institution created to facilitate a new governance structure transcending clan and the separate courts, had a separate Al-Shabaab quota. Of the ninety-seven members, Al-Shabaab commanded the allegiance of nine. Its positions in the cabinet (executive council) of the Sharia courts were even more substantial; Ahmed Aw Abdi Mahamoud Godane was appointed secretary general, he was also responsible for screening foreign visitors, and provided the writer with a visitor approval at the time. Fu'ad Mahamed Khalaf Shongola was made responsible for education and youth, and Myhedin Mohamed Omar for health.

Al-Shabaab was more unified than the other factions within the Courts and managed to use this to its advantage, putting several of its members in important tactical positions, for example getting Sheikh Abdullahi Mo'alim Ali 'Abu Utayba' appointed as a major coordinator of the effort to create a unified court militia transcending clan divisions. According to Muktar Robow, it was at this stage, in August 2006, that Al-Shabaab was created formally.[21] The new formal positions within the Courts, as well as their relative unity, also meant that Al-Shabaab got access to funding from the supporters of the Courts and the business community. In one sense Al-Shabaab was a parasite on the Sharia Courts' back, thriving from their growth.

The interaction with the Sharia Courts led to changes in Al-Shabaab's hierarchy. Members controlling the funds channeled through the Courts system gained power. Some members also gained power through their fundraising for the Sharia Courts. Two individuals were to strengthen their positions in Al-Shabaab, Ahmed Aw Abdi Mahmoud Godane as the secretary general, and Fu'ad Mahamed Khalaf 'Shongola' as being very active in collecting money for the Sharia Courts amongst the diaspora. Godane himself was a latecomer to Al-Shabaab, and a product of the Al-Ittihad al-Islamiya (AIAI) patronage network. Godane, from the Isaq Arab clan, had been one of the best students at the Omar Bin Khadaab Islamic School in Hargeisa, and won a scholarship to study in Sudan.[22] Godane received several scholarships from Saudi Arabia to go to Pakistan and study economics, but after struggling academically he travelled into Afghanistan—exactly where in Afghanistan is unknown. He returned to Somaliland in 2001, doing a variety of work. In mid-2002 he left for Mogadishu and became involved with the Islamic Court-based Ifka Halane, at the same time as Ayro. However, Godane returned to Hargeisa quickly.[23] According to the Somaliland state prosecution authority, he was involved in terrorist attacks against Western citizens. On 21 October 2003 a British couple, Richard and Enid Eyeington, were killed, and on 19 April 2004 the car of a German NGO was attacked and Florence Cheriuyot, a Kenyan citizen, was killed in the crossfire.[24] In 2004 Godane settled in Mogadishu for good.[25] Al-Shabaab defectors claimed that he had some problems explaining the fact that he had participated in a robbery close to Togu Wajale in Somaliland, and that he defended his actions by maintaining that he robbed infidels.[26]

Fouad Mohamed Qalaf was to become very important for the development of Al-Shabaab's ideology as well as its justice system. Better known as Fouad Shongola, he hailed from the Wartoble sub-clan of the Darod clan. He worked in the early 1990s as a preacher in a Swedish mosque in Rinkeby. At the time he was involved in an effort to have the first female Somali-Swedish radio reporter taken off the air, by calling the radio station and talking to the Somali community; however, the situation was resolved peacefully, through dialogue. Shongola is said to have been in Syria in the late 1990s, but to have been dissatisfied with 'the sinful society' he found there.[27] In 2004 he returned to Mogadishu. To judge from conversations Shongola had with several of the NGOs in Mogadishu at the time, his focus was preaching law and order. He was later to be in charge of important parts of the Al-Shabaab justice system.[28]

The drastic changes within Al-Shabaab, its increase in membership and power, and the shifts in the internal balance of power within the organization were bound to create challenges. There seems to have been at least two important disagreements within the young movement. The first considered a minor issue, namely how to treat the use of the mild narcotic qat. Qat, the narcotic leaf frequently chewed amongst the Somalis, was seen as sinful by all of the major Al-Shabaab leaders. However, Robow argued for allowing its use in private, only banning its public use, arguing that, as with alcohol in the time of the Prophet, it would take time to change the practice. Godane, however, argued for an immediate ban.[29] The second dispute was over the creation of a wider Islamic Salvation Front, also including Muslims of other schools, such as followers of the traditional Shafia approach of the Somalis; Robow and Shongola were more positive towards such an initiative, while Godane was negative.[30] But it should be noted that the lines were far from clear. Godane's old friend—and, according to several Mogadishu sources, Al-Shabaab's first Amir, Abdullahi Sudi Arale, later a Guantánamo Bay detainee—was engaged in similar activities, according to American documents leaked by Wikileaks, trying to create a broader Islamist umbrella organization.[31]

The disagreements within the organization were minor compared with the conflicts Al-Shabaab experienced with other parts of the Sharia Courts. The young Al-Shabaab managed to stand together in the face of rivals such as the warlord turned Islamist Sheikh Yusuf Mohamed Siyad 'Indhaadde'. Indhaade had a notorious reputation for extorting money from minority clans, the so-called 'Mokulal Maddow' ('black cat') practice. Robow raised this issue in the presence of Indahaade, nominally his superior in the Sharia Court security structure, publicly humiliating Adde.[32] Additionally Al-Shabaab seriously challenged Indahaade's attempts to gain income from Mogadishu port. In late August 2006 the situation was so tense that fighting almost erupted. Indeed, tense conflicts with the rest of the Courts system, and ultimatums to get its will, were nothing new to Al-Shabaab. According to one of Roland Marchal's brilliant reports on the organization:

Just after the defeat of the warlords in June 2006, a meeting gathering all fighting forces took place at the Ramadan hotel in Mogadishu. Al-Shabaab did not show up, but sent its requests to get included: Shari'a should be enforced without any qualifications; it should get its good share of the booty (notably of the arsenals owned by some warlords, especially 'Abdirashiid Ilqeyte, Muuse Suudi and Mahamed Qanyere); it also claimed one third of all positions in the Islamic Courts Union; and last but not the least for Western countries, it wanted the ICU to welcome foreign fighters without any conditions.[33]

All in all, Al-Shabaab demonstrated considerable unity, gaining more power in the Sharia Court structure. Moreover, it was seen as 'cool' by the youngsters of Mogadishu, and Sharia Court militias not aligned to Al-Shabaab used the brand name 'Shabaab'. There were many 'Shabaab' members who were not members of the real Al-Shabaab, but rather independent militias, by the end of 2006.

The high tide of Al-Shabaab's status was perhaps the Kismayo attack on 24 September 2006. Before the attack, hundreds of soldiers and about sixty 'technicals' were assembled around Arbiska and Lafole School outside Mogadishu (both places are now refugee camps). In an illustration of the general fragmentation in the Courts, every court contributed separately to the efforts, save Al-Shabaab. Every Islamic Court was to bring at least one technical, though it was voluntary and not all courts complied. Most of the weapons and technicals used were seized from the warlords. According to a participant, the fighters were mostly from Mogadishu and Kismayo, but included about 100 foreigners, including Yemenis.[34] The overall leader of the attacking force seems to have been Adam Ayro, with Hassan Turki leading the initial thrust. The Global Islamic Media Front claimed that a former Al-Qaeda member, Abu Taha Al Sudani, played a major role in the battle. Sudani was the commander of the Al-Shabaab forces that fought separately from the court militia, while Abdulahi Salad 'Abud Khalid' was the second in command of Al-Shabaab's own forces.[35]

The campaign itself established a pattern; it showed how Shabaab could play on fear and clanism to achieve its targets. In mid-September 2006, about half of the technicals were sent on their way to Kismayo. The forces passed through warlord-held territory around Brawa, being received as liberators by the local minority clans which had been more or less occupied by the Haber Gedir. However, the Sharia Court forces did not have the time to establish a local administration there, and headed for Jilib, which fell without a fight. The second wave of supplies and reinforcements, with Adam Ayro at their head, was behind the main attacking force—they were around Barawe when Hassan Turki was entering Jilib. Jilib itself was on the vicinity of the land controlled by the so-called Juba Valley Alliance, a banding together of warlords from the Haber Gedir Ayr sub-clan and the Marehan sub-clan. At the time the Ayr sub-clan had grown in power within the courts, and Ayr court leaders such as Hassan Dahiir Aweys and Yusuf Mohamed Siyad Indhaadde held positions of power within the court structure. The Ayr warlords in the Juba Valley Alliance in the end defected, when facing forces from their own clan. The remaining Marehan warlord Barre Hirale gave up Kismayo without a fight by 24 September 2006. One of the most stable warlord administrations in Somalia's history was destroyed without bloodshed. A combined strategy of fear, clanism and rapid movement had succeeded.

When news of Barre Hirale's withdrawal reached the ICU command, the green light was given to take the city immediately. Hassan Turki entered the city from the main road and the airport—Ayro, following, entered the city triumphantly. It was during this conquest that the new internationalist tendencies of several of the Somali Islamists were most clearly demonstrated; the Somali flag was torn down and ripped to pieces because it was seen as a 'symbol of nationalism'. Contrary to popular belief, it was Somali members of Harakat Ras Kamboni, a clan-based Islamist organization with Al-Qaeda connections, that lowered the Somali flag and tore it to pieces. Hassan Turki defended the action, saying the flag was just 'a piece of cloth'. Uproar ensued, prompting other ICU officials to distance themselves from his remarks, but the Al-Shabaab leaders remained loyal to the black flag, and defended the actions of the Ras Kamboni group.

The Kismayo incident was a clear sign of self-confidence.[36] According to an eye-witness, Ayro spoke to a euphoric crowd gathered in the central square. He declared that the Sharia Courts did indeed have non-Somali fighters, that they would be welcome, and that 'nobody could do a thing about it'.[37] The Kismayo battle illustrated a new, daring, and less clandestine version of Al-Shabaab, flaunting its international connections in the face of the Somali public. It also illustrated that Al-Shabaab had clear friends amongst the more clan-based Islamists of Ras Kamboni.

The remains of Al-Qaeda's East African cell, Nabhan, Fazul and Sudani, established a considerable fighting reputation after the fall of Kismayo. Barre Hirale was aware that most of the invading forces had withdrawn from Kismayo and gone back to Mogadishu, and he therefore launched an attack to try to take it back. They were met by forces led by the Al-Qaeda veteran Abu Taha Al Sudani, drawn from the most fanatical jihadists of Al-Shabaab, supported by Ras Kamboni militia. Mud stopped Barre Hirale's reinforcements, about thirty-four technicals, and Hirale was defeated. The Sharia Courts had expanded, and Al-Shabaab had gained considerable power and reputation in the process. Al-Qaeda veterans had aided this process.[38]

The second generation foreign fighters

It should be noted that Al-Qaeda had already declared support for the Sharia Court alliance. On 2 July 2006 Osama bin Laden made a specific call for Muslims to support the court movement, declaring, 'We warn all the nations of the world not to agree to America's request to send international forces to Somalia. We swear to Allah that we will fight its soldiers on Somali soil, and we reserve the right to punish on their own soil, or anywhere else, at the appropriate time and in the appropriate manner.'[39] In parallel to the Kismayo conquest, Al-Shabaab had organized an influx of foreign fighters. These were not Al-Shabaab's first foreign fighters. As described previously, the first were the veterans of Al-Qaeda's East Africa cell that seem to have been a part of the organization from its inception. In one sense this part of Al-Qaeda seems to have 'gone native' by 2006, taking Somali wives and settling down. The remaining Al-Qaeda members also hailed from the region, Sudani hailing from Sudan, Fazul from the Comoros and Nabahn from Tanzania.[40] However, by 2006 new fighters came to Somalia from outside the original region and without the initial Al-Qaeda East Africa connection of Al-Shabaab's first foreign fighters. These foreign fighters were clandestinely transported into Somalia; Omar Hammami, later infamous as Abu Mansoor Al-Amriki, claimed that Shongola and Abu Taha Al Sudani had organized transport into Somalia, concealed from the Courts' formal leadership.[41] Some of them were to become famous, others were to be future recruiters.

Some of the international jihadists who started to arrive in Somalia seemed quite innocent, for example Ruben Luis Leon Shumpert, an American citizen, nicknamed 'Amir Abdul Muhaimin' by his peers. Shumpert had a troubled life in the USA, committing petty crime before turning to barbering. He used his barber's shop to show films inspired by a rough 'Clash of Civilizations' thesis in which the Islamic world was seen as fighting a battle with the West. In 2004 he was arrested for threats against a businessman and the possession of an illegal firearm. However, in 2006, when he was to appear in court, he tauntingly called the FBI telling them that he was in East Africa.[42] While being radicalized in the United States, he was recruited into Al-Shabaab by Somali Americans. This illustrates a pattern for the known Western recruits to Al-Shabaab in this period—they seem to have had some connections to the Somali diaspora network.

The most famous American Al-Shabaab fighter joining in 2006 was the previously mentioned Omar Hammami (Abu Mansoor Al Amriki). Hammami also seemed to have been channeled to Somalia through personal friendship with Somalis. He was born in Daphne, Alabama and seems to have had radical beliefs even when at school, although it seems he became less political later. He was drawn to Somalia, and to Salafi jihadism when he became integrated into the Somali community of Toronto, inspired by videos from various battlegrounds around the world; videos of the Jordanian Commander Samir Salih Abdullah al-Suwaylim's 'Khattab' were said to have been very impressive, while he also stated that the Iraq resistance campaign had inspired him.[43] However, he did not travel directly to Somalia, but initially went to Egypt. It may be that his online activities in Egypt pushed him further in the direction of joining the Somali Sharia Court movement; most likely he was not aware of the existence of Al-Shabaab at the time.

Hammami joined an online forum and began communicating with the administrator, Daniel Joseph Maldonado, who was to be another famous second generation foreign fighter. Maldonado had initially moved to Egypt much earlier than Hammami, as early as November 2005, but his focus was drawn to Somalia by the achievements of the Sharia Courts and declarations on their administration in Somalia.[44] He left for Somalia in late 2006, going first to Mogadishu and then to a training camp in Jilib.[45] He was arrested by Kenyan troops in early 2007.[46] His comrade Hammami also ended up in Somalia in the same period. It should be noted that the groups seem to have been inspired by the Sharia Courts rather than Al-Shabaab, although they framed Somalia in a larger jihadist discourse; for them, Somalia was just another front in the conflict between Islam and the West.

Munir Awad, a Lebanon-born citizen of Sweden, arrested in the company of Maldonado's wife by Kenyan forces in February 2007 but later released, seems to have held similar views. Munir, inspired by the former Guantánamo Bay detainee Mehdi Ghezali, seems to have been a jihad seeker; he was arrested in Pakistan in 2009 and then again on his way to Denmark on 29 December 2010, this time for planning a terror attack.[47] Last but not least, a foreign fighter with a Jewish background was recruited. Ahmed, or 'Emir Anwar' or 'Awar,' an American, was a former resident of San Diego, California and had attended college there. He was a security guard licensed by the state Bureau of Security and Investigative Services, and had been the owner of an auto business.[48] Jehad Serwan Mostafa left for Somalia, allegedly in December 2005, and according to FBI he was later active in the recruitment of Somali diaspora members in Minnesota. Of the five, Omar Hammami was to become most important for Al-Shabaab's international recruitment efforts, and his videos were to have a proven effect in attracting American recruits.

There were also fighters from the Middle East; both Maldonado and Schumpeter claimed to have met them, and several Somalis observed them.[49] The first notable group of this sort was of Yemeni radicals, some with close connections with the future Al-Qaeda in the Arabian Peninsula (AQAP). Mansur al-Bayhani and Ibrahim al-Muqri were amongst the most prominent Yemenis. Al-Bayhani was an international jihadist 'by family ties', two of his brothers ended up at Guantánamo bay, and another brother escaped with him in the infamous Sanaa prison break of 2006, regarded as the rebirth of Al-Qaeda in Yemen. Al-Bayhani was a veteran jihadist who had seen action both in Afghanistan and in the infamous Khattab Arab brigade in Chechnya. After the death of Khattab, Al-Bayhani, later to be known as 'Abu Mansuur Al Yemeni,' travelled back to Afghanistan to fight American forces, before returning to Saudi Arabia where he was arrested and extradited to Yemen.[50] Ibrahim Muhammad Abdu al-Muqri was also an Afghanistan veteran, hailing from Saudi Arabia but born of Yemeni parents. He was arrested in Saudi Arabia when returning from Afghanistan and later extradited to Yemen.[51] Al-Muqri was by 2006 cleared of all charges, but not released before the infamous February 2006 prison break. Both of these men served time with, and escaped together with, the top leaders of Al-Qaeda in Yemen, later Al-Qaeda in the Arabian Peninsula (AQAP), including the present-day leader Nasir Abd al-Karim Abdullah al-Wuhayshi 'Abu Basir' and the ideologist Qasim Yahya Mahdi al-Raymi. During my research in Mogadishu a third Yemeni name from this period came up: that of the Bosnia war veteran Maalin Qalid 'Qasim' Hashi Abdallah, who remained active in Al-Shabaab for a few more years before he was killed. Together these three illustrate the closeness between Al-Shabaab and Al-Qaeda in the Arabian Peninsula from quite an early stage in Al-Shabaab's organizational history. However, this also suggests that some of the Yemeni recruits as well as some Americans might have chosen Somalia because of its relative safety; many of them were wanted in their home countries, and Al-Shabaab, under the Sharia Court umbrella, offered them safety and protection from the governments that were pursuing them.

It should be noted that the new internationals were kept outside the Al-Shabaab command hierarchy. The old Al-Qaeda in East Africa members, in contrast, held high-ranking positions. Abu Taha Al Sudani was even appointed to the important position of commander of the forces in Dinsor in November/December 2006.

What about fighters from the Somali diaspora? Many Somalis returned home to Mogadishu while it was controlled by the Sharia Courts, mainly because the city was comparatively tranquil. Indeed, the peacefulness of Mogadishu in 2006 must have been a major asset for Al-Shabaab recruitment in the diaspora during the following years. The achievement of creating peace was simply very impressive—people could again walk in the streets. Ordinary Somalis experienced a unique safety and the general sentiment was almost joyful.

One important point should be deduced from the above analysis: the internationalization of Al-Shabaab was well under way before the Ethiopian attack on the Sharia Courts in December 2006. Interviews with former Al-Shabaab fighters seem to indicate that Arab members could have numbered in the hundreds. One indicated that he was stationed alongside twenty-five of them in Bur Hakaba alone, a very crucial part of the front.[52] Another sign of this development was the introduction of suicide attacks against the Transitional Federal Government (TFG) in Baidoa in 2006, the first time this technique had been used in Somalia. That first attack took place only after the Sharia Courts gained power, and before the Ethiopians and their Somali allies dislodged the Courts (on 16 September). The attack targeted the president of the TFG, took place in confusing circumstances. No person or organization took responsibility; indeed it might have been an ordinary ambush. The next attack was confirmed by independent sources, however. On 30 November 2006 an Ethiopian control post on a road leading into Baidoa (at Daynuunaay) was targeted by a suicide bomber.[53] A relatively unknown individual named Mohamed Ibrahim Said Bilal claimed responsibility for the attack, but the Sharia Courts distanced themselves publicly from the attack.

Bilal's special connections with Al-Shabaab explain this difference of opinion, as he was at the time (through the Al Bayan court) working for the Afghanistan veteran Muktar Robow 'Abu Mansoor', who later became an Al-Shabaab leader. Al-Shabaab became the foremost agent of suicide attacks in Somalia after 2007; and indeed no other group has ever publicly acknowledged responsibility for suicide attacks in Somalia.[54]

These examples seem to indicate that Al-Shabaab was becoming a hard-line international jihadist organization, but this is not necessarily true. The rank and file of Al-Shabaab consisted of unemployed Somali youths, with some nebulous ideas about the global oppression of Islam, but with more important and largely correct ideas about the Sharia Courts and Islam bringing an end to warlords, injustice, and terror. Moreover, the exact borders of Al-Shabaab were unclear; some individuals were on-off members, like Aden Madobe and Hassan Turki today. Madobe especially was to prove later that some of Somalia's supposed Islamists would choose to go with their clan rather than other jihadists if forced to make a decision.

Al-Shabaab's ideology was also initially rather mixed; there was some emphasis on a wider offensive or defensive form of jihad, and many of its leaders had been veterans of the jihad in Afghanistan, but the very real suffering of the Somalis under the warlords, and a wish for Islamic reform as an antidote to this, was also very important. A short survey of Al-Shabaab's early history nevertheless shows that the organization was very different from other groups. The top leadership was clearly influenced by such actors as Al-Qaeda, and had connections with both the old Al-Qaeda in East Africa and the newer activists in Yemen. Al-Shabaab had leaders who had travelled out of Somalia to fight for the *ummah*. The early Al-Shabaab leadership, or rather its early strongmen, seem to have been driven by a mixture of ideas—reform jihadism, the idea of implementing justice in Somalia based on a more radical interpretation of Islam—but such ideas were quite popular in the crime-filled streets of Mogadishu. They clearly show that defensive jihadism was important for them, several of the highest ranking leaders having some experiences in that regard; they also respected Al-Qaeda members greatly, but often saw their actions as offensive responses to attacks against the *ummah*. Clanism, one of the major driving forces of Somali politics, seems to have been surprisingly weak amongst them, and it is noticeable that the leaders analyzed were drawn from all clans of Somali society, for they were not clan-based as almost all factions were in Somalia at this time.

According to new Al-Shabaab members interviewed after the defeat of the Sharia Courts in 2007, there was some training for recruits in 2006. Alisha Ryu, for example, describes how she interviewed Hassan, recruited to Al-Shabaab in June 2006, who claimed to have been enrolled in a training course in a former police station turned training camp called Fish Trafico.[55] She indicates a common training pattern. In several camps, new recruits were divided into small groups, and each had to complete a six-week fitness program. A final lesson focused on rapid field shooting while on the move. There is no mention of indoctrination. This does not however mean that ideological arguments were lacking when the recruits were initially approached by Al-Shabaab. One of Ryu's interviews, for example, mentions how restoring the self-dignity of Somalis, and Somali nationalism, had been used as arguments by recruiters. In the same interview it is the stressed how charisma and the stature of Aden Hashi Ayro were themselves important for those joining. Some recruits might have been sent to Eritrea for further training, illustrating the odd alliances in the Horn: Eritrea's secular regime, itself targeted by militant jihadists, employing Al-Shabaab to hurt its enemy Ethiopia.[56]

Al-Shabaab did not escape the clan realities of Somalia, but it was exceptionally good at transcending them. Take, for example, the instance in which leader Abu Utaiba collected arms from his fellow Murosade clan member and warlord Muhamed Qanyare Afra early in 2006, partly because it was expected that the arms should stay in the clan, and then distributed them widely within Al-Shabaab. However, this ability to transcend clan was challenged by youths recruited by the organization who were uninfluenced by the experiences of Afghanistan, but rather by clan wars of the early and mid-1990s, and used to the social safety net provided through clan ties.

Al-Shabaab's radical traits might have contributed to the undoing of the Courts. By December 2006 several court leaders were disagreeing in public. While some, like the present-day TFG President Sheik Sharif, were ruling out an attack against the TFG in Baidoa, Al-Shabaab's deputy head of security, Sheikh Muktar Robbow 'Abu Mansour', together with other court leaders, gave the Ethiopians a week's deadline to leave Somalia or face forcible expulsion on 12 December 2006.[57] The military escalation continued on the ground, and it seems as if a local Al-Shabaab commander took the matters into his own hands on 19 December near Baidoa, and initiated clashes that led to outright war, this while the Sharia Court leadership, including several of Al-Shabaab, was outside the country. It was the Islamic Courts frontline near the town of Bandiiradley in the Mudug province, at the courts northern flank, that fell first, and there where no mobile reserves to spare for that part of the front. This resulted in a *blitzkrieg*, in which the most inexperienced court fighters were badly mauled by the more professional Ethiopian forces. Fighting against an enemy with armor and air superiority, the Sharia Courts and Al-Shabaab forces quickly collapsed. On 28 December, Ethiopian and government forces marched into parts of Mogadishu unopposed. The fact that many of the Sharia Court leaders were outside the country while Al-Shabaab was fighting would create a split between Al-Shabaab and the rest of the Courts side.

The remnants of the Sharia Court forces, including Al-Shabaab fighters, left the city and moved south towards Kismayo. After a stand at the Battle of Jilib, the ICU abandoned the city of Kismayo on 1 January 2007 and dispersed into Kenya, or into hiding inside Somalia. Simultaneously the United States launched air strikes on Al-Shabaab as well as earlier Al-Qaeda members. Al-Shabaab suffered several losses in the following month. The supposed political leader Abdullahi Sudi Arale was arrested by the Djibouti authorities on the way to Eritrea, transferred to the Americans, and detained in Guantánamo Bay.[58] Sheikh Abdullahi Mo'alim Ali 'Abu Utayba' was also killed early in 2007. On 8 January Ayro was attacked by an American air strike that badly wounded him in the arm and killed some of his most trusted bodyguards, including a team that was armed with shoulder-fired SAMs. The Al-Shabaab command and control network died. Hundreds of new fighters returned to their homes, or lay dead on the battlefield of Somalia. Morale had suffered a heavy blow. However, over the next years, Al-Shabaab would recover and sever its last ties to the Sharia Court movement. It became active on the internet, delivering highly sophisticated propaganda, and regained control over large parts of southern Somalia, the largest area controlled by any of Al-Qaeda's nominal allies.

5

PHOENIX FROM THE ASHES

INSURGENCY (2007–08)

In early 2007 it seemed that Harakat Al-Shabaab was broken as an organization. Several of its most experienced leaders had been killed, its forces had been defeated in the field and large Ethiopian forces were in control over central Somalia. Moreover, elite members of the Sharia Courts were angry at the Al-Shabaab group, blaming it for giving the Ethiopians a pretext to enter Somalia, while members of Al-Shabaab were angry at the Courts leaders for being out of the country when the main fighting occurred.[1] However, Al-Shabaab was to rise from the ashes, and become stronger than ever. As suggested in a book allegedly written by Omar Hammami, Al-Shabaab was to reconfigure itself, to crystallize, and its membership became clearer. A border between Shabaab and non-Shabaab within the old Courts movement was to appear, and acceptance of clanist Islamists, such as Hassan Dahiir Aweys and Aden Madobe, was to decrease.[2]

Ironically, the rise of Al-Shabaab was aided by the policy mistakes of the international community. Perhaps the best known factor was the Ethiopian occupation, which created a fertile environment for recruitment amongst some clans, though those supporting the government in general continued to view the intervention positively. A factor often overlooked is the role of Ethiopian military doctrine. The Ethiopian tendency, following old Soviet strategy, to use heavy artillery in urban warfare created widespread animosity and large-scale civilian deaths. Al-Shabaab was seen by many as one of the few actors to avenge these actions.

Security reform programmes implemented by the international community were badly planned, and failed to ensure that newly trained police of the Transitional Federal Government (TFG) were paid. The TFG police became highly predatory when taking over areas cleared of insurgents, and this enabled the opposition to highlight the contrast with the peaceful and safe period of Sharia Court rule. Al-Shabaab was to focus heavily on justice provision when taking control of areas at the end of the period (late 2008), and such areas were, quite rightly, seen as peaceful oases compared with the TFG-controlled areas, despite Al-Shabaab's harsh moves against religious minorities. The lack of pay for police also enabled Al-Shabaab's, and other opposition groups, to bribe their way out of dangerous situations.[3]

However, it is simplistic to claim that outside circumstances alone were at the root of Al-Shabaab's success. It was also, for a Somali setting, a relatively efficient organization. Its operations were aided by a higher degree of unity that its rivals, the ability to transcend clan if necessary, and relatively sound battle tactics. Al-Shabaab avoided the bloodshed of the April 2007 battles of Mogadishu, but its suicide attacks and active media profile ensured that it became famous, and seen as 'fashionable'. The period 2007–08 in many ways saw Al-Shabaab go from being a marginal network to having the largest territorial control of any Al-Qaeda-affiliated organization in the world. Al-Shabaab was to gain independence from the courts, gained territorial control, and launched a highly sophisticated internet campaign.

At the start of 2007, however, the situation looked very grim for Al-Shabaab's followers. The forces of the Islamic Union had failed to defend Mogadishu. The Sharia Court forces, including the remaining Al-Shabaab militia, were fleeing towards Kismayo. In Kismayo the Sharia Courts again failed to put up a fight, and on 1 January 2007 they withdrew from there too. At the battle of Jilib the remains of the Sharia Court forces even failed to delay the Ethiopians and their allies of the TFG. There was a last stand in the traditional Islamist base areas of Ras Kamboni, close to the Kenyan border. There Al-Shabaab was bombed by Americans, allegedly to hit the local Al-Qaeda leadership.[4]

Top leaders of the Sharia Courts, such as the current president Sheikh Sheriff Sheik Ahmed and Abokor Omar Adane, surrendered to Kenya.

The Al-Shabaab leaders did not dare to do the same, probably aware of American rendition arrangements with Kenya. Al-Shabaab leaders attempted to keep the Court forces together. On 26 January 2007 the webpage halgan.net reported that Muktar Robow delivered a speech urging Somalis to support 'the Mujahidin of the Islamic Courts and defend the country'.[5] However, these moves were largely in vain; the forces of the Sharia Courts collapsed.

Mogadishu itself was calm in January 2007, so calm that some Western foreign services thought the situation was under control. The Norwegian Ministry of Foreign Affairs even told journalists that the city was safer than surrounding African capitals.[6] This was partly a result of the care taken by the Ethiopians. They approached the city of Mogadishu hesitantly, perhaps confused by their quick victories, and first stayed on the outskirts of the city, then moved into areas inhabited by clans that were defined as more friendly towards them. The Ethiopians and the TFG moved slowly into the most strategic areas of Mogadishu, by January occupying only the new harbor, the airport, the Ministry of Defense, the prison service headquarters, and Somalia's former presidential palace (Villa Somalia). However, the strategic roads into Mogadishu were controlled to the south and to the west by two Ethiopian bases.

The West was cautiously positive about the Ethiopian intervention/ invasion, seeing the Ethiopians as a new hegemon that could establish order in southern Somalia and enable the TFG to build durable institutions and rebuild its army in relative peace. By early march the TFG was also strengthened effectively by the arrival of 1,500 Ugandan African Union troops, organized in two battalions with a force headquarters. Although these forces were tasked with reconciliation, their mandate was 'Supporting the TFIs in their effort of stabilizing the country and the furtherance of dialogue and reconciliation' and to 'provide, as appropriate, protection to TFIs and their key infrastructure to enable them to carry out their functions' and 'Assist in implementing NSSP, particularly the re-establishment and training of Somali security forces'.[7] The African Union in Somalia (AMISOM) guarded the presidential palace, the new port and the airport—strategically very important locations for the TFG, enabling TFG militias to be used for other purposes. It was thus *de facto* a party in the conflict.

In the end the Ethiopians advanced into the unoccupied parts of Mogadishu. From 21 March onwards Ethiopia deployed an armored battalion from Debere Zeit. Ethiopian forces now numbered around 5,000 men. Three artillery batteries were also moved in. The TFG strengthened its forces with 1,000 men recruited from the Abgal and Saad clans, the TFG's traditional supporters in Mogadishu, under the promise of rewards in the form of positions. The new mayor of Mogadishu, the former Abgal warlord Muhamed Dheere, mobilized 500 men. These forces were used to establish bases deeper in parts of Mogadishu, advancing on Murosade clan areas, amongst other targets, as well as on Mogadishu stadium, where hostile clans dominated; these clans mobilized, and future patterns were established. In present-day Somalia the Murosade are frequently pro-Al-Shabaab, while the Abgal remained anti-Al-Shabaab until 2010.

The Ethiopians managed to establish a base at the Olympia stadium, as well as in an old police station, and attempted to collect weapons in the Shricola area. They were heavily attacked by perhaps 5,000 insurgent soldiers, drawn mainly from the Suleiman, Ayr and Murosade clans. There was a break in the fighting from 2 April to 17 April, when elders attempted to negotiate a truce, and the Ethiopians reinforced their troops, including another armored battalion. The next phase started when the new bases of the Ethiopians and the government were attacked by insurgents, now joined by Abokour Umar Adane's business militia (from the Warsangeli sub-clan of the Abgal), but the attacks were defeated. The Ethiopians used heavy artillery which caused large civilian casualties. The former warlord Muhamed Dheere then moved against the rebel stronghold of Hurriwa, supported by Ethiopian tanks, and the back of the rebel clans' resistance was broken.

What did the Al-Shabaab fighters do during these events? First, it was hard to tell what Al-Shabaab wanted, and who its members were; secondly, those members were geographically fragmented. Some Al-Shabaab activists remained in Mogadishu, but the only place they could come out in the open was the old jihadist territory of the Ras Kamboni area. If one believes the book claiming to be Omar Hammami's story, even the few training camps close to Ras Kamboni were of poor quality, hampered by lack of funds and poor instructors.[8] The quality of the camp where Omar Hammami was positioned improved when the veteran jihadist Cabdallaah Toosan took command, and allowed the students to take more responsibility. Some of the students and instructors stressed the importance of purity for the jihadists, indirectly criticizing the Sharia Courts for their lack thereof. They also emphasized the need to avoid alliances with groups adopting Western ideas.[9] The exact demarcation between those who were and those who were not with Al-Shabaab was blurred.

There were remnants of Al-Shabaab in Mogadishu, but they did not do much. Some early Al-Shabaab attacks on the Ethiopians first seem to have been quite random, as old fighters attacked on their own, for example throwing hand grenades at TFG or Ethiopian soldiers. However, a leadership structure emerged. The very loose Al-Shabaab leadership in Mogadishu was in this early phase led by Mahad 'Karate' of the Ayr clan. He was responsible for keeping contact with the middle-level commanders who were in turn responsible for keeping in touch with the low-level commanders, who would call in the most loyal fighters. Al-Shabaab stayed out of the large battles and resisted any calls to coordinate with the other Sharia Court forces. Slowly but steadily Al-Shabaab built up strength, stockpiled weapons, developed its organization. It seemed as if many of these efforts were started around the new Salaax-udiin camp in southern Somalia where veterans Afghani, Godane and 'Shongole' were reorganizing the group, which Omar Hammami contrasted with the Hassan Turki-dominated Ras Kamboni camp of Al-Shabaab.[10] The modern Al-Shabaab discarded Turki, and went with Godane and Afghani.

The organization was not entirely passive tactically. A notable effort was put into intelligence gathering, at times using allies like the Katiibatu Ansaru Tawheed Wal Jihad (KATJ), a loose insurgency movement based on the remnants of a single court.[11] Al-Shabaab also systematically attacked the softer spots of the government by killing civil servants, businessmen trading with their enemies and even civil society activists who publicly opposed them. Members of the Somali National Security, the intelligence service of the Ethiopian-backed TFG, were hunted down and killed in their homes, on their way to work, in mosques, and in every possible place.[12] Some of the assassinations were highly strategic, and motivated by advanced tactical considerations. In the Shibis and Yakshid neighborhood, civil servants were specially targeted, in order to weaken the support for the transitional government in these front line areas and the mobilization of vigilante groups, called 'Madanis', against the insurgents. In Yakshiid four heads of the district were killed consecutively, the last, Suudi Ibrahim Gacmoole, on 9 September 2007. In Shibis, Abdullahi Haji Mohamed became the second district leader that was killed, on 27 February 2008. Some killings seemed to have been highly controversial, such as the killing of Cadbuqaadir Sheikh Maxamed (Aayatulaah), as well as his assistant and two of his guards. Famous for criticizing Al-Shabaab's Sharia implementation, he was tricked into an ambush after an invitation to a meeting.[13] Al-Shabaab did not directly assume responsibility for smaller killings, but it did in cases deemed more important, as for example the beheading of Abdullahi Jahwareer, a military leader, in August 2008; video images of this act were circulated widely.[14]

From the summer of 2007 to the end of 2008, death threats were a common strategy. To participate in peace conferences, or to sell goods to Ethiopians, became dangerous. Moreover, Al-Shabaab could target the wrong people because of mistaken identity.[15] Human Rights watch interviewed a witness to such threats:

'I was not working for the government,' (he explained) 'But I used to go and do manual jobs just to get a wage—usually messenger services work for them, from one office to the other.' In January 2008 a group of men arrived at his home. They identified themselves as members of Al-Shabaab and not finding him present warned his wife that he should find another way to make a living. 'They said, "If your husband does not stop supporting the government, we are going to kill him,"' she recalled.[16]

A climate of fear was created. Many started collaborating with all groups in the insurgency in fear of retaliation. They brought information about government plans, military movements, and other members of the government security services that were not loyal to the insurgency.[17]

In the face of regular combat, Al-Shabaab would withdraw. It concentrated on small hit-and-run and suicide attacks, which gained them considerable attention. Their first known attack after 2006 was the suicide attack against an Ethiopian check-point in Darmole, and a military base in Afgoye was attacked by suicide bombers. For the first time in Somalia's history a Somali organization put a suicide video on the internet, and on global jihadist pages. In fact, Al-Shabaab launched a wave of suicide attacks during the March-April 2007 battles. On 20 and 25 April suicide bombers, Abdul-Aziz Dawood Abdul-Qader and a Kenyan, Othman Otibu, attacked Ethiopian/TFG installations. On 17 May an attack was carried out on Prime Minister Gedi, on 20 May Mohamed Dheere was attacked, but these were not suicide operations.

Al-Shabaab was a relatively marginal insurgent group, but showed a unique *modus operandi*, using suicide bombings, remote control devices and assassinations. It used fear actively. This was not a guerrilla campaign, there were few attempts to actually destroy military bases. Its tactics gained Al-Shabaab notable attention, and also sheltered it from the large-scale losses that Ethiopia inflicted on other insurgent groups, since Al-Shabaab seldom fought open battles. When the dust settled after the April-March fighting, the clan insurgency groups were crushed and the Sharia Court forces weakened, but Al-Shabaab's forces had become stronger.

In this process Al-Qaeda's East African cell played a key role. It (or rather its remnants), was actively behind the training of the few remaining Al-Shabaab fighters. It was Al-Qaeda individuals such as Nabahn who drove the development of tactics. In the wake of the insurgents' defeats in May, Al-Shabaab also spread its activities. Among others, it established a unit within Ethiopia, the Faruq Unit, which blew up a church in Ethiopia on 6 August 2007, as well as taking responsibility for several attacks in Hiraan. By August 2007, the frequency of Al-Shabaab attacks was increasing, and the organization was responsible for 60 per cent of attacks in Mogadishu at the time.

The institutional development of the TFG that was supposed to happen under Ethiopian protection failed to emerge. The UNDP, supported by Norway and the United States, trained the police, but failed to ensure its payment, over and over again. In fact the desertion rate of the unpaid police and soldiers of the TFG was growing above 100%: the number of defections was actually larger than the total amount of policemen scheduled to be in the police force. A majority of the policemen just stayed some months in the force before they defected. Donors and supporters failed to understand the seriousness of the situation before it was too late. The remaining TFG police systematically stole and pillaged to keep themselves alive, and fought other police units over the meager funds allocated to them. In the TFG army, the situation was very similar; Ethiopia equipped and trained soldiers, but failed to ensure that they received pay when they returned to the battlefront. The failure of the military reforms within the TFG became very embarrassing when the TFG lost Kismayo port without an enemy even being seen. The TFG's first brigade was supposed to be a showcase of the new multi-clan Somali army, consisting of troops from the Rahanwein, Marehan and Majerteen clans. The unit, supposed to be a flagship of the TFG, had more or less broken down by itself during the late spring of 2007, as the Majerteen commander, Colonel Abdirisak Afguduud, misused his power. In the end the Majerteens in the unit were defeated by the Marehan clan militias who served alongside them, while the Rahanwhein clan militias in the unit returned to the Rahanwhein areas, refusing to participate in what they defined, probably correctly, as clan wars. Kismayo was lost for the TFG without a single insurgent attack. Later the TFG's third brigade collapsed the same way. The TFG failed to develop credible security forces, growing more and more dependent on the Ethiopians.

Al-Shabaab commanders regrouped. After the defeat of the other insurgent forces in April 2007, Abu Mansur returned to southern Somalia. He regrouped Al-Shabaab in Bulo Marer, where he was given a safe haven by militiamen who were supposed to be TFG soldiers but were in reality insurgent supporters.[18] Bulo Marer was developed into a form of base, and was used to assemble forces that were supposed to attack Balli Dogle Airport, and to raid as far away as Beled Weyne. The raids developed into full blown attacks, and other parts of the Sharia Courts launched similar offensives. In the end Beled Weyne fell to the insurgents. The event was a sign of things to come, as Al-Shabaab ended up being influenced by clan considerations; it took over the areas of Beled Weyne dominated by the Galjale clan, which was to become a common recruiting pool for Al-Shabaab. Nevertheless, the operation was a great success, and the first territorial conquest by Al-Shabaab after the defeat in late 2006. The organization seemed to have regrouped but still seemed to be a part of a wider Sharia Court alliance.

Leaving the Sharia Courts

In parallel to this there were attempts to create peace in Mogadishu, through a clan gathering led by the former United Somali Congress leader Ali Madhi in August 2007. The clan conference failed to attract the opposition clans. The Ayr sent one of its junior representatives, rather than its highest elders, and, a sign for the future, the Douduble clan was absent from the conference. Nor did the top traditional leader of the Murosade clan, Ugas Abdulqadir Ugas Fara Adde, attend. While this was probably because he had to handle a local conflict, it left the government without means to establish deeper contact with a clan that provided many recruits to Al-Shabaab. Similarly, a dialogue with the Ayr and Douduble clans would have been important, since they were ready sources for insurgent fighters.

The opposition to the Ethiopians also attempted to organize. From 6 to 14 September a large conference was arranged in Eritrea, hosted by the Eritreans in order to take advantage of what the Eritreans saw as a second front in their cold war against Ethiopia. Ethiopia had grown into their major enemy after it defeated them in the 1998–2000 conflict between the two countries. The meeting resulted in the foundation of the so-called Alliance for the Re-liberation of Somalia (ARS), led by the former Sharia Court leader Sheik Sharif Sheik Hassan, with the warlord Hussein Aideed as secondary leader. The old secretary of the Sharia Courts, Abdirahman Janakow, became the leader of the ARS. Yusuf 'Indha Ade' Mohamed Siad, Al-Shabaab's major rival during the Sharia Court days, became head of defense. Many diaspora organizations participated.[19]

The conference was the end of Al-Shabaab's flirtation with the Courts. Ideologically, the Courts' decisions to ally with former warlords, and moves towards cooperating with secular forces, were too much for the hard-core top leadership. In several public announcements Al-Shabaab distanced itself from the meeting 'in secular Eritrea' hosted and supported by a nation (Eritrea) that prosecuted jihadists. Al-Shabaab also insisted that the mixed trans-religious marriages of several representatives—Muslim women married with atheists and Christians—were against the Koran, and that the right form of fighting was not resistance but jihad, since true Muslims could not fight for a country, only for the *ummah* itself. This was one of the clearest messages Al-Shabaab ever launched against Somali nationalism, a message repeated by most of their leaders at the time.[20] Foreign fighters, such as Omar Hammami, must have felt that the re-emerged Al-Shabaab was more welcoming of them. With Al-Shabaab distancing itself from patriotic symbols, the conflict in Somalia became a war between 'Muslims' and 'apostates', not between Somalis and Ethiopians; according to Omar Hammami's book, this provided an option and a motivation for some of the foreign fighters to stay as allies of Al-Shabaab, contributing to an internal dynamic in the organization that made it different from other insurgent organizations inside Somalia.[21]

Al-Shabaab had by now reorganized itself, and started to conduct heavier attacks. By October 2007, it was launching 44 per cent of all the attacks on the government; by November this had increased to 55 per cent. And it now became a force of its own in pure insurgency attacks.[22] By October the organization had attacked three police stations, something quite new for it. The frequency of small-scale attacks actually declined as Al-Shabaab started to fight the TFG and Ethiopia in the open. Their ranks were swelling again, fed by refugees from the fighting in Mogadishu. The Ethiopians' indiscriminate use of heavy artillery, and general clan grievances, contributed to the increase.

Al-Shabaab was thoroughly organized, consisting of squadrons of seven to eight men.[23] Its militias were paid, US$20 for a hand grenade attack, US$30 for killing a soldier, US$100 for a road bomb or a mortar attack—this in a period when the TFG's police and army failed to get any pay at all. The Eritreans also provided support, despite being aware of a considerable anti-Eritrean stance within Al-Shabaab. At this stage the organization managed to attract support from the diaspora, which in general still saw it as a part of the wider rebel alliance. In Nairobi's Somali-dominated Eastleigh district, fundraising events were organized in the Sixth Street Mosque by Sheikh Mahamed Umul, who was far from the Al-Shabaab leaders in ideology, focusing on the advantages of Al-Shabaab-supported implementation of the Sharia rather than some form of global vision. Al-Shabaab also organized an impressive evacuation route for its wounded fighters, enabling escape into Djibouti or Kenya, using bribes and border crossings with little governmental presence.

The situation in Mogadishu was a stalemate, not only between the insurgents and the government, but also between Al-Shabaab and the other insurgents. However, Al-Shabaab was to show its skills in playing the clan game. By the autumn of 2007, the eight-man Al-Shabaab *shura* council, then its highest body, decided to send Muktar Robow, hailing from the Leysane sub-clan of the Rahanwhein, back to his clan areas to establish a new front against the TFG and Ethiopia. Until now, the Rahanwhein had been seen as amongst the most stable allies of Ethiopia in Somalia, so this was a bold move. Robow hailed from Abane, deep inside the Rahanwhein areas, and he was a brother of the TFG's Colonel Robow. By November 2007 he moved 'home.' The TFG President Yusuf could probably do little to stop this, since although Abane was in theory controlled by the TFG, the real power was with Robow's sub-clan, the Leysane. The Leysane sub-clan, including the former warlord Hapsade, offered protection to its members; there was still sympathy for the TFG, but clan loyalties trumped other political loyalties. Stories even tell how Robow entered the capital of the TFG, Baidoa, without any reaction.[24] Although these stories may be false, they indicate how Al-

Shabaab played the clan card, and could find shelter amongst clans if it needed to. The new front survived and thrived, a wedge had been driven into the supposed capital area of the TFG. By 27 December 2007, Al-Shabaab-affiliated sites started to announce that Ahmed Abdi Godane 'Abu Zubeyr' had become Al-Shabaab's new leader, and simultaneously it became clear that Muktar Robow was functioning as a press spokesman for the whole organization.[25]

Al-Shabaab developed several techniques in this phase of its struggles. One technique was the so called *koormeer*, in which forces would attack outlying TFG posts, or non-occupied cities, and hold them a couple of days and then withdraw. These attacks were advertised in the media and often included formal speeches, attempts to make peace between clans, and short periods in which Al-Shabaab militias and *qadi*s arrested and sentenced criminals. The latter action was often highly popular, as the TFG police often did the opposite, committing crimes to sustain themselves.[26] As the International Crisis Group (ICG) said at the time, one of the boldest takeovers was that of Jowhar, the capital of middle shabelle, on 26 April 2008. Government troops and officials first fled the city in front of advancing al-Shabaab forces. The town was held for two days, and then abandoned. The insurgents held the town for two days, and then abandoned it. By spring-summer 2008, such attacks were getting more and more common.[27]

There were setbacks. The killing of the Afghanistan veteran Aden Hashi Ayro in the central town of Dhuusa Mareb on 1 May 2008 by a US missile was a disaster that damaged Al-Shabaab in central Somalia, as he was popular with his own sub-clan, the Ayr Absiye. It also removed one of the organization's most extreme ideologues. However, by that time he was not Al-Shabaab's leader and could easily be replaced.

Going global?

By the autumn of 2007, the organization also took its war online. The break with the courts was mainly conducted on the internet. Articles by Omar Hammami, in which he distanced Al-Shabaab from the Courts, were circulated through the Al-Qaeda affiliated Global Islamic Media Front, while the speeches of Fuad Shongola and Godane on the subject were distributed through Youtube, as well as Al-Shabaab's own web pages. The internet, and sites as Hegan and Kataaib, enabled the group to speak more directly to potential jihadists or sympathizers all over the world, and to the Somali diaspora.

Why did Al-Shabaab develop its internet capacities? Two structural factors might explain this. First, it was an insurgent organization in the period 2007–08; it did not control any traditional media outlets, because it did not control any territory, and so the internet was a good alternative for disseminating propaganda. The fact that Al-Shabaab was now independent from the Sharia Courts alliance meant that its old guard could allow its more international jihadist leanings to emerge in public, as the need to compromise with other factions within the Courts became less prominent. An important factor was that Al-Shabaab was still small, making it easier to maintain ideological unity. Al-Shabaab's internet communication targeted three audiences. It spoke to potential international followers, using pan-Islamic symbols, depicting the struggle in Somalia as a part of a wider 'Clash of Civilizations'. In contact with the Somali diaspora Al-Shabaab stressed the theme of Crusader/apostate occupation, in general referring to Ethiopian forces in Somalia. Al-Shabaab's propaganda effort was indirectly supported by Al-Qaeda and the Global Islamic Media Front, the latter providing comments on events in Somalia, encouraging volunteers to go there and potential financial supporters to provide funds.

By April 2007 battle reports from Al-Shabaab were distributed to jihadist forums across the world. The messages themselves were short, summing up Al-Shabaab's small hit-and-run and suicide attacks, depicted in language unfamiliar to Somalis: the language of global jihad. Slowly Al-Shabaab also started to host its own web-pages, and its allies/sympathizers hosted others. The first of the new homepages was http://www.Hegaan.net, opened during the winter/spring of 2007 by a Norwegian Somali, but it changed its contents over the summer of 2007, adopting a more global focus. The webpage then offered biographies of 'martyred' Al-Shabaab leaders, pictures of soldiers, and news updates on operations in English, Somali and Arabic. Also uploaded was a video depicting desecration of dead Ethiopian soldiers. The stories of the 'martyrs' celebrated death in a way unknown in Somali culture, but in a language very familiar in Al-Qaeda videos. Death worship was best illustrated by Abu Mansoor's words:

Our brother Ma'alin and our brother Umar Dheere alias Abu Jabal. Many of those who were present during the formation of the group have also been martyred. Those who are still alive are also looking forward to death, in order to die for the same cause that others before them died for. Shabaab ideology, much more refined than its Somali predecessors, also provided stronger justifications for suicide attacks.[28]

Before August 2007, the page still directed itself towards Somalis, and was written in Somali. However, the content of the page changed, and by August 2007 the symbolic content had turned towards international jihad, with depictions of Osama bin Laden, and Arabic was used. In the end Hegaan served as a mirror for the Almujaahid.com website, which contained animated images of Osama Bin Laden, Dr Ayman al-Zawahiri, Abu Musab al-Zarqawi, and various Somali suicide bombers. This site again became a mirror of the infamous Kataaib (http://www.kataaib.info/ www.kataaib.net) set up from the town of Marka Caday in south-western Somalia on 13 April 2007 but hosted in Vancouver in Canada.

Kataaib put the struggle in Somalia in a larger context, containing the speeches and works of Abdullah Azzam, Osama bin Laden and Ayman al-Zawahiri. However, Kataaib also celebrated an older generation of Somali jihadists that had fought against the Americans in Somalia in 1993–94. It still contained the stories of Al-Shabaab martyrs, and the speeches of various leaders, mostly Godane and Shongola. The site also offered the Somali-language *mujahedeen* newsletter *Nashrada al-Jihad*, and even the possibility to submit questions directly to Godane.[29]

The use of symbols struck a chord with the audience, both Somalis and non-Somali jihadist sympathizers, and several other sites emerged, probably unaffiliated with Al-Shabaab, but bringing news from them. Ultimately, Al-Shabaab had to distance itself from these, and declared Kataaib its public site. Al-Shabaab also distributed information through other channels on the internet, often organized by the Al-Qaeda-affiliated Global Islamic Media Front.[30] The spokesperson Abu Mansoor also became 'interactive' on the internet, even appearing on the chat service PalTalk.

It is hard to evaluate the effect of these sites. They were clearly aligned with other Al-Qaeda-affiliated web pages, and drew attention towards Somalia. However, contrary to popular belief, Al-Shabaab had been relatively successful in attracting foreign fighters before launching these sites. It also seems as if other webpages and speeches influenced the recruitment. Some foreign fighters indicated that they had been motivated by Anwar al-Awlaki's speeches, and those of the Al-Qaeda leadership could also have contributed. Notably, some of the few remaining original Al-Qaeda in East Africa members, especially Nabhan, were also engaged in online recruitment. Nabhan even swore allegiance to Osama bin Laden in July 2008: 'My greetings to the courageous commander and my honorable leader: Sheikh Osama bin Laden (may Allah protect him and his followers).'[31] This created some commotion in the press as it was read as an Al-Shabaab pledge of loyalty to Al-Qaeda, but the event has to be seen as a declaration of loyalty from a veteran Al-Qaeda operative to the central leadership of Al-Qaeda. The distribution of the film of the event was perhaps more interesting. It was carried by four Al-Qaeda-affiliated web-pages, Ekhlaas, Al Boraq, Al Hesbah and Al Firdaws. Al-Shabaab messages were by now widely distributed through the internet, and read by an online jihadist community. Images from Somalia now reached a global jihadist audience.

Al-Shabaab also received more attention from international jihadists. For example, a video issued by the senior Al-Qaeda leader Abu Yahya al-Libi, later to be definitively an Al-Shabaab favorite, in April 2007 carried a specific address to 'the *mujahedeen* in Somalia.' Al-Libi (later killed in 2012) in fact became a common name on Al-Shabaab-affiliated web-pages, and he was praised publicly by Al-Shabaab leaders.

What kind of purpose did online activity serve? These outlets, and Al-Qaeda-affiliated ones also, were vital in enabling Al-Shabaab to distinguish itself from the Sharia Courts. This process started with Shongola's speech in October 2007, targeting a Somali audience, claiming that the Sharia Courts were an infidel movement. It continued with general statements targeting both an Arabic speaking and English speaking audience, for example statements written by Omar Hammami (Abu Mansoor Al-Amriki). The flirtation with Al-Qaeda also drew local Somali support, making Al-Shabaab seem more important through its international ally, and showing it to be indirectly engaged, through its alliance with Al-Qaeda, in the struggles in Iraq, Afghanistan and Palestine, including the symbolically important Jerusalem. These places and conflicts arouse strong feelings of solidarity amongst many Somalis. The global aspect of Al-Shabaab's internet efforts were stronger than many believed, as expressed by the often explicit anti-nationalist rhetoric.

Al-Shabaab's online presence from the summer of 2007 onwards took a surprisingly anti-nationalist stance, for an organization commonly seen by southern Somalis as fighting an Ethiopian invader. Abu Ayoub declared, 'O my people, know that I am doing this martyrdom operation only for the sake of Allah and his religion… not… for nationalism, tribe, and money.'[32] Muktar Robow, later claimed rather ironically to be Al-Shabaab's chief nationalist, clearly attacked nationalism directly, stating that 'a nationalistic, patriotic bond is against the (Muslim) brotherhood bond', as well as criticizing other Somali Islamists for replacing the jihad with 'patriotic resistance'.[33] Symbolically, Al-Shabaab even refused to use the Somali flag, removing the flag from areas under their occupation. In this sense Al-Shabaab, or at least most its leaders, depicted themselves as fighting a global war, a front in a wider civilizational struggle.

Since four of the eight leaders in the *shura* council in 2007 had a background in Afghanistan, such a focus seemed natural. The leadership's rhetoric was nevertheless surprisingly anti-nationalist. It tapped into a perception of a general threat to the *ummah*, and not only to Somalia. The suicide videos from the summer of 2007 and onwards, for example frequently commented on world affairs, such as the cartoons in Denmark, and showed pictures from Iraq.[34] Ideologically, Al-Shabaab leaders often declared the need to resurrect the pan-Islamic Caliphate, putting their local conflict in a global framework of good versus evil. In this sense, the enemy was not only Ethiopia but also the West. In many ways, their rhetoric strongly echoed Al-Qaeda's focus on the global *ummah*. Several doctrinal documents were distributed. Publicity given to Muktar Robow Abu Mansoor by the Global Islamic Media Front was an interesting case as he was allowed to present some kind of ideology, claiming that:

Concerning goals, we attempt to revive the spirit of jihad among Muslims, unite their ranks in adherence to the truth, and implement the Shari'ah rulings on the people. The jihad in Somalia is therefore, completely the same as the global jihad in everything. However the jihad in Somalia lacks immigrant Mujahidin, as there are not enough numbers of non-Somali brothers. We are in need for Somalia's Zarqawi, Khattab, and Abu-al-Layth. O heroes, how long should we wait.[35]

In one sense Al-Shabaab's global rhetoric was a paradox. Its local recruitment was not based on global ideas; it recruited from youth hostile to the Ethiopian intervention and with a nationalist/clanist motivation for joining the organization. Some clans such as the Murosade became very friendly to Al-Shabaab as they were exposed to Ethiopian human rights violations, and to what were fundamentally commercial disagreements.

Could the global rhetoric have been a strategy to get foreign support? In the autumn of 2008, Al-Shabaab issued videos showing foreign fighters giving speeches in Arabic, English, Somali, and Urdu, asking Muslims around the world to join them in their jihad.[36] The symbolism in the videos also drew on a global jihadist narrative, the 'Ambush at Bardal' video, for example, including a section entitled 'Join the Caravan', reassembling Abdullah Azzam's seminal work.[37] It should be remembered that pan-Islamism comes in different versions, of which one version accepts religion as an identity marker. The exact border between pan-Islamism and a form of local patriotism easily becomes blurred, and this confusion, combined with a lack of knowledge of the organization, probably helped Al-Shabaab to gain local acceptance, as did its heavy emphasis on bringing justice to Somalia, to prevent crime.

The influence of non-Somali ideological elements could clearly be seen in frequent Al-Shabaab suicide bombings. It was the first Somali actor to employ this strategy, overcoming Somali cultural inhibitions about suicide attacks. Those attacks served Al-Shabaab well in that they gained it attention at low cost. At the start they were also militarily effective: suicide attacks targeted Ethiopian bases and led to a large number of casualties.[38] A study of the attack pattern in 2007 and 2008 suggests that suicide attacks were a tool used by Al-Shabaab to gain attention, especially at critical times. An Al-Shabaab defeat often led the organization to launch such attacks: 'Even the release of suicide videos tended to be timed with political events, showing Shabaab strength and commitment in public during critical periods.'[39] It was also used for VIP assassinations. As quoted from one of my previous articles on the subject:

During the summer of 2008, the TFG started negotiating with a powerful and popular faction (as it was then perceived) of the opposition in Djibouti. At first these negotiations were cumbersome and few believed that they could succeed, but by the autumn of 2008 the talks produced tangible results. On 26 October 2008, the two parties in the Djibouti process—the Alliance for the Re-liberation of Somalia, Djibouti group (ARS-D) and the TFG—announced a ceasefire. At the time, the agreement was popular within Somalia and was supported by the United States as well as by several of the veteran Islamists within the old SCIC.

The mood amongst diplomats in Nairobi was frantically positive. As the focus shifted onto the Djibouti process, the insurgents lost media attention and were threatened politically and militarily. Even worse, increased military deployments from the African Union and United Nations forces were seriously discussed. The insurgents' response was swift: they attacked the city of Merka. Almost simultaneously, a suicide video of Abdulaziz Bashar Abdullahi's attack against the African Union forces in April 2008 was released. Then Somalia's largest and most well coordinated wave of suicide attacks began on 29 October 2008.

The wave of attacks succeeded in shifting attention away from the diplomatic triumphs of the new negotiation process and back to the insurgency, and contributed to the deterrence of the potential UN and AU peacekeeping contingents for Somalia which was discussed within the United Nations and the African Union. However, the Djibouti peace process was not derailed by the 29 October attacks.[40]

For Al-Shabaab, suicide attacks were a way to gain attention, to maintain its reputation when facing defeats, both militarily and diplomatically. However, they were also inspired by Al-Shabaab's ideology, quite unique in a Somali setting, justifying suicide attacks in themselves, explaining why Al-Shabaab was the only organization using such strategies.

In one sense the media efforts and suicide attacks indicated that Al-Shabaab was interconnected with the wider jihadist community.[41] The international recruitment could also indicate this. However, a major part of this recruitment brought in members of the Somali diaspora. Some of these suicide bombers gained fame through the internet, and through articles written about them in the West.

The suicide bombers tried directly to recruit followers from the diaspora in their suicide videos. Did it work? The period 2007–08 was definitively a time when Al-Shabaab attracted many fighters from the Somali diaspora. Fighters from the United States became especially famous. The first group of Somali-American men seemed to have had a connection with the Abubakar As-Saddique Islamic Center in Minneapolis, and had different backgrounds.[42]

The second group of fighters that left for Somalia were on average younger than the members of the first group. Several of them had a more successful past than the average members of the first group. With one exception, an American convert to Islam, they were mostly raised in the United States. Troy Matthew Kastigar was one of the few non-Somalis recruited in this group. Kastigar had a criminal record, but also an impressive athletic record; he played basketball in a travelling team with young Somalis and was a black belt in karate.[43]

Another Seattle resident, Omar Mohamud, died in an attack in 2009, in which two stolen UN vehicles were detonated at Mogadishu airport, killing more than a dozen peacekeepers of the African Union. Some Somalis in the US went to Somalia and returned, deciding Al-Shabaab had nothing to interest them. Salah Osman Ahmed and Abdifatha Yusuf Isse went home again in 2008, after discovering that Al-Shabaab was not what they had expected.[44]

What did these individuals have in common? It seems that most of them were what Stevan Weine, John Horgan, Cheryl Robertson, Sana Loue, Amin Mohamed and Sahra Noo referred to as the 1.5 generation.[45] The recruits had a background in refugee camps, but had been brought to the United States in their teens. The second common denominator seems to have been that they were exposed to a highly organized recruitment network. Organizers in Minnesota as well as Somalia handled the recruitment process, through a network that included the previously mentioned Jewish American 'Ahmed', 'Emir Anwar', and several fighters who previously had fought in Somalia and returned to United States. Sympathizers who previously had raised funds for Al-Shabaab also played a role. Thirdly, nationalism seemed to have played a role, as Somalia was seen to have been suffering under the Ethiopian occupation. However this nationalism was formed and shaped by religion, that being a vital cultural identity marker for Somalis, a trait of Somaliness vs. Ethiopianness. According to the United Nation arms embargo commission a last factor that intervened, at least in the Minnesota cases, was clan; it was claimed that half of the recruits were of the Harti clan confederation.[46] However, this may not have been because of actual clan motivation; social interaction patterns are often formed by clan considerations, as clan members meet in the same places, more easily getting to know each other, often forming their own distinct perception of reality by insulating themselves from other clans.

There was also recruitment in Canada, where the 'Toronto Six Group' gained fame. Most of the six seem to have attended the Abu Haraina mosque in Toronto. The most famous of these was Muhamed Ibrahim Elmi, who ran his own blog, 'The Gardens of Paradise'. The blog offered insights into the minds of a future jihadist, commenting upon the Danish cartoons incident, Gaza, and the obligation of jihad. Following the pattern of one of the American jihadist, Mohamoud Hassan, Ibrahim Elmi also read and quoted jihadist material on the internet and listened to lectures by the Yemeni cleric Anwar al-Awlaki.

Denmark also saw its first returning migrant becoming a suicide bomber in Somalia in this period, Abdi Rahman Mohamed. He originally came to Denmark at the age of five and settled in a suburb of

Copenhagen. He became a more ardent Muslim, even condemning friends for un-Islamic practices, and in 2008 he moved to Merka, Somalia, bringing his small family with him.[47]

What drove the recruits from the Somali diaspora? It was definitively a sense of humiliation driven by Ethiopian human rights violations, but some, like Ibrahim Elmi, also put this definitively in a larger ideological framework, seeing the Somali struggle as a part of a wider 'Clash of Civilizations', between Islam and the rest. Importantly, most of them were exposed to harsh indoctrination when arriving in Somalia, indoctrination generally based on Al-Qaeda ideology, and most, perhaps under pressure, stayed even after the Ethiopians withdrew in 2009.

The turning of the tide, from guerrilla movement to territorial control

During 2009 Al-Shabaab actively created a strong image of itself. Through suicide attacks and guerrilla campaigns, it engaged TFG forces, as well as the Ethiopians, in a high-profile struggle while conserving its resources. Through the maintenance of strict unity in its ranks, it managed to keep a unified image that stood in contrast to the other factions in south central Somalia, as well as keeping clan fragmentation at bay. TFG policies, as well as the failed rule of law project managed by the UNDP, had more or less prepared the stage for Al-Shabaab by creating a highly corrupt and predatory police force despised by many Somalis.

It was nevertheless the Djibouti negotiations that were to hand large parts of southern Somalia to Al-Shabaab. However, even before those negotiations, Al-Shabaab was to take strategically important towns by a combination of well coordinated attacks and local allies. The most important victory was perhaps the seizure of Kismayo. The port city was of strategic value, as it served large parts of southern Somalia, taxes could be collected, and weapons could be imported, but proved an easy target. The Al-Shabaab attackers had local allies, in the form of the perhaps most radical clan-based Islamist organization in Somalia, Harakat Ras Kamboni, Hassan Turki's old group. This group was drawn from the Ogadeen clan, which had felt alienated and humiliated by the previously described victories of the Marehan clan fighters in Kismayo in the spring of 2007. The Marehan takeover had meant that the Ogadeen clan members were alienated from control over the city, and in many cases had to pay more taxes. Al-Shabaab thus had important clan support locally, as well as an ally with considerable clan ties.

A second factor lay in the distance between Kismayo and Mogadishu and the TFG, as well as the Ethiopians, who felt no need to help the Marehan, which had effectively ousted the TFG from the city in 2007. On 22 August 2008 joint Al-Shabaab and Ras Kamboni forces attacked, first from the south through Kismayo airport. According to the defending Marehan clan, the first attacks were made by Ras Kamboni, while the second wave was composed of Al-Shabaab troops commanded by Muktar Robow 'Abu Mansoor'. The two groups were heavily supported by militia from the Ogadeen clan, as well as by other local clans, which had felt dominated by the Marehan. In this sense, the battle was clan-dominated. The fighting, between Islamic insurgents and clan militias, started on 20 August, but developed into a stalemate, and Al-Shabaab and its Ogadeen/Harti allies suffered severe losses. However, the tide turned, and on 22 August the Marehan clan militias withdrew from Kismayo.[48]

Kismayo indicated the start of a pattern. Al-Shabaab, in alliance with the Ras Kamboni group, immediately purged ideological enemies. The first group exposed to such policies was the Sufis, widely seen by Al-Shabaab leaders as apostates because of the role of 'saints,' founders of various Sufi schools, had in their ceremonies. Sufis prayed to Allah through the 'saints', as well as worshipping around their tombs, a practice condemned by Al-Shabaab leaders. Several Sufi sheikhs were imprisoned, including senior ones—Sheik Abdullahi Buraale, Sheikh Abdi Shafat and Muhammed Sheik Fayo—and sheikhs from all clans in Kismayo (except the minority clans). Over the next months Sufi shrines were destroyed. Al-Shabaab rapidly transformed Kismayo, first demonstrating a disregard for its clan-based allies by marginalizing the representatives of the local clans, while establishing a power-sharing agreement with the Ras Kamboni group. Al-Shabaab itself appointed Sheikh Abubakr Sayli'i, *a nom de guerre* for the Al-Shabaab veteran Ibrahim Afghani, as mayor of Kismayo. The city council of seven was comprised of three Al-Shabaab members (of whom one was from Hassan Turki's group—Filu, the head of security), three weak actors from the former Sharia Court group, and one representative from the local clans. Al-Shabaab also created a new Somali media celebrity in its new local information secretary, Hassan Yaqub Ali. The new administration improved local conditions drastically, and moved against crime, which had been rampant under the Marehan militia; support was actually forthcoming from the locals.[49]

The next offensive by Al-Shabaab was against Qoreole, Merka and Brawa in October-November 2008. The situation in Merka was rather confused, with similarities to the situation in Kismayo. The old war chiefs of the warlord Indaadde had seemingly turned their backs on their former leader and sided with the TFG in Mogadishu. In reality they worked with Indaadde, who remained a part of the Sharia Court alliance at the time, and was a part of the insurgency. There was strong rivalry amongst the Merka leaders, and the internal killings and rivalry within Merka made it very vulnerable to outside attackers.

The attack on Merka was perhaps Al-Shabaab's best-planned operation. They first planted a road bomb that killed the Deputy Governor and his rival the deputy security chief in the region as well as eight policemen.[50] This was a severe blow to the TFG in the region since its forces depended on the charisma of the local leaders, now dead. Al-Shabaab proceeded to move slowly towards Merka. There were setbacks, and severe clashes between Ethiopian forces and Al-Shabaab in the close Lego and Yaq Bariweyne occurred on 27 October. However, on 13 November 2008 the final blow fell—two Al-Shabaab columns, one from the south and one from the north, rolled into the city. The forces were received as liberators by the local Biyemal clan that had been at the receiving end of oppression by the Ayr clan for years.[51] Al-Shabaab quickly took over Merka's police station and government buildings.

The Ethiopian response was feeble, despite Merka only being 60 km south of Mogadishu. Troops attacked Al-Shabaab positions close to Mogadishu, but nothing more. Indeed, by 2008, Ethiopia was losing interest in its Somali adventure. In Mogadishu, the Ethiopians' strength was scaled down; local sources indicated that only 2,000 soldiers remained, often of Somali origin.[52] The frequency of patrols was reduced. This resulted in the first Al-Shabaab victories inside Mogadishu, including the withdrawal of government forces from Abdi Wayel Cinema, and SOS Hospitalet in Heliwa, in September. However, the government returned later, supported by Ethiopian forces.

The hesitant Ethiopian reaction to Al-Shabaab activities might have been due to general war fatigue, but probably also had something to do with increased international activities in the direction of making a new peace agreement with the remains of the Sharia Courts, organized in

Asmara during the autumn of 2007. Much of the hope put into the peace process was based on the assumption that the major factor enabling Al-Shabaab to exist was recruitment encouraged by national resentment of the Ethiopian occupation. A negotiated settlement between the remnants of the Courts within the Alliance for the Re-liberation of Somalia (ARS) was also to create an Islamist alternative, which would sway recruits away from Al-Shabaab.[53] However, such views neglected the organizational discipline of the group, combined with its ideology, which for many leaders went further than the Ethiopian-Somali conflict. Moreover, Al-Shabaab leaders were emboldened by their victories, and hesitated to negotiate with the new cabinet created after the Djibouti process; there were attempted negotiations with the new President, Sheik Sharif, but they came to nothing.

The TFG entered into a process driven by the United Nations Special Envoy to Somalia, Ahmedou Ould Abdallah that was to produce major territorial gains for Al-Shabaab. This began in May 2008 when the representatives of the TFG and the ARS participated in a peace conference in Djibouti, but the first meeting ended after a week. A second round, ending on 9 June 2008, led to an agreement including a cease-fire. The agreement, though hailed internationally as a big breakthrough, was highly problematical in the sense that the remnants of the Courts were split over participation in the negotiating process, and parts of the Courts movement felt excluded. The meeting had also been driven through very fast, and the circles around 'the grand old man' of Somali Islamism, Hassan Dahir Aweys, were discontented. Hassan Dahir Aweys, as well as other leaders skeptical about the Djibouti process, established an alternative to the Sheikh Sheriff-dominated ARS faction, the so-called ARS Asmara, based in Eritrea. Nevertheless, the process moved forward, and there were two new rounds of negotiations in October and November 2008 (Djibouti III & Djibouti IV), again creating a frenzy amongst diplomats in Nairobi, which saw the negotiations as a tool to destroy Al-Shabaab, and as taking an advantage of splits inside Al-Shabaab to draw out moderate leaders. A new parliament was agreed upon, with more than 550 representatives.

In parallel to this, Ethiopia and the TFG went on the offensive, perhaps to improve their position in the negotiations. Al-Shabaab's Eldon base, closely associated with the forces of Muktar Robow, was attacked and fell quickly. On 23 October, attacks were launched against Bardale,

Ufurow, Buurhakaba, Qansah-Dheere, Wajid and Huddur. The largest offensive in Bay-Bakool ever launched by the Ethiopians had started. Al-Shabaab forces in the area melted away into the bush, and did not attempt to meet the Ethiopians in open battle. Indeed, Al-Shabaab seldom chose battle, but when it did, it attempted to maximize the media coverage, warning local media before the attack. It did, however, continue with an intensified bombing and assassination campaign against TFG officials. Both Ethiopia and the TFG had shown their strength ahead of the continued Djibouti negotiations, showing that they could still mount offensives. There was also considerable synergy around the Djibouti process. Suddenly, Turkey and Bangladesh warmed to sending forces to Mogadishu, and the AMISOM forces were increased to 3,400 soldiers. There were hopes that the positive results in Djibouti could sway neutral city administrations towards the new TFG/ARS-D alliance.

However, there were ill omens. Merka, Brawa and Kismayo were still partly or wholly under Al-Shabaab control, and Al-Shabaab forces under different commanders came to each others' aid, transcending clan lines in a way quite unique in a Somali setting. Al-Shabaab again managed to withdraw most of its forces in the face of superior enemies; they were not destroyed. The attacks against Merka described earlier, and suicide attacks in northern Somalia, all showed that Al-Shabaab was still militarily strong, and it released a couple of videos on the internet to show its strength. Al-Shabaab also had peaceful victories, such as the establishment of a police (Hisba) force in Guri-El. Last but not least, international society failed to notice that the crack forces of the TFG were almost exclusively from President Abdullahi Yusuf's clan, and loyal to him, not to the TFG; this meant that a negotiated settlement not giving top positions to his clan would effectively neutralize large TFG forces. It was probably hoped that these units could be replaced by ARS Djibouti forces, but those were much fewer and less organized than was widely believed; they were also based around charismatic leaders, and if those leaders were to disappear, severe blows to ARS-Ds military strengths would result.

There was a large discrepancy between predictions, in general highly positive, and what was to happen. Foreign analysts claimed that Al-Shabaab was racing towards annihilation and fragmentation.[54] This was believed in part because what was supposed to be the main factor contributing to Al-Shabaab's popularity, the Ethiopian presence, was dwindling, and by February 2009 even this disappeared, except for raids and support for some factions. Fragmentation within the organization was also highlighted.[55]

However, the Al-Shabaab leadership's ideology and its well developed problem solving mechanisms probably made it the most unified actor in southern Somalia in 2008, a factor that was neglected by most observers, except for the Somalis themselves. The organization also showed that it could govern, and could implement a more transparent form of justice; in the area of justice the government had failed utterly, which lent it popularity. The Djibouti process and the Ethiopian withdrawal were not signaling the demise of Al-Shabaab, but quite the opposite. Al-Shabaab was to grow into an organization controlling an area equal to the size of Denmark, with perhaps five million inhabitants. It was to become the only self-proclaimed Al-Qaeda ally controlling large territories. Ironically, the practical needs of governance were also the source of Al-Shabaab's perceived problems in 2008. When Al-Shabaab controlled territory it had to engage clans and recruit locally; this in turn meant that clan became more important inside the group. The rapid territorial expansion also meant a stronger focus on Somalia and governance, and a weakening of Al-Shabaab's emphasis on the global struggle, as well as the enrolment of recruits motivated by opportunism, the quest for justice based on the Sharia, and clanism; Al-Shabaab was to become a victim of its own success.

6

THE GOLDEN AGE OF AL-SHABAAB (2009–10)

The Djibouti agreements achieved an Ethiopian withdrawal from Mogadishu in January 2009. The territorial gains that followed the withdrawal were the largest that Harakat Al-Shabaab ever experienced. The former capitals of the Transitional Federal Government (TFG), Baidoa and Jowhar, fell; the city of Beled Weyne was fully conquered. Al-Shabaab had to establish local governance structures. Several clan groupings attempted to join *en masse*, as did mere bandits. The group expanded but was in uncharted territory. Its Al-Qaeda connections could offer little in the way of guidance. Governance and administration were something beyond Al-Qaeda's experience, except for the brief encounter with Taliban governance in Afghanistan, and the examples of the four righteous caliphs and Muhammad in the classical era.[1]

Local governance, the policy dilemmas facing decision makers with a responsibility towards a population, fast organizational growth and the presence of weakly committed recruits were to create severe problems for the Al-Shabaab. Moreover, old conflicts within the organization increased, as differences over governance styles as well as differences in strategies for defeating enemies emerged, and Al-Shabaab was to face its most serious splits ever. It was also in the end to face intensive urban warfare, slowly sapping Al-Shabaab's strength in Mogadishu, where the forces of the African Union in Somalia (AMISOM) had military superiority.

In January 2009 the Ethiopians withdrew from Somalia. Mogadishu actually became more peaceful, but only until May 2009. The new TFG, led by Sheikh Sheriff, the former head of the Sharia Courts Union, had wide support in Mudug, Hiraan and Galguduud, and seemingly among the Ayr, Saad and Abgal clans in these areas. Many expected Al-Shabaab to collapse, seeing it as a form of nationalistic resistance organization targeting Ethiopians, because of the age-old enmity between Ethiopia and Somalia.[2] It was not in decline, however, but rather playing for time, feeling out its new opponents, re-positioning its forces towards the war leaders of the Sharia Courts who had joined the Djibouti process. There were defections amongst Al-Shabaab soldiers. Some felt their struggle had ended when the Ethiopians withdrew. But by and large these tendencies were kept under control, partly by the regular payment of wages, partly by a common ideology amongst the leadership, an ideology that went beyond Somalia and the Ethiopian occupation, and partly also by fear, often created by Al-Shabaab's newly established secret police, the Amniyat. The families of defectors were systematically targeted by the Amniyat, and former members who had left were hunted down and killed, inducing fear in potential defectors.[3]

Al-Shabaab also played propaganda games on the internet and in the media, increasing its high profile suicide attacks, a cheap way of maintaining media interest. New commanders were rising through the system. Some new mid-level leaders, such as Macalin Qalid Hashi Abdallah, were attracted by Al-Shabaab's focus on unity, and repelled by the extensive conflicts within other groups. Macalin Qalid (also written as 'Khalid') was born somewhere in Somaliland around 1975. He joined the Ras Kamboni group around 2004, and received military training. In March 2006, when Ras Kamboni came to Mogadishu to help their fellow Islamists, he fought in the Battle of Galgalato. After that battle, he became an instructor at the Nasrudiin training camp in Mogadishu (this camp, near Ramadan Hotel, was used to train members of the Abgal clan).[4] After the Islamic Courts Union was defeated, he hid in Ras Kamboni. However, he joined Al-Shabaab when a dispute within the Ras Kamboni group caused a split within the latter. The incident illustrated a general point; Al-Shabaab avoided the large public splits that its enemies, even its nominal allies, experienced. It managed to keep a unified face before the media, the only southern Somali faction that managed this.[5]

Foreigners were also still coming to Somalia, amongst them Rajah Abu Khalid. Rajah was a Yemeni member of Al-Qaeda in the Arabian Peninsula (AQAP). He is said to have entered Somalia in late 2009 by way of Kenya to become an Al-Shabaab instructor and to have brought new ideas from Yemen to Somalia. Khalid was, together with an Egyptian named Khattab, put to work on planning defensive countermeasures inside Mogadishu, after the TFG forces collapsed many places in Mogadishu when Ethiopia withdrew.[6] The plan involved digging anti-tank ditches similar to those constructed around Moscow in 1941, but in Somalia they were camouflaged. The 'Khalid-tactic' also involved closing roads in front line areas to civilian traffic, and ordering civilians to evacuate homes near the front lines. However, Khalid met the same fate as Abdallah. He was killed at the front in Mogadishu in December 2010 by a shell that hit his position as he was leading an attack.[7] The story of Khalid illustrated how tactics from Al-Qaeda were adopted by Al-Shabaab and how Al-Qaeda members had an instruction and planning role inside Al-Shabaab, their experience being still respected. There were many like him, such as Sheikh Mohamed Abu Faid, Al-Shabaab's financier, and famous commanders and advisers such as Abu Musa Mombasa, allegedly from Pakistan, and Mohamoud Mujajir from Sudan, who worked on the recruitment of suicide bombers.[8] Many worked as instructors in training programmes. These programmes, only implemented at specific training facilities, were more than mere weapons instruction courses; they taught recruits to look at the world through the lenses of Al-Qaeda, distinguishing good and evil in Islam and the West respectively. How well did this work? This is a question not easy to answer, but clan leaders would maintain that the recruits retained clan loyalties.[9]

Al-Shabaab also attracted outright bandits, such as Mohamed Saed Timojele 'Rambo', a former child soldier turned bandit and then part-time jihadist. In many ways Rambo was a bandit still when he rose through the ranks. He was seen as ruthless and highly efficient, but also as still maintaining his businesses on the side, which included kidnappings.[10] Rambo was to perish early in 2009. He participated in Al-Shabaab's rapid expansion in the Mudug area, but faced the counter attacks in January 2009, and was killed together with several Kenyan Al-Shabaab fighters on 10 January 2009.[11] He was symptomatic of a particular category of Al-Shabaab fighter, the '*shifta*' (bandit) Shabaab: fighters joining the group because it was winning, and because of a need to get protection for their criminal activities. Both the dedicated Al-Qaeda-inspired international fighter and the bandit existed in the new Al-Shabaab, in addition to the mere opportunist and the genuine idealist focusing on local law and order.

In December 2008 Al-Shabaab got a new enemy: Aluh Sunna Wah Jamaa (ASWJ). This was widely claimed to be a part of the ASWJ organization established in 1992, based on religious leaders of the Sufi schools of Somalia, always opposed to Al-Shabaab, which called them 'idol worshippers.' However, the nominal leaders of the 1992 organization did not even know who was fighting in Galguduud and who was against the struggle.[12] From the start ASWJ became something more than a Sufi organization, and central clans such as the Hawadle, parts of the Ayr, and the Abgal-Waisle joined en masse, making the ASWJ field forces an odd mix of Islamist and clan fighters.

Nonetheless, the popular support for ASWJ militias amongst the clans they drew on for recruitment made them formidable, and by December 2008 they won large victories in Mudug-Galguduud. Al-Shabaab counter-offensives in January 2009 failed to dislodge ASWJ. The Al-Shabaab fighters involved were mainly from the Murosade clan. In this region Al-Shabaab often mobilized Murosade clan fighters using clanist arguments, claiming to defend them against clan intrusion, mainly by the Ayr and Hawadle, into Al-Shabaab/Murosade held areas. As Al-Shabaab expanded, it became embroiled in clan conflicts around Somalia, at times involuntarily, at times deliberately. In Kismayo, for example, Marehan fighters attempted to join Al-Shabaab in order to offset the dominance of the Ogadeen clan around Kismayo.[13] Al-Shabaab now had to deal with the clan-based realities of Somali politics, and at times chose to play the clan games, supporting one sub-clan against others at a local level.

The change of power in Mogadishu had confused many of the TFG commanders. Many such commanders shared the clan background of the ousted President Abdullahi Yusuf and had lost interest in war after his removal. Several other commanders were confused about who their enemies were, partly because their old enemies from the Sharia Courts were now supposed to be their new allies. Shabaab managed to take advantage of the confused situation. On 1 April 2009 Al-Shabaab forces entered the strategic town of Bulo Burte and held a popular meeting. ASWJ forces launched an attack against the Al-Shabaab stronghold of Mahas, and the latter replied by deploying reinforcements. However, the TFG-appointed governor in Hiiran refused to participate, declaring himself neutral, showing how little loyalty he felt towards the new TFG leadership. The TFG's problems continued when it tried to collect taxes in Beledweyne by the end of April 2009, when clan militias attacked them.

Al-Shabaab successfully blocked the bridge in Bulo Burte to prevent the TFG reinforcements from reaching Beled Weyne. In this city, the Hawadle clan ended up supporting Hisbul Islam, the rest of the clans supported Al-Shabaab; the city changed hands when the Hawadle changed their mind, and probably after Al-Shabaab paid a bribe to the former Hawadle governor.[14]

Al-Shabaab's largest victory was perhaps the conquest of Baidoa, the interim capital of the TFG, after the withdrawal of the Ethiopian forces on 26 January 2009. It seemed that the TFG police more or less melted away on its own—in one sense it was rather a TFG collapse than an Al-Shabaab victory. Before Al-Shabaab entered the city, TFG militias were heavily engaged in looting various TFG bases, including the presidential palace, the parliament building and the central bank.[15] When it became clear that the TFG forces had collapsed by themselves, Al-Shabaab sent forces into Baidoa. Again indicating the importance of clan allegiance in Somali politics, regular TFG forces deserted the TFG. Al-Shabaab instead met clan-driven resistance. Fighting took place between Al-Shabaab militia and the security forces of the speaker of the parliament under the TFG, Sheik Adan Madobe, who came from a different sub-clan from Robow, the commander of Shabaab's advance into the city. Robow's own clan members within the TFG, such as Muhamed Ibrahim Hapsade and Ibrahim Yarow, did not fight, and Rahanwhein traditional elders intervened to get them free passage, which Robow granted; this was later to create serious internal problems for Al-Shabaab.[16]

Robow and his interim Al-Shabaab administration immediately started implementing the Sharia, with the first death penalty carried out just four days after the takeover. There were many sad cases, as when five poor Somali girls were arrested on 5 May because they could not afford the veils that Al-Shabaab had ordered all females to wear.[17] The registration of NGOs started almost immediately, and the media crackdown started in April 2009, when a Shabelle Media Network (A Somali news-server and radio station) reporter named Muhiyidin Hassan Mohamed (Husni) was arrested by Al-Shabaab accused of reporting an incident in which bandits looted public transport in the Bay region. On 26 April 2009 the popular FM Radio was closed down by Al-Shabaab, for allegedly spreading false information about the arrest of several local bandits. Although three reporters were released, most fled the area, and by the end of June the last independent local radio station, Radio Baidoa, was closed. Al-

Shabaab also started a crackdown on human rights organizations, which led to many of them fleeing the area; one, Alin Hillowle Hassan, was severely tortured. However, there were also clear advantages to Al-Shabaab rule. Locals claimed that it was providing better justice than the TFG, and rapes, killings and robberies declined.[18]

The fall of Baidoa had several consequences. First, it brought the internal tension within Al-Shabaab to the forefront. This tension was quite natural since Al-Shabaab, after gaining so much territory, now had to interact with the Somali clan system. Interaction with local elders and clan leaders, combined with Al-Shabaab's old tactic of using fighters from a clan to lead attacks in the areas of that clan, made the organization vulnerable. Al-Shabaab's counter-measure—appointing local post-takeover leaders from non-resident clans, something sensational in the Somali setting—did not fully serve as a remedy to this, as local clan groupings had to be accommodated. There had been practical differences on management issues before, for example on how to deal with qat, but with the renewed expansion of territories to govern, and the interaction with clanism, such issues were to come to the forefront.

Many commentators have argued there was a deep ideological division within Al-Shabaab in 2008–09, partly because of the events in Baidoa between a group of 'moderates' around Abu Mansoor-Muktar Robow, and Godane. However, this is too simplistic.[19] There were problems between Godane and Mansoor back in late 2008, but these problems were of a more peaceful kind, such as disagreements over the future of the Mogadishu airport blockade—Robow in a *shura* setting argued for lifting Al-Shabaab's blockade of the airport, which he alleged was causing harm to the civilians, and in the end he got his way. However, it was Robow's actions relating to his own clan member Hapsade, described earlier, that were to spark the first larger disagreement within Al-Shabaab. From the outside this could be interpreted as a clan-based move by Robow, but it should be remembered that in Somalia there is a fine line between clan politics and *realpolitik*, as clan considerations influence factional politics. Hapsade had supported the nucleus of the Sharia Courts during 2006, by putting pressure on the TFG, and more than one Rahanwhein member has claimed that Hapsade directly protected Robow after his return in 2007.[20] Hapsade's release can also be seen as a strategy to ease the transition of power in Baidoa. Outside observers predicted a full split over this issue. It is easy to understand the confusion it created, aided between the clandestine nature of Al-Shabaab and lack of primary sources.[21]

The idea of deep Al-Shabaab divisions was partly driven by too much reliance on TFG-friendly sources, partly by existing divisions, but those divisions were relatively easily handled by Al-Shabaab, and the fact that they were handled so fast and efficiently is perhaps the biggest surprise. In contrast to all the other factions in Somalia, these conflicts did not spill into the open, they were contained by Al-Shabaab's factions, and were largely (with the exception of a critical speech by Fuad 'Shongole' criticizing Robow) kept secret—quite an achievement in a Somali setting.[22] Moreover, the top level *shura* still met, and there were attempts to solve the disagreements that did exist through mediation within the *shura*. Indeed, most remarkably, one conflict was solved through mediation by a Al-Shabaab sheikh, with a decision that Robow should step down as spokesperson. Robow kept considerable power within the organization, commanding forces in Mogadishu, keeping his position in the top *shura* council, as well as remaining important in Baidoa, although the leadership in the city was formally under another commander.[23]

Indeed, according to one witness in Baidoa at the time, the indoctrination of Al-Shabaab soldiers had simply gone too far for a split to occur. Local sources confirmed that Robow's fighters had been trained in special courses, and indeed were subscribing to a global jihadist view rather than clan-based view. At the time they predicted that it would be impossible for Robow to move against the central leadership.[24] In this sense, Al-Shabaab had something that other Somali factions lacked; it had institutions and ideology, albeit both were relatively confused. It should also be kept in mind that Al-Shabaab was the winning side and there were few rewards for individuals who wanted to defect.

Al-Shabaab was to expand its territories even further, first securing Bay and Bakool. On 25 February it dislodged the remnants of the TFG in Hudur, attacking with an impressive 800–1,000 men. However, an ill omen was that these forces were clan segregated; local sources suggest 70–80 per cent of the fighters came from the Rahanwhein clan. Another interesting fact, illustrating another trend, was that perhaps as many as seventy of the fighters were non-Somali East Africans, Shirazis from Tanzania and even Muslim Kikuyus from Kenya.[25] Al-Shabaab's victories did create a clan dilemma for it. Clan could be used as a tool to achieve easy victories; but clan conflicts could also fragment the organization. Roland Marchal produced an excellent account of how Shabaab used clans instrumentally:

The capital city of Middle Shabeelle (Jowhar) was taken by a coalition of Ogaadeen and Murusade (plus a few 'Ayr and Abgaal/Reer Mataan) militias. To a large extent, the Shura became an instrument in settling old scores. The Shura was including Daarood and Rahanweyn representatives plus Gaalje'el and Jareer beyond the usual Abgaal sub-clans. In particular, the Harti Abgaal sub-clan that used to dominate the region throughout the civil war got as many representatives as the Jareer![26]

In this sense Al-Shabaab tried to play the clan game when it was in its interests to do so. However, at the top administrative levels, an officer from an outsider clan, a clan alien to the area, in theory remained most important. Al-Shabaab had two faces, one clanist but pragmatic, one anti-clanist. Showing the clanist face could have been a pragmatic approach to conquer new areas, but often there was a price to pay: Al-Shabaab became a part of clan conflicts.

Al-Shabaab's sweeping victories left other radical Islamists sidelined, and made it pressing for other relatively radical Islamists to organize themselves; in one sense they drove the formation of the Islamic Party (Hizb Islamiya, Hisbul Islam), initially led by Sheikh Omar Iman. This was in many ways formed as an alliance between weak but radical Islamist fronts in Somalia. The strongest party in the alliance was the Alliance for the Re-liberation of Somalia—Asmara wing (ARS-A). This branch of the ARS did not accept the Djibouti process. It was led by Sheik Hassan Dahir Aweys, and was dominated by the Ayr clan. The second organization joining the party was the so-called Jabhatul Islamiya (Islamic Front). These organizations were joined by the Anole group, consisting of a small number of fighters from the Harti clan. The last partner was the Harakat Ras Kamboni, led at the time by the veteran Islamist Hassan Turki, a close friend of many Al-Shabaab leaders. The loose alliance became more cemented when the ARS-A leader, Hassan Dahir Aweys, a man who supported many Al-Shabaab leaders during the early stages of their careers, returned to Mogadishu on 23 April 2009. His return came amid problems within Hisbul Islam; two of its organizations, the Kamboni (based on the Ogadeen clan) and the Anole (based on the Marehan), clashed close to Kismayo. However, Aweys managed to pull the fragmented organization together. Hisbul Islam nevertheless faced

serious problems during the autumn of 2009. One of its member organizations changed as Hassan Turki, who was stricken with diabetes and
old age, lost power to his son-in-law, Ahmed Madobe Mohamed.[27]

Mu'askar Kamboni was always based on the Ogadeen clan, but the
strong ideology of Hassan Turki himself had moved it closer to Al-Shabaab. Madobe led the organization to drift towards clanism rather than
Islam. Many members of the Ogadeen clan felt challenged by Al-Shabaab's increased focus on creating a multi-clan governance structure in
Kismayo, which was seen as an Ogadeen city. This set the stage for the
October 2009 combat between Ras Kamboni and Al-Shabaab.[28] In the
end Ras Kamboni's forces under the command of Madobe, and their
allies in Anole, were crushed, and Al-Shabaab took sole control; the rest
of Hisbul Islam failed to send reinforcements. Hisbul Islam's problems
again highlight Al-Shabaab's efficiency and relative unity.

Al-Shabaab leaders also understood the dynamics underlying the new
TFG and were actually attacking the TFG politicians commanding forces
on the ground (often commanding them because of their charisma rather
than their formal positions). The suicide bomber Muxamed Deerow
Shiikh Aadam (Zubayr) targeted the new government's head of security
Omar Hashi Aden on 18 June 2009. His attack seems to have been thoroughly planned and caused chaos in the government's security apparatus, paving the way for Al-Shabaab's tactical victories during the summer
of 2009. Omar commanded large forces by force of personality, and many
defected after his death.

The TFG nevertheless felt strong enough to initiate an offensive in
Mogadishu on 22–23 May 2009, followed by a second offensive in early
June, attacking Hisbul Islam.[29] Al-Shabaab then initiated a large scale
counter-offensive. It was again playing the clan game, as it targeted the
parts of Mogadishu inhabited by the Abgal clan; it chose a new governor (*wali*, or *waliga* in Somali), Ali Mohamed Hussein, from the Abgal.
In a fast-moving campaign Al-Shabaab forces swept to the coast, in the
process conquering the Abdulazis area, which had been TFG-controlled
since January 2007. However, the campaign also illustrated the realities
of the group's new situation; it was facing the limit of its capacities. On
11 July, Al-Shabaab advanced on the Ugandan-protected presidential
palace, seeing this as having major symbolic value. The Ugandan forces
were, however, vastly superior; they struck back with T55 tanks and APCs,
and quickly reconquered areas such as Karan, Shibis and Bondere. Only

at this stage did Al-Shabaab take advantage of its biggest asset: its mobility and ability to reinforce its fronts, overcoming clan difference. Reinforcements arrived from Gedo and Bay. At the same time the Ugandan forces retreated, leaving the TFG forces to hold the newly conquered areas. On 13 July Al-Shabaab and its allies in Hizbul Islam, launched a new offensive, and the TFG forces in their way collapsed, but the offensive was again blocked by Ugandan forces.[30] Al-Shabaab used foreign fighters; local sources estimated the number to be around 200–400, but their presence did not help. In the end 250,000 refugees fled Mogadishu.[31] The fighting illustrated a very important point: from 2009 and onwards, the military situation in Mogadishu was turned into a bloody stalemate, not unlike the World War I trench battles. Al-Shabaab simply did not have the forces to dislodge the Ugandan and Burundian AMISOM forces, while the latter lacked the mandate to expand their areas. The TFG forces were largely irrelevant, despite arms supply and training from the West; they were ill motivated and poorly commanded, and lacked the armored support of AMISOM. Al-Shabaab, weak in numbers and resources, suffered huge financial and human losses.

However, when AMISOM forces were not present, Al-Shabaab victories continued. The group also drove the TFG from the strategically important Hiran valley. Despite the trench war in Mogadishu Al-Shabaab now felt strong, strong enough to challenge one of its old allies, Eritrea. Eritrea-Al-Shabaab relations had been very troubled from the time the group formally separated from the Courts in 2007 and publicly denounced Eritrea. Eritrea nevertheless chose to support Al-Shabaab, but relations were at times tense. During the summer of 2009 two French security advisers were kidnapped and sold by the TFG police to Hizbul Islam. Al-Shabaab put Hizbul Islam under pressure, aiming to get control over one of the hostages; according to Roland Marchal, this was not without internal disagreements, Muktar Robow stating that he refused to follow Godane's orders to attack Hizbul Islam in order to capture the two hostages.[32] However, in the end Al-Shabaab succeeded. Eritrea, on the other hand, attempted to use leverage to achieve the release of the hostage, but failed. So the relationship between Eritrea and Al-Shabaab was not one of affection and loyalty, but rather characterized by the maxim 'My enemy's enemy is my friend', and Al-Shabaab leaders openly criticized Eritrea for fighting against its own Islamists.

Governing Somalia

By mid-2009 Al-Shabaab controlled most of southern Somalia. Its victory had been built on mobility and—quite contrary to popular belief—its unity, and its forces were small, perhaps only 5,000 men; this was too few to have more than a rudimentary control over the areas, but slowly Al-Shabaab started to build up governance structures. These structures were far from perfect, some of them were clearly corrupt, and there were parallel chains of authority within the organization. However, parts of the governance structures were highly important, and the Al-Shabaab institutions dealing with implementation of the Sharia created a relatively stable legal regime in larger cities.

Al-Shabaab was still dominated by an inner circle of eight to ten members forming an executive *shura*, while a larger *shura* of thirty-five, later fourty-five, could be summoned according to need.[33] Centralized institutions also grew. The most important was perhaps the Maktabatu Amniyat, the Ministry of Intelligence and Internal Security that became the most famous, headed by Sheikh Muktar Abu Seyla'i, who belonged to the Isaq clan. The Amniyat in the end had an almost mythical reputation. According to a local respondent from Mogadishu in a somewhat broken English:

Amniyat, these are kind of secret police, intelligence that carry out...they carry out the orders of execution in any place, in anywhere. They assassinate, they shoot. Sometimes they can even go beyond the borders and carry out functions...they can execute or can carry out an order outside the country. And nobody knows how they are connected and who are their bosses. To some extent people seem that they are connected to the big commanders and all kind of things, but nobody can specifically say that they are connected to that place or that place. And they can do anything in anywhere at any time without fear. They can single-handedly do...take care of things. Sometimes they normally hide...when one of them is being killed, they what normally do, they cut off his face or his head so that in case of...in case the second person...they don't want anybody to notice them. If they enter into a fight, or in a battle and one person who belongs to amniyat group is killed, what they normally do is they chop off his head and run away with the head, so that nobody can notice them.[34]

The Amniyat was to handle internal justice, and functioned as a form of intelligence agency; it was the main tool to create unity, and was feared inside Al-Shabaab. In one sense it acted outside the group, and recruited spies in all Al-Shabaab-controlled areas, as well as in Nairobi for example. It was, and is, directly controlled by Al-Shabaab Amir Godane, and was to be one of the few centralizing mechanisms for Al-Shabaab during the period of trouble in 2010–11. In one sense it was an important tool for centralization of power, with wide jurisdiction, including the ability to circumvent the Al-Shabaab Sharia courts in cases of spying.

The Maktabatu Da'wa was the ministry responsible for spreading Shabaabs own brand of Islam, their interpretation of Sharia and Islam, in this sense it had a standardizing and thus centralizing function, homogenizing the religious interpretations of various sub-leaders of the organization. In one sense the activities of this organization were extraordinary in a Somali setting, organizing training in the various jihadist ideologies for local sheikhs, re-indoctrination programmes for elders in Kismayo, and various events where ideology was discussed. According to NGO sources, they even attempted to standardize the curriculum in the schools in southern Somalia, putting more emphasis on Islamic and Arabic studies.[35] The veteran Al-Shabaab ideologist Fuad Shongola headed this department. Significantly, the institution is highly important for the formulation of *fatwa*s, regulating local justice. In one sense this is the closest to a legal office Al-Shabaab has. According to a local sheikh: 'They act as *mujtahideen* [*mujtahid*], they make new *tafsir* which is not known to the community and wasn't applicable to specific situation. For example when they are doing ijtihad, one explains some verse of the Holy Qur'an. They prefer to apply how it is to people who lived one thousand years ago.'[36]

The law and order aspect of Al-Shabaab governance structures was perhaps the most overlooked by Western media, but it was the strongest card in getting local support. A recent refugee from Kismayo in Nairobi told me in 2010: 'The good that they do is that you cannot be robbed in the street in Mogadishu, actually, the part they control. You cannot be robbed. You can walk openly with a lot of money, if you are not a target [of Al-Shabaab]. So, they do policing. They protect against thieves, they protect property, they do guard.'[37]

While many Western observers believe that Al-Shabaab's imposition of the Sharia is widely resented by ordinary Somalis, its relatively successful law enforcement and justice system generated sympathy among locals who were used to predatory warlords or the ineffective and corrupt governance of the TFG. Indeed, justice provision was the trait that really created local support, although it became more resented over time.

Interviews conducted in Norway indicate that it is just this perspective—seeing Al-Shabaab justice providers, as Islamist reformers—that still attracts diaspora Somali support for the organization. The contrast with the TFG was in this regard very noticeable. The advantages of Al-Shabaab governance for the local population could be seen at the checkpoints that Somali militias typically used to fund themselves by taking money from local and international travellers. Amazingly, Al-Shabaab managed, at least until 2011, to limit this practice. One Somali told the writer that during a journey from the Kenyan border to Mogadishu in 2009, he was stopped at sixty-seven checkpoints, sixty-one of them controlled by Al-Shabaab. The militiamen manning all but one of the non-Al-Shabaab checkpoints demanded money from him and one of them even stole his mobile telephone. Only one Al-Shabaab-controlled checkpoint demanded payment, but he noted that road construction work was going on at the post, so he presumed the money was being well spent. But, there were differences within Al-Shabaab areas—the minorities remained more exposed to harassment, and respondents interviewed by the writer spoke of cases in which rapists had gone unpunished. However, the Al-Shabaab justice system functioned by and large, and was a notable relief for Somalis used to the predatory police of the TFG and warlord rule.

The justice system could be divided into three parts: the militia commander, a local level and a regional level. The average checkpoint commander/militia commander was the first level. He could hand out punishment for a variety of minor offences such as Western-style haircuts, 'indecent clothing', playing music, walking or sitting with a member of the opposite sex and not having a beard. All these were and are minor crimes for Al-Shabaab that can be handled at a low level.

The local Al-Shabaab commander only implemented relatively light punishments for minor offences. As reported by a refugee from Al-Shabaab-controlled areas around Kismayo, 'For wrong haircut, they will cut the hair. For wrong dress/clothes, they will cut the trousers. If you have music on your phone they will take the phone and whip you. If you are seen without a beard they will whip you.'[38] The implementation of these punishments varied from militia to militia, and low-level Al-Shabaab commanders seemed to have little knowledge of the Sharia. There were also cases of outright corruption amongst them, some commanders were outright bandits, but many were at some stages punished.[39] At times Al-

Shabaab also had to employ former warlord militias; in Kismayo, it appointed Sheikh Abdirahman Nuur Fiilo as one of two deputy commanders of the Hesba. Fiilo was a member of the Jubba valley administration led by a diehard enemy of Al-Shabaab, the warlord Barre Hirale, but switched sides when Al-Shabaab emerged as winners. The fighting between Al-Shabaab and the larger clans of Ogadeen and Marehan forced Al-Shabaab to rely on small clan leaders, and Fiilo was from the small Talho sub-clan. However, the most important point was Al-Shabaab's 'reinvention' of religious institutions by appointing individuals with no religious training who just took the title of Sheikh and started to implement the Sharia at a low level.[40]

With local commanders coming from so different backgrounds, it is not surprising that sentences varied, and that Al-Shabaab also designated two other levels for Sharia implementation. It was these levels that dealt with more serious offences. Al-Shabaab established both regional (Wilaayada) and district courts, as the major tools for administering justice. District courts often, though not always, have their own militia, the Janjawiil. The courts of Baidoa might serve as an example. The Baidoa court consisted of a president/judge (*Qaali*), deputy president/judge and court clerk. It functioned effectively and passed sentences every day. In Baidoa there was a regional court (the court of the *wali*) as well as a district court. Both courts actually had possibilities for appeal.[41] The various courts under Al-Shabaab were operational and local observers noted how the Mogadishu courts and Baidoa courts were highly popular amongst the local population in 2010, with long queues of Somalis wanting to take civil cases to court; another respondent in Kismayo reported the same phenomenon in 2010. Clearly the Al-Shabaab justice system was relatively popular.[42] There was clear division of labor. According to an additional Mogadishu respondent: 'One who commits a murder, which will be taken to high court, in Bakara. If you are disturbing people, me and you fighting in the street, or parents saying…they accused becoming stubborn, something like that, you go to the low court [animal market].'[43]

The lower courts handled other tasks, such as marriage ceremonies. Justice could be random, and not exactly based on Al-Shabaab ideology, partly because it was short of recruits.[44] It seems as though Al-Shabaab tended to use councils of local sheikhs to issue *fiqh*s on property cases, but emphasized what fitted with their own ideology, according to the

Hanbali code, or more specifically the Wahhabi version of that code. There was a general lack of standardization of punishments, but there was also cooperation in interrogation; prisoners were for example sent from Baidoa to Mogadishu for torture in 2010. The diversity of punishments did not follow any political lines, there was no specific *wilaya* that was more lenient than others, and it rather varied among governorates. Some Al-Shabaab courts would tolerate aspects of Somali culture, such as *diya* (blood money) payment, but others did not.

The court system was a challenge for Al-Shabaab; it had simply expanded too quickly, and had to recruit new members to fill the new posts. This meant that another group of Al-Shabaab members emerged, the administrators, with ample administrative knowledge but little ideological understanding; some of these were outright reformists and idealists, fighting for justice in a new society. The low level commanders and the two levels of justice are what urban Somalis usually related to when it came to Al-Shabaab justice; rural Somalis most usually depended on the traditional clan system for justice, so that for them Al-Shabaab governance did not exist.

Importantly, there were, and are, justice functions outside this system. First, the battle commanders, as well as the previously mentioned Amniyat, could and still can inflict punishments on spies without summoning them to a Sharia court, and this is often done with alleged spies, though if a high-ranking commander is found guilty of spying, the case has tended to go to the Al-Shabaab *shura*. In addition, the *fatwa* council within the Maktabatu Da'wa could receive requests from ordinary citizens for a *fatwa*, which overrules all other courts. The *fatwa* council of the Maktabatu Da'wa also attempted to oversee military fronts and their implementation of justice, but lacked the capacity to do so fully.

There was more to local administration than the lower courts. The regional administration, the *wilaayada* or Islamic governorates, was the major formal governance structure of Al-Shabaab. It was of variable strength around Somalia, in some areas just weak structures, but governance was in general one of Al-Shabaab's strong cards. Although it was weak, its predecessors, the warlords, and its rivals in the TFG were even weaker. As early as 2008, the group began establishing a series of eight local *wilaayada* to govern the provinces that it only sporadically controlled at the time. These administrations theoretically consisted of a governor (*wali*), Office of Social Affairs, Office of Finance, Office of the Judge and

Office of the so-called Hesbah Army, Al-Shabaab's equivalent of a police force. These offices were initially *pro forma*, with little power. However, in 2009 the administrations started to become more functional to varying degrees and the Hesbah Army became increasingly effective in enforcing law and order.

Local low level administrations emerged. In July 2009, administrations were established in Yaaqbari Weyne and in Leego, and Sharia court was established at Walanweyne, headed by Al-Shabaab's Aadan Macalin Muuse. A separate head of humanitarian affairs, Sheikh Hussein Fidow from the Isaq clan, was also appointed, and Al-Shabaab took the initiative of forming a charity council consisting of businessmen in the middle of June. These developments meant that a new Al-Shabaab local administrative elite emerged, consisting of individuals like Muhammed Omar Abdikharim, Al-Shabaab's *wali* in Bay-Bakool, Ali Dheere, the spokesperson in Shabelle and Ali Mohammed Hussein, the Benadiir *wali*. Global jihad had little meaning for these parts of the organization; they were rather technocrats chosen for their ability to organize.

In Baidoa courts and administrative positions were filled with individuals nominated centrally by the Al-Shabaab *shura*, in general for six months only. The process was surprisingly centralized. Parallel to this, the Islamic governorate—*wilaya* (Arabic) or *walaayada* (Somali)—was established. This was first headed by Sheikh Hassan Mohamed Mo'alin alias Abuu Eyman, who was later replaced by Sheik Mahad Abdikariin. The *wilaya* had a relatively clear organizational structure, with a Deputy Governor/Deputy Regional Administrator, Abdulaahi Gaab, and a senior commander (Amir) of the Amniyat, Sheikh Hassan Deerow (later replaced by commander Dagare). The *wilaya* also had a head of social affairs and Islamic mobilization; in Baidoa the highly efficient Mo'alin Gaduudow was put into that position, later to be replaced by Sheikh Yusuf Sheik Balcad 'Bashiir.' A financial officer, Bakar Sharif, was appointed, as well as a Qadi for the Al-Shabaab Islamic court, Sheik Adan Adare.[45] Al-Shabaab also had a local district commissioner, the head of the Baidoa area, Sheik Hussein, with a deputy, Sheikh Mohamud (Abuu Basiir), a head of social affairs, Sheikh Yusuf, and a financial officer, as well as a head of Hisbah (police), who was the infamous Hassey Moalin.

The situation in Kismayo was special. Al-Shabaab originally had to rule in cooperation with its allies in the local Ogadeen clan, as well as the Ras Kamboni and Anole organizations. Ironically, Al-Shabaab was at the same time headed by one of its more extreme leaders, the veteran Ibrahim Afghani. However, ideology did not create friction, which arose rather from economic questions. The most important problem between the group and its allies was that of the import taxes from Kismayo port. In April 2009, a compromise seemed to have been reached: Al-Shabaab took 40 per cent of the harbor taxes, Ras Kamboni got 30 per cent, and Anole 30 per cent. Ras Kamboni also got the governorship, and a formal power sharing agreement for control of the city was established. But this was not enough for Al-Shabaab, and it established its own parallel *waliya*, which was highly active in upholding 'public morals,' amongst other things screening films from Afghanistan, Gaza and Pakistan, while the destruction of Sufi tombs also continued.

The strength of the Al-Shabaab administration, it must be stressed, also varied according to its local strength. Al-Shabaab administrations were an urban phenomenon, and were more ideologically streamlined in the larger cities. Outside the cities the group simply did not exist, or consisted of local clan militias. The Al-Shabaab governance structures were nevertheless revolutionary, and functioned better than other, Western-backed, institutions in the south of Somalia. High turnover rates indicate the personnel problems the organization faced when trying to establish new administrations, but there were attempts to standardize.

Al-Shabaab's administrative drive has also included courses for Muslim clerics working in territory controlled by the group. In its propaganda, Al-Shabaab announced several such courses held at the Abdullah Azzam Centre (named after the influential Palestinian jihadist ideologue) to teach the students the hard-line Salafist interpretation of Islam.[46] The courses were supervised by Sheikh Fuad 'Shongola,' who was seen by many as a leading ideologue within the organization.

The Al-Shabaab governorates engaged in development work too. In Kismayo, it ordered work on the long asphalt road in Kismayo city that connects most parts of the town, the Kismayu-Jilib road, the road between Kismayo police station and the airport, the road between Mugambo and Koban towns along the tarmac under Jamame district of lower Juba, and the Dobley main road.[47] The Kismayo Governorate also organized (indeed, still does) many successive seminars in the towns of the Waliya in which it aimed to create awareness of Al-Shabaab policies and ideologies. These seminars, called *uluumul Muslim ummah* (teachings of the Muslim *Ummah*), have been part of Al-Shabaab programmes throughout the country, led by a sheikh with a PhD, Muhyadiinul Khartoum, who used to teach Islamic studies in Sudan. He also introduced courses for Qadis and imams and an extra curriculum for schools. Indeed it seemed as if there was a massive ideological campaign taking place within Kismayo. According to one local observer:

There is a *Da'i* [Preacher] in every mosque and village who has started teaching Islamic Sharia, which has brought new practices different from the centuries old Sharia interpretations. Since they [Al-Shabaab] came to the region they have overtaken all existing schools and created new ones. Old curriculums have been replaced by new ones. All mosques administration came under their programme and people have been forced to attend morning class at the mosque (both males and females). In some villages and towns in Lower Juba everybody takes at least one lesson every morning, failing to do so will result in a penalty for next morning. There are separate *madrassa*s run by the Imam and there some which are incorporated into the primary schools and separate ones. *Madrassa* students needs the Imam's promotion to join good *madrassa*s. For example the Al-Harameyn *madrassa* used to be a technical college and has good boarding and decent residential halls. There is a separate education programme center in Sheik-Nor village which used to be the largest and oldest pilgrimage of the Somali-Sufi center for centuries. Since Al-Shabaab took over it has been converted to an educational college where they teach all Imams and elders and former Sheiks of the villages and rehabilitate according to them.[48]

There were other centralized institutions also. Al-Shabaab took steps to prepare a new generation; it did cadre training. Located in the mosque of Munaaradaha near the animal market in Mogadishu was the training center for new Amirs, young leaders, trained in ideology and decision making.[49]

Al-Shabaab also built up a system to promote information targeting the Somalis. Maktabatu I'laam became the Ministry of Information. A network of several FM radio stations was organized, and took over several TV and radio stations. In the regions it controls its main radio stations are known as al-Andalus, but I number them I, II, III, IV and V, meaning Mogadishu (until August 2011), Baidoa, Kismayo and lower Juba, and Buulo Haawa (until early March 2011) and Eel Buur for Galgaduud. The Andalus stations coordinated their broadcasts, and at least one hour of broadcasts was the same across all stations; the Kismayo based radio station seemed most important. New websites also emerged, not controlled by Al-Shabaab but at least sympathizing with them: Somalimemo.net; AmiirNuur.com; Somalimidnimo.com; and alqimmah.

net. In general these webpages (with the exception of the last, Al Qimmah), were more locally focused than their predecessors, and more commonly appeared in Somali.

The Maktabatu Siyaasada iyo Gobolad, the Ministry of the Interior, was another centralizing mechanism.[50] The department was supposed to have control over the *walis* (the Islamic governors) and the local administrations. Huseen 'Ali Fiddow (Murosade/Foor'ulus/Haber Mohamed/ Hilibi) was put in charge of this, while Godane kept close control over the appointments to the local administrations.

How could all of this be financed? Al-Shabaab created the Maktabatu Maaliya, the Ministry of Finance. The Maktab was chaired by Ibrahim Afghani (Abuu Zalma). Al-Shabaab's Islamic administrations were financed by an increasingly efficient taxation system. Like all Somali militias, Al-Shabaab took payments from workers, businesses and aid organizations. One non-governmental organization (NGO) manager in Mogadishu told the writer on condition of anonymity:

In the regions where the Shabaab has absolute control, they demand a percentage of the total project cost. It may range between 5 and 15 per cent depending on the administration and the influence of the local partners implementing the project. A demand is also made on landlords [and] vehicle owners working under a contract with the UN or international organizations. Around 15 per cent of the rent must be paid to the Shabaab if you lease your property to an international organization or the UN. Employees are also instructed to reimburse roughly 5 per cent of their salary on a monthly basis.

At times it seemed that local staff of international NGOs were aware of the taxation and tried to cover it up. One respondent said: 'I know a case with MSF in Middle Juba: Al-Shabaab told them to pay US$10,000 in contribution for being allowed to stay there. They refused, but they agreed about paying tax in the form of qat. They are still there, doing their work.'[51]

Business activity and employment generally increased in Al-Shabaab-controlled areas before 2011, owing to the relative security. This, in turn, allowed for a more regular tax revenue stream for Al-Shabaab. For example, by 2010 Al-Shabaab charged every ship that docked at Kismayo's port US$2,000 and US$1,000 for a dhow. The group also taxed the imported goods unloaded at the port, with US$0.60 levied on every 50 kg bag of imported food, US$200 for every car and between US$400 and US$500 for every truck. But ordinary Somalis were also taxed, according to a respondent from Kismayo: 'Al-Shabaab does collect and manage taxes like other administrative services they perform in the region under their rule. They tax 10–15 per cent on everything from land property—both plots with houses or small land plots, to commercial centers, stores, livestock, farms or any other place that engages business activities.'[52]

Tax rates in Kismayo, 2010

Camel	– 180 000 Shillings
Cow	– 90 000 shillings
Goat	– 50 000 shillings

In Kismayo Al-Shabaab taxed business, hawkers, residential houses, new houses, and even the construction sector. However, the rapid expansion also meant that it faced problems when collecting taxes. Taxation was seen as too important for the 'new Shabaabs', the new administrators to handle, so old-fashioned Al-Shabaab adherents, ideologically indoctrinated, young, but not necessarily trained for their new tasks, were employed. According to a local respondent: 'All taxes and administration employees are former fighters given short training of one month, and the Al-Shabaab taxation system was generally unpopular and troublesome, mainly caused by the lack of proper accounts.'[53]

Al-Shabaab managed to transfer strategic taxes, such as the taxes from Kismayo port, to the central organization. This was not done without resistance from members of the Kismayo administration, but was aided by the fact that Ibrahim Afghani, the head of finances who was also prominent in the Kismayo administration, could oversee the process. The group also managed to centralize some of the other forms of taxation. During the 2010–11 period it seems income from Eritrea decreased.[54] But Al-Shabaab also diversified its income; contrary to popular belief, its major sources of funding were domestic—local taxes, and taxes from the various ports became the main sources of income.

The new military structure

The organization mania within Al-Shabaab also resulted in the establishment of a variety of training camps. Many were constructed in 2009, but many also rapidly disappeared. The leadership became painfully aware that the plethora of training camps was draining its resources, and decided to focus on more concentrated and larger training camps. In the southern areas the Khalid bin Walid base, previously known as the Badmadow base (The Black Sea base), close to Kismayo, became the most famous, although one near Jilib, a camp named Shuhadaa Al Khayr (the holy ones who die in jihad), also became prominent.[55] Close to Brawa, the Haawa camp, a combined militia base and training facility, grew in importance and hosted diaspora Somalis, including some from Scandinavia. In the Hiran region, a camp was constructed between Buqda and Eel Ali, a jungle area, which hosted numerous foreign fighters.[56]

In Mogadishu the training became concentrated in the bases around the Daynile, which hosted the Amniyat, and recruits from the Puntland area. The Nabhan training center in the villa of the late General Mohamed Sheikh Osman was commanded by Omar Hammami, alias Abu Mansoor Al-Amriki. This camp was rumored to be the most internationally focused, training East Africans, and also to have the strongest ideological indoctrination routines.[57]

In Bay Bakool, the El Bashir camp close to the Borame sub-village in the Kor Kara Madina area of Buur Hakaba District was perhaps one of the most famous. The El Bashir camp was the first camp that this writer is aware of that engaged in forced recruitment, mainly of children, and the remote location was said to have been chosen to keep children away from their families. In Baidoa the former Bay Project compound known as Siliga American was used to train volunteers supporting Al-Shabaab. The courses focused on military tactics, which included suicide tactics, as well as mobilization, orientation and motivation. Courses in Bay Bakool would normally last three to six months, after which trainees joined the fighting in different regions of Somalia such as Mogadishu, Gedo, Bakool and Galgaduud. In this sense, at least in the period 2009–2010, the military camps of Bay acted as a forces reserve for all of the Al-Shabaab, enabling it to reinforce on all fronts. African, Arab, Afghan and Somali instructors sought to instil a particular world view amongst recruits, akin to Huntington's 'Clash of Civilizations'—painting a picture of a world divided between good and evil. On one side stood bin Laden, and on the other Bush and Obama.

However, the very location of the camps led to several problems. First, it encouraged clanism. Recruits to the various training camps were recruited locally, and thus had a clan bias, and when these recruits were enrolled in their respective units, mostly raised locally, these units also became clan-based. In one sense there was tension between the clan-based recruitment and the indoctrination taking place during training, which stressed the unity of the *ummah*. The recruits in the camps were not necessarily motivated by either a desire for global jihad or Somali nationalism, money could be enough. Around Brawa one Al-Shabaab militiaman reported that he was recruited on the promise of a start-up bonus of US$400 and regular pay.[58]

In Mogadishu, according to AMISOM, Al-Shabaab was organized on three fronts. The first front stretched from Lido sector of Abdi-Aziz District to Godey Elementary/Intermediate School. The militants deployed in this site were assigned to mount attacks to vicinity of the Lido sector, the Hotel Global, and sectors in Behani, while they got logistical supplies from a building in Suq-Ba'ad which used to be an administrative sector of Suq-Ba'ad district. According to AMISOM officials, these forces were under the direct command of Sheikh Ali Mohamad Rage. A second group of Al-Shabaab fighters operated from Sinai up to Howlwadag; this group was assigned to launch attacks against Villa Somalia, the May 15 School, and a depot of the former Wardhigley police station, and were commanded by Muktar Robow, even after his supposed fall from grace in 2009. The third group operated in an area covering Howlwadag, Casa-Populare, Bermuda and Dabka, all in the Hodan and Howlwadag districts. Their logistical supplies were in the Daynille district. This group's main job was to harass the bases of AMISOM and government forces defensively lining up from Km-4 to the monument of Sayid Mohamed Abdulle Hassan, and it was commanded by Sheikh Fuad Mohamed Shongola.

In one sense these units, the most important under Al-Shabaab command, were a product of the Mogadishu trench war. They also demonstrated Al-Shabaab's unbelievable centralization in 2009–2010; together they were reinforced and contained recruits from the whole of Somalia. In times of crisis, they would be reinforced from all the governorates, and the reinforcements would accept the command of one of the three sub-commanders. But they also demonstrated the double face of Al-Shabaab, since two of the three units mainly drew upon forces from their respective areas, and so were largely clan-based. Although there was recruitment from the whole of Somalia, the distribution of recruits amongst units inside Mogadishu was influenced by clan.

Fighting was not only limited to Mogadishu. In Galguduud and Mudug, Al-Shabaab still had an open fight with the forces of Alhu Sunna Wah Jamaah. In this region, the fighting deteriorated into mere clan clashes, in which the Murosade, on the side of Al-Shabaab, fought traditional enemies in the Hawadle clan. The front lines roughly followed the clan borders, with the largest Al-Shabaab base roughly corresponding to the largest Murosade clan controlled city in the area. However, there were also attempts to centralize in this area, and the commander in the area, who was also the nominal Mudug Governor, Yusuf Sheikh ise Sheikh Ahmed 'Kabatukade' (meaning 'the one who prays with shoes'), was a close friend of Godane. As another illustration of the shades of ideology within Al-Shabaab, Kabatukade, a nominal ally of Godane who was supposed to represent the pan-Islamism of the organization, was nevertheless one of the leaders with strongest local focus, characterizing Al-Shabaab as a local resistance group.

Continuing internationalization?

The Al-Shabaab expansion actually led to a weakening of the international offensive jihadist strand in the organization, with the arrival of new recruits, administrative leaders, bandits, and individuals attracted to the perceived justice and order brought by Al-Shabaab. In 2009–2010 there was a hollowing out of the organization with regard to ideology.

Al-Shabaab's rhetoric retained aspects of its highly international focus, for example threatening the soccer World Cup in South Africa in 2010. It also praised Al-Qaeda and pledged support to various Al-Qaeda affiliates, and even threatened to send reinforcements to Al-Qaeda in the Arabian Peninsula (AQAP).[59] After the killing of two Iraqi Al-Qaeda members, Abu Ayyub al Masri and Abu Omar al-Baghdadi, Al-Shabaab indicated that some attacks in Mogadishu were revenge for their deaths.[60] There were many other examples: Fuad Mohamed Khalaf for example claimed that Islamists would carry out attacks in the United States if President Barack Obama and American citizens did not convert to Islam.[61] On 2 February 2010 Al-Shabaab's Amir Godane publicly swore to 'connect the horn of Africa jihad to the one led by Al-Qaeda and its leader Sheikh Osama Bin Laden.'[62] The rhetoric of the top level leaders of the organization, as well as of the propaganda outlets (including those intended for a Somali audience only), were surprisingly pan-Islamic. This also went for the supposed moderates such as Muktar Robow, vowing to re-establish the Caliphate as well as to send direct help to AQAP.[63]

However, the focus of Al-Shabaab's tactical campaigns, its military focus, remained in Somalia. There were exceptions such as the threats against the World Cup, which made South Africa engage with Al-Shabaab in dialogue.[64] There was a strange incident where the Kenyans alleged that an Al-Shabaab militant had blown up a bus in Nairobi in 2010.[65] However, in general Al-Shabaab attacked targets explicitly involved in Somali warfare.

Al-Shabaab's most spectacular attack so far, the 11 July 2010 suicide bombings that killed seventy-six people watching soccer on TV in Uganda, was in fact an example of the local focus. The Ugandan and Burundian AMISOM forces were tactically very powerful within Somalia, and by 2010 were the only thing that stood between Al-Shabaab and total victory in the south; The TFG forces simply did not function, most of the units that were trained defected,[66] but Uganda and Burundi had more plentiful and better quality forces in Somalia, with armor and artillery support. It is too easy to take this as a sign that Al-Shabaab was isolated and unprofessional; in a Somali setting it was not, and had a surprising level of organization and sophistication by comparison with other Somali actors. Indeed, the attack was indicative of operational sophistication in that it demonstrated how Al-Shabaab was able to inflict causalities outside Somalia, and how it could use the international jihadist narrative to enlist support within Uganda. The Ugandan authorities claimed that Ugandans had been aiding Al-Shabaab.[67] There were ample warnings that the latter was attempting to persuade foreign jihadists to support it tactically outside Somalia. On 9 July 2010, two days before the Kampala blasts, Al-Shabaab issued a statement that encouraged other jihad organizations around the world to attack Ugandan and Burundian embassies, as a revenge for the countries' support for the TFG.[68] However, the focus of the attack was purely tactical, it was against targets selected because of the situation in Somalia, and the aim was to drive Ugandan and Burundian forces out of Somalia.

There were no indications that international recruitment, of both ethnic Somalis and non-Somalis, declined after the Ethiopian withdrawal. Ethnic Somalis were still recruited all over the West. In Scandinavia a pattern was established, where first recruiters based in Rinkeby, then recruiters based in Gothenburg, spread their nets beyond Sweden and into Norway and Denmark as well. Norwegian Somalis alleged that it was Swedish recruiters that swayed Norway's first 'martyr' from Somalia to leave Norway in 2009, to act as an instructor for Al-Shabaab.[69] The individual in question had received training in VIP protection, in the vehicle protection unit of the Norwegian royal guard, and used this skill for training purposes in Mogadishu. He was born in Somalia in 1984, but arrived in Norway in 1994. His parents had divorced, but he was highly popular with his friends and a capable football player before he joined the Norwegian army in 2005–2006. After national service he got a relatively well paid job. By late 2009, he was alienated from his own family, losing contact with his father and mother, becoming involved with Swedish Somalis. He disappeared, and his father was told about his new whereabouts by a surprise call from Beled Hawo in 2010.

In Sweden it seems that Shuaib Ali Sheikh Mohamed, born in 1981, was a key figure in establishing the recruitment channels, but Ali died on 2 July 2009, fighting for Shabaab. Two other Swedish Somalis, Mohamoud Jama and Billé Ilias Mohamed, were charged, and admitted travelling to Somalia and joining Shabaab training programmes, but were acquitted in court, mainly because the link between joining the Shabaab and collaborating in terrorism could not be proved.[70] One of the accused had been an active blogger (http://abumuminah.bloggspace.se/3/), and showed an international rather than purely Somali engagement. The internet pseudonym for Mohamoud Jama was also active on Islamic awakening publishing entries as 'I love the trio bombers for Allah sake.' Another document, '44 ways of supporting Jihad' written by Anwar al-Awlaki, was found on a memory stick belonging to Billé Ilias. The two had wider connections, and one of them had been living with Munir Awad, who was arrested both in Pakistan and in Ethiopia for alleged attempts to link up with Shabaab and Pakistani jihadists.[71]

Shabaab also gave Denmark its first suicide bomber, when twenty-four year-old Abdi Rahman Mohamed blew himself up at a graduation ceremony for Somali medical students in Mogadishu. Indeed it seems that many of the foreign recruits became suicide bombers.

The Norwegian and Swedish recruitment followed the patterns established by US recruitment; the 1.5 generation was still over-represented. Several members of the Minnesota group also left as late as October 2009, including Farah Mohamed Beledi. Beledi was a football player, but was convicted of stabbing a man in the back in 2007 (during a football match), and imprisoned. Upon his release, he worked on rehabilitation of criminal youth at the Abubakar Center, which actually sent several fighters to Somalia. Al-Shabaab also claimed on its website that a Somali American from Minnesota, twenty-five-year-old Abdullahi Ahmed, had joined it; on 2 June 2011 he attempted a suicide attack on Mogadishu port. Two American citizens, Mohamed Mahmood Alessa, a twenty-year-old US citizen of Palestinian descent, and Carlos Eduardo 'Omar' Almonte, aged twenty-four from a Dominican background attempted to go to Somalia. However, the two were arrested when they attempted to board separate flights that was scheduled for Egypt, which was planned as a stop on their way to Somalia. It seems that they had been impressed by the Yemeni American jihadist Sheikh Anwar Awlaki (killed in Yemen in 2011).

What motivated the ethnic Somalis to go to Somalia? The factors could have been many. In an interview with Al-Shabaab recruits in Nairobi conducted in 2010, several factors were highlighted, including the feeling of alienation from their host countries, partly because of blocked opportunities and discrimination, and a wish to implement the Sharia in Somalia and elsewhere, to help people; one recruit still stressed the Ethiopian role. A single Kenyan Somali who was interviewed stressed money as a factor.[72] They had all been recruited through groups within mosques or *madrassas*, which seem to have reinforced a narrative stressing discrimination.

There was definitely an apparatus waiting for them in Nairobi. They were given an address at the airport, and preparations were made for their travel to Mogadishu. At times travel took place through Hargeisa in Somaliland, an easier entry point than through the Kenyan border since controls were fewer. The recruits were destined for specific training camps. Some camps such as one in the Brawa area were specially designated to handle foreign recruits, and some standardized instruction materials, such as books *The Morals of the Mujahedin* and *Black Flag of the Mujahedin*, were given out.[73]

The Al-Shabaab recruits were not necessarily from the margins of society. However, recruitment was very often aided by the situation of the diaspora community. In Scandinavia, the Somali community was heavily criticized in the media, and this created a defensive posture among the various Somali communities, where information was kept secret and the dialogue with the police was weak. The effect was not created by jihadism, but rather by skepticism towards the press in the various countries as well as the police. Facts that circulated in the Somali diaspora community simply did not reach the greater community outside it because of this effect. There were large segments in Denmark, Norway and Sweden that in Somali settings expressed support for Al-Shabaab, usually seen as a provider of justice and discipline inside Somalia, but these elements were simply not the Somalis that the press and the various governments in the countries talked to, and they were hesitant to speak to outsiders.

The recruitment pipelines, organizing recruitment and providing practical advice to potential jihadists, were of major importance. In Sweden, such networks seem to have existed in several radical mosques in Stockholm, Gothenburg and Malmø, perhaps because of the large size Somali communities there. In Denmark the role of mosques seems to have been less important, and in Norway virtually non-existent. However, the environment in Gothenburg seems to have been important for the recruitment in both Denmark and Norway (see the last chapter), and it also seems that roving Tabliqi missionaries were infiltrated by Al-Shabaab sympathizers in Norway and used for propaganda purposes, a technique seemingly used in Somaliland too. There were also Al-Shabaab fighters who wanted to leave Somalia and to escape the group. According to the Swedes charged with supporting Al-Shabaab, there was a formal procedure for dealing with them, whereby the group isolated a person in a house, with no communication with his surroundings, while taking a decision that could be bad for the suspect.[74]

What about international non-Somali recruits? The flow of recruits from the Middle East continued, but the older generation of foreign fighters, the old guard of Al-Qaeda's East African cell, was dying out. In 2009, Saleh Ali Saleh Nabahn was killed in 'Operation Celestial Strike': an American helicopter attack.[75] Only one of the Al-Qaeda veterans, Fazul Mohamed, was now confirmed alive and free. Another, Issa Osman Issa, might have been active, but was rumored to have been arrested by the Americans. The dynamics had changed; Al-Shabaab was centralized, allied to a new generation of Al-Qaeda fighters, large and bloated, containing opportunists, dedicated jihadists, and reformists, the border being sometimes highly blurred between these groups, and even within individuals. It was this organization, large and impressive in some ways, that was to take on the African Union in an all-out battle in

September 2010, the so-called Ramadan offensive, also known as Nahayatu Muxtadiin ('the end of the apostates'), an operation that was to see Shabaab encountering its largest losses since 2006, and seriously fragment the organization.

Nahayatu Muxtadiin

Strategically, the AMISOM forces were a thorn in the side for Al-Shabaab, and the Al-Shabaab leadership was perfectly aware that the 1,500 men actually serving in the TFG's forces would be easily defeated without the presence of the AMISOM forces numbering between 7,200 and 9,200. However, the AMISOM deployment was militarily vulnerable, roughly following an 'L' shape, where the tip of the 'L,' the north eastern bases around Villa Somalia, had limited logistical connections with the airport, mainly via the Makkah Al Mukaramah road. This was correctly estimated by Al-Shabaab to be a strategic weakness.[76]

Al-Shabaab was in a strategically vulnerable position; it was extended and vulnerable to the military harassment of Ethiopian forces conducting border raids, such as that in el Berde on 1 June 2010. Around Dolow and Beled Weyene, TFG forces based inside Ethiopia and Kenya also conducted frequent raids.[77] It must have been tempting to try to change the threatening situation by initiating a decisive battle in Mogadishu, where the AMISOM forces could in theory be defeated; to stop Ethiopian supported raids would have meant an invasion of Ethiopia, an act that would almost certainly have ended in defeat. Al-Shabaab's 21 May offensive inside Mogadishu had given it an advantageous position for a larger offensive within Mogadishu, and the possibility of commanding a position from which it could shell the harbor. An additional asset was its newly formed and highly professional Kataaib.[78]

For Al-Shabaab's Amir, Godane, the situation was so advantageous that it seemed reasonable to attempt to sway the leadership into an all-out offensive. An operation, targeting the Makkah al Mukaramah road could, if successful, isolate the forces of AMISOM in Villa Somalia; roughly 40 per cent of AMISOM's forces would have been surrounded. The top *shura* of Al-Shabaab, which now included Al-Qaeda's Fazul Muhamed, was not convinced. According to local sources Shongola and Robow, as well as Al-Qaeda's representative, questioned the military wisdom of an all-out battle against AMISOM, claiming that Al-

Shabaab's strength had been related to insurgency tactics rather than conventional warfare. Shongola and Robow also opposed the plan for religious reasons, as it was problematic to launch an offensive during the Ramadan fast.[79] However, the centralization of Al-Shabaab had strengthened Godane's personal authority, and in the end Godane's views were pushed through.

The preparations for the Ramadan offensive were massive, and indeed impressive, far superior in planning to what other southern Somali actors had achieved. Simultaneously Al-Shabaab reinforcements came from Juba, Hiran, Gedo and Bay. According to a participant, 1,800 fighters were brought to Bali Doogle alone, for orientation and preparation; Ahmed Osoble and Omar Hammami, aka 'Abu Mansoor Al-Amriki' were in charge of indoctrination there, showing films of the various humiliations of the Islamic *ummah* around the world, and giving speeches—according to a witness, 'Fighters became emotional and started crying after viewing the videos and listening the speeches.'[80] An opinion was issued by the Al-Shabaab *fatwa* council to exempt their soldiers from the fast. There were also reports of forced conscriptions.

On 23 August, following a statement by spokesman Mohamed Ali 'Raghe', Al-Shabaab launched an offensive in the Hawalwadag, Hodan, Bondehere and Whardigley districts of Mogadishu.[81] Infiltrators dressed in TFG military or police uniforms gained access to the Muna Hotel in Hamarweyne district, behind enemy lines, and created confusion, attacking more than 100 or so TFG politicians and civil servants. Al-Shabaab killed at least thirty-one people, including six parliamentarians and five soldiers.[82] A suicide attack was also launched against the presidential palace just before the offensive. Similarly, Al-Shabaab was actively using Improvised Explosive Devices (IEDs) to disrupt AMISOM and TFG logistics.[83] However, it was Muktar Robow's front that was to bear the brunt of the fighting, it was simply best positioned to try to wrest control over the Makkah Al Mukaramah road from AMISOM and the TFG. Al-Shabaab was not without tactical successes, and even managed to surround a unit of AMISOM soldiers in the Jubba Hotel in Shangani for a couple of days.[84] Moreover, several TFG units deserted because of the lack of pay.[85]

However, AMISOM was strong, and Uganda had just brought in 300 men as reinforcements. Al-Shabaab was not militarily strong enough to prevail, Uganda's main battle tanks proved more than a match for Al-

Shabaab fighters. Robow's unit was lured into an ambush, losing forty men; his fighters had been invited to participate in a Ramadan feast, but had been tricked. After two weeks, Al-Shabaab's strength showed signs of weakening, and AMISOM intelligence estimated that it lost around 500 to 700 fighters and approximately 2,000 others were wounded when the month-long pitched battles in Mogadishu ended. Al-Shabaab was publicly humiliated when a gathering of the traditional elders of the dominant Hawiye clan publicly declared that Al-Shabaab had lost the offensive on 13 September.[86]

The units commanded by the individuals who had argued against the offensive, Robow and Shongola, took the heaviest losses. As a result, Robow withdrew his forces before the battle had ended. There was widespread dissatisfaction with Godane's strategy, expressed by Shongola among others. Adding to the discontent was the fact that one of Robow's friends, Sheikh Ayub, who had been badly wounded in the street battles, ultimately seems to have been killed by the Amniyat, in what seemed to have been developed into an ordinary practice amongst Al-Shabaab, the killing of badly wounded soldiers to enable them to achieve martyrdom. In many ways Al-Shabaab was in a state of disarray; according to AMISOM sources, it had more than 25 per cent of its fighters put out of action and many top leaders were dead. It had also spent large sums on the Ramadan offensive, and increased both its taxation and the use of forced recruitment. Al-Shabaab was in turmoil.

7

THE ERA OF TROUBLES (2010–)

After September 2010 Harakat Al-Shabaab was a changed organization. The failure to gain a decisive victory against the African Union in Somalia (AMISOM) in Mogadishu, the clan-based recruitment, and Robow's conflict with the rest of the organization after the release of Hapsade in 2009 all indicated that the organization had some problems, and Godane's centralization drive ended. In fact, for a period Al-Shabaab became fragmented into smaller local parts with little centralized command. Nevertheless, its achievements were still impressive for a faction operating in Somalia, with less internal conflict than most of its rivals, appearing much more unified in the media, and being much more able to coordinate its attacks. By 2012 centralization efforts were continuing, and Godane again gained power.

The Ramadan offensive led to the most serious crisis in the history of the organization. The fact that it was Godane who planned the ill-fated offensive, and was the strategist behind the centralization efforts, meant that the September defeat damaged his status as a leader, and his leadership was now contested. This was more serious than Muktar Robow's old conflict with the other leaders, since the skepticism about Godane was shared by other Al-Shabaab veterans, including Hassan Yaqubi and Fuad Khalif 'Shongola'. Some commentators have said the conflict was ideological, between the trans-nationalists and nationalists within the organization.[1] However, the ideological differences were smaller than perceived, the boundaries between the different groups were blurred, and a compromise had been reached: all members of Al-Shabaab, as well as affiliated Al-Qaeda members, held that Somalia, and the establishment of Islamic governance structures, should have priority, ahead of international attacks.[2] It should be noted that such an arrangement also provided Al-Qaeda with notable advantages, as Al-Shabaab camps could be used as channels to promote their world view.

Unsurprisingly, disagreements over tactics and the disposition during the first Ramadan offensive became the first major challenge for the organization.[3] Al-Shabaab's major victories had been won by a combination of speed, flexibility, hit and run attacks, terror—not the Stalingrad-like warfare that had taken place in Mogadishu under the Ramadan offensive. The second major disagreement concerned the Amniyat and its status as outside of the regular Al-Shabaab justice structures. Under Godane, the Amniyat had become a separate entity independent of the Al-Shabaab executive *shura* council and the supreme guidance *shura*, an entity dominated by the person who was to become perhaps Godane's main opponent within the group, Fuad 'Shongola'. The reactions were serious, as both Robow and Hassan Yaqubi withdrew their forces from the Al-Shabaab command hierarchy in the aftermath of the battles.

There was serious speculation about splits; the anti-Al-Shabaab Puntland affiliated webpage wrote for example that Muktar Robow and the leader of Hisbul Islam, Hassan Dhair Aweys, planned to leave Al-Shabaab and take control over most of southern Somalia.[4] The many rumors forced Robow himself to go out in the Somali media and reconfirm his commitment to Godane, as well as addressing Osama bin Laden directly: 'We are sending a message to our group leader—Al-Qaeda leader Osama Bin Laden that we are still continuing fighting until we join our fellow brothers who killed by American troops in other countries.'[5] Robow was actually stepping up his anti-American rhetoric, perhaps in an effort to reassure Al-Qaeda leaders in East Africa as well as outside supporters.[6] Al-Shabaab leaders, or at least Ali Dheere and Robow, also attempted to organize parades of fighters in Mogadishu, and smaller scale attacks on the presidential palace continued.[7] The various attacks conducted by Al-Shabaab, and the various declarations of loyalty and unity, could not hide the existence of strong tensions within the organization; the leadership still met, but there were still issues that had been left open.

Several meetings were held to resolve the situation.[8] One Somali newspaper, the *Sunna Times*, claimed that Robow initially requested four concessions.[9] He allegedly demanded that Ahmed Godane should resign from his position of leadership and that aid workers on the ground should be given full access to Al-Shabaab-controlled areas.[10] More important, he was also said to have demanded that the Amniyat should be disbanded and all killings of Al-Shabaab military personnel at the frontlines by Amniyat agents should be investigated, and that the leadership in charge of intelligence should be fired.[11] The Amniyat was a centralization tool, and directly under Godane's control. To a certain extent it functioned as a separate organization. In its rhetoric Al-Shabaab stressed heavily the role of the Sharia courts, but were circumvented by the Amniyat, which had powers of 'instant' prosecutions outside the court system for relatively serious crimes. It was no surprise that Shongola, one of the leaders of the emerging Godane opposition, and holding responsibility for the courts, was against this development.[12] His decision to voice his anger in public was sensational in revealing the organization's disunity.

The incident also illustrates the existence of one specific and important group of dissidents within Al-Shabaab—a group of reformist Islamists, who saw the group as a tool to improve security and conditions inside Somalia through implementation of the Sharia. Al-Shabaab's increased use of forced recruitment and taxation was alienating this group, and high-ranking members even contacted AMISOM forces in order to facilitate a deal that would enable them to leave Al-Shabaab while at the same time maintaining security. Indeed, in this period AMISOM and TFG officials reported that at least two top *shura* members wanted to defect. Moreover, Al-Shabaab's allies in Al-Qaeda continued to suffer; on 6 December the Yemeni-born fighter Rabah Abu-Qalid, rumored to be number two in Al-Qaeda East Africa, was killed.[13]

These problems encouraged mid-level Al-Shabaab commanders to position themselves in what many believed to be an all-out power struggle, increasing the tension between clan groupings, for example between Ayr and Rahanwhein commanders. And according to aid workers there were instances in which the Amniyat had to snatch its prisoners from regular Al-Shabaab forces.[14] The leadership had to settle the crisis fast, but it took time; between October 2010 and February 2011, the situation was one of tense coexistence and weakening of the centralization processes that had taken place inside Al-Shabaab in early 2010. Solutions were eventually reached through intensive meetings and mediation involving local Al-Qaeda followers.

According to local sources, the Amniyat was disbanded for a period— in other words, Godane's centralization tool was abolished—but Godane remained in power.[15] Moreover, there was a large-scale campaign against the spread of corruption and abuse of power within Al-Shabaab. Some Amniyat officers were even executed.[16] Godane himself delivered a speech that contained several important points, instructing that the militias should not overreact and that the Al-Shabaab administration must protect property rights.[17]

Some observers claimed that these steps failed to solve the problems, as illustrated by the February execution of Ahmed 'Ali Huseen Keyse by Al-Shabaab. In Nairobi many claimed that this perceived act of revenge proved Robow's hostility towards Godane. As Roland Marchal has said, this explanation overlooks several facts. Keyse was himself not close to Godane, and at the time was on the fringe of Al-Shabaab, closer to the more loosely network-based Al-Ittihad al-Islamiya (AIAI) organization, and the accusation leveled against him, that he was a spy, was believed even amongst Godane's close confidants.[18]

Nevertheless, Godane had been weakened, as had Al-Shabaab itself. The first consequence was that the 'magic' of the organizations had been lost. Until 2010, Al-Shabaab had suffered some setbacks but not any large defeats since December 2006. It was in general feared and seen as unbeatable. After the Ramadan offensive this changed, aided by the various, very often overdone, stories of coming Al-Shabaab disintegration, which had been predicted by outsiders since 2008; now such rumors were for the first time taken seriously in Mogadishu.

AMISOM and the TFG also launched a major offensive against the Al-Shabaab forces in Mogadishu on 22 February 2011. Al-Shabaab was for the first time chased away from the symbolically important former Ministry of Defence (Gashaandiga) and its old positions in the former Warshadda Caanaha Milk Factory. AMISOM suffered heavy losses, as did the TFG, but Uganda and Burundi had the will and the resources to endure the losses, and the TFG received financial support that enabled it to replenish its losses, while Al-Shabaab was not able to re-supply itself.[19] It lost severely in the fighting; its finances were on the verge of collapse, and its pool of volunteers had dried up; as people saw that Al-Shabaab was unable to deliver victories, forced recruitment became more common.

The problems were serious indeed, but Al-Shabaab still had major advantages in dealing with them. It managed to convene a meeting in Kismayo as early as September to deal with the serious problems facing the organization, again an amazing show of unity by comparison with other factions in Somalia. The international fighters seem to have acted as a kind of glue, negotiating between the various parties, and gave Al-Shabaab a clear advantage; this did not settle the leadership problem, but the dialogue was started. When Fazul Mohamed was killed, for example, top AMISOM intelligence officers claimed to have found letters from Abu Yahya Al Libi of Al-Qaeda, encouraging Ahmed Godane to moderation. And in the crisis in the autumn of 2011, sources close to Al-Shabaab maintained that six Al-Qaeda officials had been sent to create unity in the face of the Kenyan advance.[20] At the same time AMISOM noted mediation efforts by Jehad Mostafa and Omar Hammami (Abu Mansoor Al-Amriki), while the former also gained more prominence in the Al-Shabaab media.[21]

The top level dialogue was, however, not enough to hide the fact that it was an altered Al-Shabaab that emerged; the weakening of the centralization of revenue as well as of the Amniyat, meant that some of the glue that kept Al-Shabaab together had been lost, and private contractors in Mogadishu, for example, started to report how Al-Shabaab forces were unwilling to aid each other.[22] Defectors also claimed that Muktar Robow had started to train his own fighters in the Jemame camp in Juba.[23]

On the diplomatic front, Al-Shabaab did achieve some victories, mainly through union with the remains of their nominal allies Hisbul Islam, which had originally been a somewhat ramshackle alliance of four Islamist organizations—the so-called Asmara group of the Alliance for the Re-liberation of Somalia (ARS-A, a group that disagreed with attempts by the other part of the ARS to negotiate with the TFG in 2009), the older Jabatulla al Islamiya, the veteran Somali jihadist Hassan Turki's Ras Kamboni, and the small Anole organization. These four organizations never became fully integrated, and two of them, Ras Kamboni (Ogadeen clan) and Anole (Harti clan), were clearly clan-based. The four had entered into an uneasy marriage on 2 February 2009. The various parts of the alliance showed disunity from day one. Their disunity might have prompted the only warlord of Somalia who turned Islamist, Siad Yusuf Indaaddes, to defect from the alliance in 2009. More seriously for the fragmented and ill-fated Hisbul Islam was the falling out between Al-Shabaab and the Anole and Ras Kamboni forces in September 2009.[24] Numerically, Ras Kamboni was the largest faction of Hisbul Islam, but Al-Shabaab easily defeated the two organizations. Nominally, Ras Kamboni's leader,

Hassan Turki, joined Al-Shabaab, but in reality, a majority of the Ras Kamboni forces either defected from Hisbul Islam because they felt it failed to protect them, or were killed in action against Al-Shabaab.[25] The first group joined under Turki's son-in-law, Ahmed Madobe, and still exists and continues to fight Al-Shabaab, in an alliance with Kenya. After the victories in Kismayo in 2009, Hisbul Islam was a mere shadow of itself, organized around the person of Hassan Dahir Aweys and his followers and their headquarters in a refugee camp in Elasha Biye, in the Afgoye corridor outside Mogadishu.

During 2010 the organization regained some power, partly by capturing the pirate port of Haradrere and re-establishing the makeshift port of Mogadishu in the 1990s, the El Maan port.[26] However, it was frequently under siege, and its local administration in Beled Weyne, for example, defected wholly to Al-Shabaab. In November 2010 Hisbul Islam was only in control of Luuq (Gedo), Haradhere (Galgaduud), Buur Hakaba (Bay), Afgooye (Lower Shabelle) and a few districts of Mogadishu.[27] After the Ramadan offensive, there were signs of a rapprochement; Hisbul Islam changed its rhetoric to become more internationally focused, praising Al-Qaeda and inviting it to come to Somalia. Sources within Al-Shabaab also claimed that a negotiated merger was close to succeeding, the final points being not points of ideology, but rather how to allocate positions within the Al-Shabaab *shura* to Hisbul Islam members. However, attacks by elements within Al-Shabaab continued, and there were several attempts to kill Hassan Dahir Aweys.[28] In December, Al-Shabaab launched an offensive against Hisbul Islam. Buud Hakaba fell after fierce fighting on 1 December, Toro-Torow fell on 14 December, Luuq on 18 December, and last, Afgooye on 21 December.[29] This was the military end of the movement.

Hisbul Islam therefore had to merge with Al-Shabaab in order to survive. The merger was declared on 28 December through formal Al-Shabaab media channels, and took place at a ceremony which emphasized the international dimension of the organization through its many references to Al-Qaeda and the international struggle.[30] Ahmed Godane, alleged to advocate a hard-line strategy towards Hisbul Islam, was in the end forced to accept the remnants of Hisbul Islam as a part of Al-Shabaab, and publicly endorsed the merger.[31] The exercise was equally humiliating for Hisbul Islam, as it negotiated from a position of being effectively defeated and failed to achieve any positions in the executive *shura*, and had to accept Harakat Al-Shabaab as its name.[32] In many ways Hisbul Islam was swallowed whole by Al-Shabaab, but Aweys, as Somali Islamism's veteran, still carried respect and considerable symbolic power, and probably saved his life by entering into the union. Hisbul Islam also carried one important prize to Al-Shabaab: the pirate city of Haradere.

Shabaab joins in piracy

Piracy had in general been met hitherto with a mixture of understanding and condemnation by Al-Shabaab. It argued that piracy was protecting Somali shores, but also that it was un-Islamic. Muktar Robow said once, 'It is a crime to take commercial ships,'[33] but could be found praising the pirates on other occasions.[34] It has been suggested by several observers that Al-Shabaab had an intimate relationship with piracy, the first allegations surfacing as early as 2008.[35] Most of these allegations were wrong, and some suggestions were very odd, for instance that Al-Shabaab trained some 2,500 men for piracy (which would have amounted to around 80 per cent of the estimated total number of pirates in 2008).[36] As I have noted elsewhere, Somali pirates were first and foremost profit seekers, and to persuade them to share revenue, something had to be given in return, protection from violence (including violence by Al-Shabaab), supplies, or resources of some kind.[37] Before 2010, Al-Shabaab had been largely irrelevant for the pirates. The fact that until 2010 it lacked a military presence in pirate ports indicates that pirates probably had little motivation to pay shares to them, and Al-Shabaab few means to pressure them to do so.

Some Al-Shabaab commanders, such as the deceased Timojele Rambo and Hassan Afrah, admittedly had some early connections with various pirate groupings. Afrah was connected to the pirates through his Suleiman clan background. However, the Suleiman in general did not support Al-Shabaab. Recruitment within other clans engaged in piracy—the Saad, Ayr and the Majerteen—was also limited (an exception would perhaps have been Ayr until the killing of Aden Hashi Ayro in 2008). The two commanders mentioned were not high-ranking in Al-Shabaab and Rambo died in 2009. Around Kismayo, pirates used the island of Koheima to re-supply, probably aided by businessmen from the Majerteen and Ayr clans from Kismayo, and it is likely that there were some payments to Al-Shabaab from this business. The last connection was through Ayr pirates who managed to launch a few attacks out of the Merka-Brawa area. But by and large, Al-Shabaab-controlled territory was surprisingly free of piracy, and until 2010 no hijacked ship was led into an Al-Shabaab controlled port or makeshift landing place.

However, this was to change. On Sunday 25 April 2010, newspapers reported that elements of Al-Shabaab had entered one of Somalia's four major pirate ports, Haradhere.[38] It came about after a strategic victory in which it routed a large proportion of the fragmented Aluh Sunna Waah Jamaa (ASWJ) group. By 21 April Al-Shabaab scored another important victory, evicting ASWJ forces from the towns of Galcad, Masagaway and Eldeher. Symbolically it was an important victory, as Massagawa was the birthplace of Sheikh Ibrahim, one of ASWJ's spiritual leaders. However, it was also an important tactical victory, as the Abgal Waisle section of the ASWJ had been sizeable and was now routed.

Nevertheless, Alhu Sunnah forces in Dhusamareb remained strong, and could have threatened Al-Shabaab on the flank. The latter withdrew and Hisbul Islam took their place on 2 May. Hisbul Islam set out on a lightning move, not unlike the Russians' race to Pristina airport in Kosovo in 1999. Forces were mobilized from the Hiraan and Mogadishu area and set out on an arduous trip, avoiding Al-Shabaab troops, and finally reaching Haradhere, snatching it in front of Al-Shabaab.[39] Haradhere remained loosely controlled by Hisbul Islam until Al-Shabaab swallowed up that organization in December 2010.

The first sign of a change within Al-Shabaab however came before December. A taboo was broken in October, when for the first time a ship was taken into the areas controlled by Al-Shabaab, as no hijacked vessel had been before. The South African yacht *Chosil* ended up in the Merka-Brawa area. The *Chosil* case also turned out to be quite a special one, as the small ransom demanded was said to have been just to cover food and accommodation for the hostages, and a political statement was demanded by Al-Shabaab, requiring South Africa to distance itself from the United States. According to local sources the hijacking simply involved an Ayr pirate leading *Chosil* to the coast, and a confused local Al-Shabaab commander conveying a message to the *shura*, which sanctioned the mission.

By December 2010, Al-Shabaab became even more entangled in piracy when it occupied Haradhere with some 200 militiamen. The occupiers' presence was much more centralized than it had been under Hisbul Islam.

The latter's forces had consisted mostly of its local clan-based supporters, but the Al-Shabaab militia was multi-clan, including members of
the Rahanhwein clan, not from that area at all. Al-Shabaab, it should be
noted, was in no condition to wield absolute power in the area, as it was
still present in limited numbers; it was nevertheless able to take advantage of clan conflicts in the local areas, establishing relatively good control. Al-Shabaab then moved to tax the pirates, allegedly at a rate between
15 and 20 per cent, partly by having a presence in Hazarder, but partly
also by threatening Ayr pirates operating outside Haradere with violent
action against their relatives within Al-Shabaab-controlled areas.

There were immediate reactions on behalf of the pirates, and late 2010
and early 2011 saw many pirate leaders—the infamous Mohamed Abdi
Hassan 'Afweyne', Abdulkadir Mohamed 'Afweyne' and his son Mohamed
Abukar 'Gafaje', and Abdi Qarani—relocating to Hobiyo; some, like
Mohamed Abdi Hassan 'Afweyne', tried to maintain operations outside
Haradhere without going ashore while some, such as Gafaje, attempted
to ally with Al-Shabaab's enemies in Galmudug state.[40] The clan dynamics among the Haradhere pirates seemed to change radically; the Ayr,
often associated with Hisbul Islam before, now had clan connections
within Al-Shabaab, since many Ayr members had joined when Hisbul
Islam merged with Al-Shabaab. This led to a boom in Ayr piracy; according to one Somali researcher as many as ten out of fifteen major Haradhere
syndicates were led by Ayr leaders. Al-Shabaab did, however, still fail
largely to tax pirates outside their area of control, including those in the
major pirate city of Hobiyo, although this situation improved for Al-
Shabaab when the 'Afweyne' cartel again showed an interest in Haradhere,
because of a need for a seasonal base.[41]

Al-Shabaab gained control over Haradhere when it was in a vulnerable period, as the southern pirate groups had become increasingly unsuccessful in their attacks, and the pirates of Haradhere had large losses, with
twelve teams getting lost at sea during the spring of 2011 alone; so the
areas Al-Shabaab controlled were the pirate areas that were in decline.[42]
It is important to stress the 'Somalia first' policy of Al-Shabaab, and that
pirates, including the ones in Haradhere, are profit seekers who want to
avoid involvement in the wider War on Terror. Thus local pirates, as well
as Al-Shabaab commanders, so far seem uninterested in using Haradhere to launch maritime terror attacks, suspecting trouble for piracy in
the form of United States counter-moves and pirates having to flee from
Haradhere.

The conquest of Haradhere and Al-Shabaab's involvement did however mean a sacrifice for Al-Shabaab fighters who focused on juridical reform; a compromise was reached on the relevant Sharia principles, in which (non-Muslim) foreign ships were considered legitimate targets. This was the biggest concession to the criminal elements within Al-Shabaab so far.

Offensives, counter-offensives, internal tension and drought

Al-Shabaab's military troubles were not over by the spring of 2011. A loose alliance of Somali militias, with the military support of Kenya and Ethiopia, went on the offensive in Gedo province, and these forces managed to take control of Beled Hawo, Luuq and Dhoobley. In Dhoobley, Al-Shabaab faced Kenyan artillery, and the local clan-based forces were supported logistically by the Kenyans.[43] By the end of April the town of Garbaharey also fell.

Al-Shabaab could not concentrate its forces to meet the threats in Gedo and in Mogadishu, but had to fight a 'four front' war; it was engaged in combat in Hiraan and Galguduud as well, although successfully defending itself in these places, even launching the odd offensive around the town of Dhusamareb. On 10 May AMISOM and allied TFG forces attacked in the direction of the Bakara market of Mogadishu. Almost simultaneously the alliance in Gedo, supported by two Ethiopian battalions, renewed the offensive.[44] The May AMISOM offensive in Mogadishu had been planned for some time, and aimed to strangulate the economic center of Mogadishu, the Bakara market, by surrounding it, thus removing one of the main sources of income for Al-Shabaab. The position of Al-Shabaab in this area had been left quite vulnerable by previous AMISOM advances, leaving it as a bulge, surrounded by AMISOM on three sides. AMISOM and its TFG allies were quite successful, Al-Shabaab was again bleeding. By the end of the offensive AMISOM gained control over roughly thirteen out of Mogadishu's sixteen districts.

The defeats in Gedo and in Mogadishu put pressure on Al-Shabaab, sub-commanders within the organizations became demoralized, new militias had to be forcefully recruited, and revenue was lost. Violent clashes within the organization occurred for the first time. Around Dobiley, an Al-Shabaab district commander and his replacement fought a small war.[45] The precariousness of Al-Shabaab's situation was also apparent as it accepted that at least one of its district commanders organized clan militias.

Al-Qaeda's losses, it should be noted, were also Al-Shabaab's losses, as the two entities were connected in the minds of many Somalis. On 8 June Abdullah Fazul, then Al-Qaeda's East African leader, drove in a wrong direction in Mogadishu and was killed; the event was blamed on his rivals amongst Al-Shabaab, who allegedly had supplied him with wrong directions, but it was probably an accident.[46] The killing of Osama bin Laden on the night of 1–2 May 2011 was equally a humiliation for the Al-Shabaab leadership, because of their foreign allies' loss of prestige. Interestingly, in a public show of unity, Al-Shabaab launched a form of funeral ceremony outside Mogadishu, in Afgoye on the Bin Jabir farm.[47] The ceremony, called 'We are all Osama', was aimed at showing sorrow for the death of the supreme Al-Qaeda leader. At the ceremony Sheikh Muktar Robow delivered a speech explaining the main relations between Osama bin Laden and the Somali people that could, according to him, be traced back to the 1990s when Osama was in Sudan. He mentioned that bin Laden had helped the Somalis in their fight against General Mohamed Farah Aideed, American forces and UNOSOM in 1992–94. Sheikh Muktar Robow further shared his experience with Osama bin Laden from the time he was in Afghanistan. The ceremony was attended by prominent Al-Shabaab personalities including Hassan Dahir Aweys, Fuad Shongola, Sheikh Nuur Moallim Abdirahman, Sheikh Mohamed Abu-Abdalla (Wali of Lower Shabelle Region), Sheikh Mohamed Hassan (Wali of Banadir Region) and Omar Hammami (Abu Mansoor Al-Amriki). A number of other foreign fighters were also present. The whole session was duly filmed, photographed, and put on the internet.[48] Many Al-Shabaab leaders expressed their sorrow for the death of Osama bin Laden. Spokesman Mohamed Rage proclaimed Al-Shabaab's loyalty to the new leader of Al-Qaeda Ayman al-Zawahiri; interestingly, he did so in a Somali radio show, primarily intended for Somalis.[49]

Ironically the Arab Spring, which was viewed very positively by Al-Shabaab, drew foreign fighters back to their home countries. In May 2011, for example, sources inside Mogadishu reported that Libyan Al-Shabaab fighters had set out on an arduous trip to Libya in order to support the rebellion against Gaddafi. American drone attacks also created problems; on 23 June 2011, the United States launched drone attacks against Al-Shabaab leaders alleged to be linked with Al-Qaeda in the

Arabian Peninsula (AQAP), which resulted—much more important for Al-Shabaab—in a rapid decline in the vital import/export businesses conducted from Kismayo port.[50]

The spring of 2011 was thus a time of trouble for Al-Shabaab. Nevertheless, the organization also showed strengths. It was still able to transport reinforcements across clan divisions, and managed for example to use reserves from Baidoa in Mudug and Mogadishu. These efforts were relatively centralized, the organization using the Maslah building a form of arrival center. Moreover, Al-Shabaab increased its taxation and recruitment efforts. In the Afgooye District, for example, it imposed new taxes on local businesses. Small business stalls were from April and onwards to pay US$20–40 per month to the movement, while bigger business concerns had to pay US$100–200 per month. People living in public buildings, potentially including at some point a large number of IDPs in the Afgooye Corridor, were to pay US$10–20 per month as rent. Al-Shabaab was also changing its strategies, employing more assassinations and suicide attacks as well as road bombs in a form of asymmetric warfare, in order to counter the superior forces of AMISOM. In one sense this was 'back to the roots'—Al-Shabaab was again invoking the strategy that had brought them success in 2007.

Al-Shabaab also seemed to continue its attempts to indoctrinate the society under its control, for example organizing training for NGOs, and continuing to ban qat, even in the Bay Bakool area, which was supposed to have a moderate regime. Elders were also trained in order to help the recruitment efforts. Al-Shabaab's very organization gave it advantages. As Roland Marchal states, 'Al-Shabaab, at the opposite of all factions including the TFG, has put in place a system of rules and regulations that provides the fighters with a salary that is not symbolical. Although figures varied in the interviews, this earning is between US$60 and US$200 for a fighter or low rank officer. The point is that this is paid not once a year but every month of the year.'[51] In late June 2011, it again seemed that Al-Shabaab was resurfacing, according to a field researcher in Mogadishu:

The current situation of the Harakat Al-Shabaab is getting better compared to two months ago. Two months ago there was a plan of escape, foreigners and important weapons were taken from El-Maan port and Elbur airport, at that time, now they reorganize and they have a chance if the TFG do not attack. The nomination of the new foreign Shura member, a Yemeni was very good, the began to regroup, orientate, give salaries, he came to Somalia few days before Nabhan was killed. He stopped all attack and accepts only defense.[52]

Al-Shabaab continued its road construction and aid programmes, and it still had major sources of income. The sugar and charcoal trade through Kismayo port was considerable, the UN arms embargo enforcement body estimating the taxes from sugar trade at between US$400,000 and US$800,000 annually.[53] Charcoal, illegal according to Al-Shabaab's own regulations, also provides a huge income. The key to the charcoal trade, highly damaging to the environment inside Somalia, is Al-Shabaab's control over the ports of Merka, Brawa, Buurgabo, El Maan, and Qudha, where according to the UN arms embargo commission, it taxes 2.5 per cent over the whole logistical chain. However, much of the income comes from more trivial sources; the group also taxes houses, farms, shops, and transport. It also collects its largest taxes from ports it controls, taxing more ordinary commodities such as small cars (US$500), big cars (US$1,000) and consumer electronics. Other items such as building materials are also taxed. NGOs and UN organizations/local partners that operate in Al-Shabaab-controlled areas are also taxed. Perhaps the most underestimated source of income is the transport taxes, as Al-Shabaab from 2010 increased the number of its checkpoints. A minibus (*matato*) going from Elasha outside Mogadishu, for example, has to pass four checkpoints, paying US$27.70 altogether, and an estimated fifteen buses were going back and forth per day, while at least thirteen other such routes are in operation.

Inside Mogadishu, Al-Shabaab established cooperatives for minibuses, which probably still exist, taking 50 per cent of their income. The figures are impressive, but there are several facts that should be kept in mind. Not all of this money reached Al-Shabaab commanders, there were clear incidents of corruption, and the increased tax pressure also decreased the group's popularity. And there are questions as to whether the taxes ended up with the central leadership or went to individual sub-commanders. Kismayo taxes did indeed go to the central Al-Shabaab Ministry of Finance, since it was physically located in this town. Interviews with Al-Shabaab leaders in Merka and lower Shabelle also indicate that there was some centralization and the tax surplus that was gained above a specified sum of money was sent to Mogadishu. However, little information was available about taxation in Muktar Robow's home town, Baidoa, or in Galmudug, and it is highly unlikely that the taxation here was centrally governed from 2011 until the Al-Shabaab withdrawal.

It seems that Al-Shabaab had a short rebound in the early summer of 2011, and its sound finances and its old ties managed to keep the leaders together. Al-Shabaab, as well as its opponents, had nevertheless changed. The disorganization continued, and the centralization of training collapsed. Hassan Dahir Aweys, for example, rebuilt his Al-Shabaab militias, drawing from the Ayr clan, giving him almost as great independent military power as when he was the leader of Hisbul Islam. Robow's militias were not fully integrated into Al-Shabaab's structure of fighters. Moreover, Al-Shabaab was to face a major propaganda defeat, due to the widespread East African drought.

The international press soon claimed that Al-Shabaab failed to allow drought relief into the areas under their control.[54] This was inaccurate: Al-Shabaab was highly favorable towards many international and Somali aid organizations such as UNICEF, the International Red Cross/Red Crescent, Islamic Relief, the Zam Zam foundation, the Norwegian Refugee Council and several others, although some of these later ceased to operate in those areas.[55] At least one of the local leaders of the above mentioned organizations actually expressed appreciation of Al-Shabaab, as it still held enough control locally to implement deals with the NGOs, at least in the Merka area. I also met several Somali aid organizations that were highly impressed by Al-Shabaab, which organized a refugee camp council and increased tax to fund aid to drought victims. Al-Shabaab did however have a very troubled relationship with the largest actor on the humanitarian scene, the World Food Programme (WFP). As early as 2010 Al-Shabaab had fallen out with the WFP, accusing the latter of ruining the local market by dumping cheap food aid and ruining business for local Somali farmers, as well as distributing food that had passed its expiry date.[56] It was the WFP that was banned first from operating inside Al-Shabaab-controlled areas in 2011, but the WFP was a large actor, and so this led to a reduction in food distribution. Moreover, those areas were most severely hit, and many Somalis wanted to flee to the refugee camps within Kenya. Some Al-Shabaab commanders attempted to prevent this, and the issue of taxing aid organizations (not only directly, but also through contractor tax), problems with the WFP, and preventing refugees fleeing to Kenya, all created disagreements. By early August the disagreements within Al-Shabaab again gained momentum, dividing the organization into two—one Mogadishu based, one Baidoa based. When Muktar Robow was interviewed for this study, he admitted divisions, but also claimed that it would be solved through *shura* meetings, and that he could still travel safely through Al-Shabaab-held lands.[57]

The withdrawal from Mogadishu on 4 August 2011 was an important step that removed one of the disagreements between these two groups; the whole *shura* now agreed that Al-Shabaab should focus on insurgency strategies rather than open warfare, and though this was a defeat for Godane, even he agreed to the decision. Al-Shabaab did still have major advantages on its side. Its opponents were highly divided and highly corrupt. The Kenyan intervention in October 2011 did not change this; the Kenyans brought with them clan-based allies, drawing from Al-Shabaab's old allies in the Ras Kamboni group led by Ahmed Madobe as well as clan-based forces from the Ogadeen clan and smaller units from the Rahanwhein. Paradoxically this can be seen as a weakness, as it will enable Al-Shabaab to base its recruitment on local clans opposed Ogadeen dominance, as well as increasing Ethiopia's reluctance to support the Kenyan effort—Ethiopia has been fighting Ogadeen based Somalis for several hundred years.

The Kenyan entry into Somalia was in one sense the start of a series of important territorial defeats for Al-Shabaab into 2012 (until the time of writing). Most of them were inflicted by Ethiopia, which took the strategically important city of Beled Weyne on 31 December 2011.[58] By 22 February 2012 Ethiopia, pressing on rapidly, entered Baidoa with some fifty tanks.[59] By the end of the month, the Ethiopians seemed to have deployed around 5,000 men inside Somalia, and they managed to attack the second largest city in Bay Bakool on 22 March 2012.[60] The Kenyan offensive stalled, however, and has at the time of writing failed to capture any important part of Somali territory, though it forced Al-Shabaab to evacuate Afmadow on 31 May. Simultaneously, the African Union forces were strengthened and given a changed mandate, enabling possible expansion out of Mogadishu. First AMISOM was to be strengthened to 17,000 soldiers, including the Kenyan forces, but excluding the Ethiopians in the hope of preventing anti-Ethiopian nationalistic recruitment to Al-Shabaab. Newcomers to AMISOM, Djibouti and Sierra Leone, were to boost its strength, and the Djiboutians were even to take control over Hiraan and the central Somali areas. Ethiopia was to be phased out of Somalia, being replaced by fresh Burundian and Ugandan troops. Simultaneously, a big increase in the forces of the TFG was to take place; members of the Somali parliament claimed that of the 22,000 soldiers of the TFG, 5,000 were paid directly by the United States and 3,500 directly by the European Union, while the TFG special forces, the so-called Delta 1, Delta 2, and Delta 3 groups numbering some 900 men, were also to be paid by the United States.[61] Several private military corporations, most notably Bancroft, were involved in the build up and had advisers in the front line. The new mandate was transformed into action, and on 15 February AMISOM launched an offensive on Afgoye, a small city close to Mogadishu; there were also several offensives against the last Al-Shabaab-held areas in Mogadishu, specifically in the Dainile area.[62]

The situation was seemingly grave for Al-Shabaab, perhaps prompting it to declare a merger with Al-Qaeda on 14 February 2012, a coup to gain attention, perhaps made possible by the new Al-Qaeda leader Zawahiri's increased sympathy with more localized outfits, but also by a change of heart by several Al-Shabaab leaders who had been skeptical towards Al-Qaeda, under pressure of outside events. The help Al-Shabaab could get from Al-Qaeda was limited, but it had very good advantages, amongst them the intervening powers' lack of understanding of clan dynamics within Somalia.

Kenya's intervention had clear potential to promote Al-Shabaab recruitment through clan dynamics. Top positions inside the Kenyan police, intelligence, and army were staffed by Ogadeen clan members, including the defence minister, Osman Haji Hussein. Observers including the researcher Ken Menkhaus claimed that the Kenyan intervention in Somalia was created by Ogadeenis through manipulation.[63] Such a theory does not take into account Kenyan interests in protecting their tourist industry from Somali bandits, and the fact that the October intervention started with the pursuit of kidnappers who had attacked tourists and Western NGO workers. Nor does it takes into account the strength of non-Ogadeen politicians such as the late George Saitoti and President Kibaki in the process, and the massive support of the Kenyan population for the effort. It does, however, illustrate a vital point: that the Kenyan intervention has strengthened the Ogadeen clan, and some of the factions recruited from it, at times branded as part of the TFG but only paying lip-service to it, have been greatly strengthened, for example the Ras Kamboni militia, which increased in size from some 500 men to 3,000 to make perhaps the strongest fighting force in Somalia. Such a development will of course scare off the traditional rivals of the Ogadeen, and can create support for Al-Shabaab, based not on any ideas of global jihad but on clan solidarity.

Similar mechanisms were at work in central Somalia, where a clan conference intended to make nominations for the new parliament in the summer of 2012, failed to properly integrate two sub-clans, the Galjale and the Douduble, and only weakly integrated a third, the Murosade.[64] The Galjale clan, of the Hawiye, was always marginalized from political and economical life during the civil war, and saw a major Al-Shabaab deployment relatively early in the war; Al-Shabaab gained support from its elders. The Douduble, a sub-division of the Gorgate sub-clan of the Hawiye, had their lands controlled by Al-Shabaab at an early stage and were friendly towards them later, as well as being marginalized in Somali clan politics.[65]

Al-Shabaab can be viewed as an internationalist outfit, and this is an important element, but its strength is perhaps its local focus and its previous image of being an alternative to warlords and crime. Today (February 2013), the Somali government also fails to perform, with soldiers and police in Mogadishu getting only occasional pay. It was the predatory practices of the warlords that enabled Al-Shabaab to grow in the first place, and the current predatory practices of the Somali army and police can enable it to grow again. It is however a clear drawback for Al-Shabaab that Mogadishu was by the summer of 2012 becoming relatively peaceful; except for districts as Huriwa and Dainile, peace was being felt by Somalis, but not peace implemented by allies of Al-Shabaab.

Al-Shabaab is not militarily defeated, it has withdrawn from the major areas of the AMISOM/Kenya and Ethiopian offensive, and the international allies facing it in the south do not have the strength to control the countryside yet, so that Al-Shabaab, even if defeated in the larger towns it still controls, is able to wage a long guerrilla war. Somalia's conflict has developed into a race, in which AMISOM has to stay until the TFG is mature enough to bring security to the countryside, otherwise the victory will be Al-Shabaab's.

8

LOSE SOME, WIN SOME?

Harakat Al-Shabaab was by 2012 experiencing severe military setbacks in south central Somalia. It was, however, expanding in other areas, seemingly taking control in new areas inside Somalia and gaining ground in Kenya, Tanzania, Uganda and Ethiopia. There are also indications that Al-Shabaab has managed to reinforce its allies in Al-Qaeda in the Arabian Peninsula (AQAP) with fighters. It has in many ways become a supporter of jihad movements in Africa, as well as some in Asia.

Inside Somalia, Al-Shabaab has also gained new ground owing to clan grievances and network connections. The first area in which it grew was along the northern coast of Puntland and adjacent Sanaag, early in the 1990s a hotbed for the old Al-Ittihad al-Islamiya (AIAI). Puntland itself consisted of the northeastern part of Somalia, an area that had been plagued by war in the early 1990s but had earlier been spared from the showdown between Siad Barre's forces and rebel groups that devastated Somalia in the period 1988–91. The rebel faction of the area, the Somali Salvation Democratic Front (SSDF), easily took power there, although it faced problems both from AIAI and Muhammed Farah Aideed's militias in the south.[1]

As described previously AIAI had strongholds in the Sanaag province in the early 1990s, and this was to have a lasting impact on the dynamics of that organization, as well as influencing Al-Shabaab's dynamics. However, Al-Shabaab's influence in the region from 2006 onwards illustrates the way in which clan politics can create openings for Al-Shabaab in solving local grievances and using them to gain influence. Al-Shabaab

gained ground through a process that started with clan wars and disagreement over mineral resources. At the center of these disagreements
stood Puntland's attempts to harvest oil and mineral resources in the territories of the Warsangeli clan. The Warsangeli clan elders, led by their
nominal head, Sultan Said of Warsangelia, had participated in peace processes both in Puntland and in neighboring Somaliland, and both entities actually claimed the Warsangeli inhabited areas; however, the
Warsangelis had played a wise double game, often having two administrations from both Somaliland and Puntland, living side by side peacefully in the same city. By 2006 Puntland, in partnership with non-Somali
oil companies, began to take interest in what they believed to be oil and
mineral rich Warsangeli territories. Unsurprisingly there were local coun-
ter-reactions: some Warsangeli leaders attempted to solve the issue with
dialogue, others organized themselves in groups fighting the Puntland
forces to protect what they deemed to be Warsangeli resources.[2]

It seems that the initial struggle was led by Ahmed Jeni Tag, and names
as 'the defenders of Sanaag resources' were used.[3] However, the focus
increasingly shifted to the territories of one of the sub-clans of the
Warsangeli, the Dubais, and the balance of power between the leaders
of the movement changed. Mohamed Said, nicknamed 'Atom', became
one of the leaders of this movement. His background is relatively well
known in Puntland. He gained a degree from the East African University in 1993 in Islamic Studies, and was probably a member of AIAI in
the early nineties.[4] He was giving speeches in local mosques, and at least
some local witnesses claimed that these speeches were rather moderate.[5]
He was also an investor, engaged in business such as arms smuggling to
the south, and had connections to the Sharia Courts through this work;
after the Ethiopian intervention in 2006, he kept these connections. In
one sense it was natural that these connections led to a relationship with
Al-Shabaab, and his prominent local position, based on fame and wealth,
also enabled him to enjoy a prominent role in the struggle to protect
what many saw as Warsangeli resources.

The struggle itself in many ways recalled the Houti rebellion in Yemen,
taking the form of rounds of fighting followed by attempts to negotiate
peace. In most of these rounds the Warsangeli militias, now largely drawn
from the sub-clan of Dubais, were the underdogs, militarily weaker than
the Puntlanders, but taking advantage of the mountainous terrain of the
region and the many places in the mountains where they could hide when

on the run. Nevertheless, Puntland was slowly weakening the insurgents. The Puntland government also worked on incorporating clan leaders from Warsangeli into their governance structures, including notable figures such as Abdullah Jamaa (Ilkajir), the current Minister of the Interior. In 2010 the group suffered heavy losses, as well as defections, and Yasin Said Osman Kilwe (later leader of the Al-Shabaab-aligned Galgala militia), Yuma, and Ali Karshe were amongst the few sub-commanders who remained loyal to Atom. Atom and other Warsangeli activists were losing ground. Even Atom was forced to enter negotiations with the Puntland authorities.[6] The arms embargo monitoring group of the United Nations highlights Kilwe's increasing position in the Galgala militias as well as the prominence of a newcomer, Muhamoud Faror, an Al-Shabaab veteran from the northern Haber Jalo Isaq clan, as indications of the growing power of Al-Shabaab.[7] From July to September 2010 the larger Puntland forces again got the upper hand, killing Commander Jaama Osman Du'ale in the process. The Galgalas were not beaten and were able to launch ambushes, even attempting to kill the Deputy Minister of Security on 7 January 2011, and over the next month Al-Shabaab-style targeted attacks on elders and leaders affiliated to Puntland followed. In February a Puntland-friendly mayor was targeted, the RCIED attempt on a Galgala elder at the beginning of March followed, and then, on 28 March, another Warsangeli elder, Ahmed Salah Hairab, was targeted; the latter had a son in the dreaded Puntland intelligence service, and this might have been one of the reasons for the attack. However, the attacks illustrated a growing animosity between the insurgents and Puntland-friendly members of the Warsangeli elite. By 11 May 2011 the Galgalas were able to ambush Puntland forces in Galgala, taking hostages as well as overrunning several Puntland posts. The attack was well planned, reinforcements sent from Karin by the Puntland authorities were ambushed on the road, and the use of IEDs expanded; the strategy was successful, and Atom was back in power in Galgala.

The Farole administration attempted to bring the militia back to the fold of Puntland, and initiated an amnesty, as well as negotiations through local elders. However, by the autumn of 2011 the clashes started again, and inter-clan violence escalated when the Galgala militia used force against other Warsangelis in El Laqoday, when attempting to establish a base on 18 November. The arms monitoring group of the United Nations had already drawn attention to the links between Al-Shabaab and Atom's militias, but this link was far from clear-cut. If one studies the attack pattern of the Galgala, one can clearly see that the conflict over natural resources still influenced their agenda. On 14 December a car was targeted in a bomb attack. Later in December, a bomb offensive in Bosasso was initiated. Atom and the Galgala rebels still denied Al-Shabaab links.[8] Indeed it still was a clan-based militia, and not an Al-Shabaab affiliate as suggested by the arms monitoring group. It did, however, have ties to the organization. The tension between the clan dimension and the Al-Shabaab link could most clearly be seen when a part of the group declared its allegiance to the latter in February 2012. Another part of the rebels, led by a self-proclaimed leader of the Galgala, Dhair Muhamed Ali, denied any Al-Shabaab links, and claimed that he was leading the largest group of the insurgency.[9] It nevertheless seems as if what started out as a clan conflict had become 'Shabaabified'; it had created an opening for Al-Shabaab influence.

The exact degree of Al-Shabaab influence in the conflict is however open for discussion. Several analysts have suggested that Al-Shabaab leaders would evacuate to the north because of the pressure the group faced in the south, overlooking the fact that the African Union in Somalia (AMISOM) forces in the south lack the resources to fully control the southern countryside, and that their southern allies have large problems with corruption and discipline amongst their troops, making them unable to secure the countryside as well.[10] Al-Shabaab thus has considerable possibilities for guerrilla warfare in the south, and so far no senior Al-Shabaab leader has been proved to have moved to Galgala. The discussions amongst senior Galgala leaders over the exact status of their links with Al-Shabaab showed clearly the internal discord on the issue. In February 2012 the more Al-Shabaab-friendly Yasin Said Osman Kilwe declared allegiance to Al-Shabaab, but this was publicly criticized by another leader—Sheik Muhamed Abdi—which was relatively embarrassing even though Al-Shabaab publicly endorsed the merger; later another Galgala leader, Dahir Muhamed Ali, also expressed opposition to the links.[11] The confusion over those links clearly shows a confused organization, perhaps more correctly a loose network, consisting of subgroups often drawn together because of clan affiliation.

This does not mean that Al-Shabaab is without influence, and its propaganda outlets, such as Radio Andalus, have frequently claimed that it has sent reinforcements to Galgala.[12] The influx could also have been connected to the human trafficking routes to Yemen, and AQAP's need for fighters in its push to control the Abayan province in that country; Somali jihadists left for Yemen in large numbers, to the extent that the American Ambassador to Yemen estimated that they were the largest foreign fighter group in that country.[13]

The Puntland authorities were said to claim strong Al-Shabaab links, but also links to AQAP, and several foreign leaders—Sheikh Ahmed Ali from Yemen, Salem Sayeed from Yemen, Sheikh Fuad Ismael from Sudan, and lastly Ibrahim Ahmed from Egypt—have been listed as evidence of such connections. Several other Somali individuals with roots outside the Warsangeli clan areas were also taking part in the Galgala insurgency, such as Sheikh Abdulqaadir Muumin, a known ideologue and, equally important, a member of the neighboring Ali Suleiban clan, and Saleban Sharif who was from the Haber Jalo clan of Isaq, or an Ogadeeni Darod.[14] In this more multi-clan situation the rebels operated more outside the core areas of Dubais, sometimes the home areas of the Dashishle and Ali Suleiban clans. However, these could have been mere raids. From February onwards the militia again intensified its attacks, perhaps because of the Puntland authorities' arrest of Ahmed Said Mohamed, Atom's brother. Nevertheless, the targets in general followed old patterns from 2011, with checkpoints attacked on the road into Bosasso, the major port of Puntland.

It is beyond doubt that the links between the Galgala and Al-Shabaab have strengthened; these links are blurred and confusing, as often happens when clan politics has been involved, but clearly clan grievances allowed an opening for Al-Shabaab to fill a void. It should be noted that grievances over oil and mineral related issues still have the potential to strengthen the Galgala militias, while there is an elite Puntland force, the Exploration Security Unit, trained by the private security cooperation Pathfinder—a force that will face the Galgalas in combat. The upcoming Puntland selection of a new president in 2013, where the neighbors to the Galgala, the powerful clan of Osman Mahmoud of the Majerteen, might be tempted to ally with the former in order to swing the selection against the current president, might empower the Galgala as well. Such moves will inevitably strengthen Al-Shabaab in the north.

Al-Shabaab clearly used clan politics to expand, but ironically its strength also lay in its ideology, the belief that it was based on a global force defending itself. Al-Shabaab was to expand outside Somalia, disproving the claims that it was defined by Somali nationalism. Its strongest area of expansion was perhaps Kenya, showing the strength of Al-Shabaab's global ideas.

Shabaab and Kenya

Kenya was important to Al-Shabaab logistics from the start. Ethnic Somalis living in Kenya had functioned as a logistical hub, channeling funds and money into Somalia. However, from 2009 onwards, Al-Shabaab transcended ethnicity and non-Somalis were to become important.

Kenya has traditionally been a country where religious cleavages were of little importance; after its independence politics was dominated by Christian elites, but this domination did not, with some notable exceptions, manifest itself in wider political divisions.[15] The conflict between Muslims and Christians became more intense after 9/11, when Kenya became a front line in the War on Terror. Kenyan counter-terrorism issues, as well as rendition, became controversial and contributed to a rise in tension.[16] However, by 2008 this tension was declining again, when Barack Obama, of Kenyan origin on his father's side with roots in Kenya's Muslim community, was elected. At the same time Kenyan Muslims got an ardent leader, Najib Balala, into the government (although he had to leave in 2012). Kenyan Muslims were also granted advantages, or original privileges were confirmed. In the new constitution, section 130 allowed Qadi courts for Muslims, and section 24 (4) exempted Muslims from the Kenyan bill of human rights, thus allowing the Sharia to be applied, for example regarding inheritance, weakening women's rights.[17] Although Kenya was initially skeptical towards the Bush presidency, its relations with the United States improved when President Obama came into power. Obama was widely seen as a 'son of Kenya', by the Muslim community and others.

Nevertheless, the general unimportance of religious issues in Kenyan politics did not prevent Al-Shabaab from developing quite a substantial organization within the country, and today perhaps as many as 10 per cent of its members are of Kenyan origin.[18] Links between Kenyan Muslim leaders and Al-Qaeda had developed even in the mid-1990s. Several Islamic charities connected to Al-Qaeda, such as the Saudi Al Haramain foundation and Mercy, which was later alleged to be financing terrorism, operated in Kenya.[19] Al-Qaeda also managed to launch some of its most notable and successful operations in the region, using Kenyan contacts, and taking advantage of corruption inside the Kenyan police.[20]

A key figure in the early radical Islamist environment in Kenya was Sheikh Aboud Rogo Muhamed, who according to the Kenyan government was to become vital in the Al-Shabaab recruitment process in Kenya. Rogo, a radical cleric based in Mombasa, was alleged to have used funds from Haramain to aid Al-Qaeda in East Africa's attempt to attack targets in Kenya in 2002.[21] Sheikh Rogo was also accused by the Kenyan police early on of complicity to the Paradise Hotel/Arakia airlines attack launched by Al-Qaeda in East Africa, partly because his number had been found on telephones belonging to the Al-Qaeda in East Africa leader Fazul Abdullah Muhamed, mentioned earlier.[22] The subsequent court case ended in acquittal, but Rogo and the Kenyan authorities were to go several rounds in court over other terror related court cases.[23] According to the Kenyan authorities he became too famous to have any operational role in Al-Shabaab recruitment, but until 2010 he served such a role.[24] He remained important ideologically until he was killed in Mombasa in late August 2012.[25]

His rival, also fulfilling the role of an ideologue as well as an organizer, was perhaps the now deceased Sheikh Samir Hussein alias Shamir Hashimu Khan alias Abu Nusaybah. He was a Kenyan of Indian descent.[26] Hashimu Khan was highly active on the internet with speeches on global jihad distributed relatively widely; in some of his speeches he established a theme that was to recur in the future rhetoric of the Kenyan Shabaab, namely anti-Americanism and the belief that the Muslim community globally was under attack. The West was portrayed as the old colonial oppressor, continuing the tradition of Muslim oppression in Somalia.[27] The odd mix of a narrative stressing the global 'Clash of Civilization' with the local colonial past was to appear later in Al-Shabaab publications.[28] The exact link between Nusaybah and Al-Shabaab is a matter of speculation, although he definitively endorsed Al-Shabaab in his speeches, and probably was involved in well organized recruitment efforts as far away as Hadramauth in Yemen, and was due to face a Kenyan court in 2012 on charges of having brought in and trained Al-Shabaab recruits inside Kenya.[29] Kenyan police claimed the operation was quite advanced, involving a Yemeni sheikh, Shaykh al-Bashir of Sheher in Hadramauth province, collecting the recruits, including six Yemenis and one Pakistani, smuggled into Kenya for training.[30] Hashimu

Khan was however found dead in a morgue, castrated with his body severely mutilated; it is unclear who was behind the killing, but Rogo, and other radical sheikhs, later spoke of Hashimu as an example of a martyr in the struggle against the Kenyan government's oppression of Muslims, choosing to accuse the Kenyan police of his death. The Kenyan police have been known for breaches of human rights, and rumors pointed to Rogo as the two were rivals in the radical Islamist movement in Kenya. The death did, however, create mobilization against the police amongst more moderate Kenyan Muslim clerks; if it was the work of the Kenyan police, it would be another example of the police's insensitivity towards the consequences of their use of violence.[31] Al-Shabaab used the killing to illustrate the suffering of the *ummah*, highlighting his work against poverty and his work to free Muslim prisoners inside Kenya, creating a metaphysical pantheon of martyrs in Kenya, as it had done in Somalia.[32]

Over time Al-Shabaab developed direct contacts with several Kenyan organizations, amongst them the now infamous Kenyan Muslim Youth Centre, established as a response to the harsh conditions facing Muslim youths in the Majengo area of Nairobi, initially by a former student of Rogo, 'Amir' Ahmed Iman Ali 'Abu Usama'.[33] The center provided help for youths in need of support but also had a dark side to it, dominated by the view that Muslim solidarity was needed at a time when the whole of the *ummah* was under direct attack from the West. It was perhaps natural that one of the Muslim Youth Centre activists became active in Al-Shabaab as early as 2008, where the Kenyan Mohamed Juma Rajab alias Qa Qa aka Kadume joined Al-Shabaab and in the end died at Bardale;[34] a martyrdom video was subsequently produced by Omar Hammami.

The links grew more serious when the leader of the Muslim Youth Centre, Ahmed Iman Ali, left for Somalia in 2009 and established a sizeable Kenyan contingent in Al-Shabaab, numbering between 200 and 500 fighters in 2011. Several other Kenyan sub-commanders, most notably Wahome Tajir Ali 'Abu Jafar' and 'Ikrima' Mohammed, were also active, and Kenyans were rising in the Al-Shabaab hierarchy, although not receiving top positions; in the end, in February 2012, the Muslim Youth Centre blog declared that it had joined Al-Shabaab, praising the latter's merger with Al-Qaeda in the process.[35]

Kenya's Shabaab recruits came from a variety of backgrounds; many of them were converts, for example John Mwanzia Ngui alias Yahya, killed on 3 December 2010 when attempting to infiltrate Kenya after military training inside Somalia.[36] Yahya, who was allegedly involved in the 2010 Uganda attack, was born in 1984 in Mwingi, and converted to Islam as late as 2008.[37] Some recruits were lured into Somalia by offers of scholarships and jobs and then even forcefully recruited, some went because of poverty and a sense of adventure. However, a notable trait was the presence of former petty criminals, first amongst the Kenyan Shabaab fighters inside Somalia, later also amongst Al-Shabaab members based inside Kenya. One example was Ayub Otit Were 'Taxi Driver', who according to his own father joined Al-Shabaab through the Muslim Youth Centre, having joined the latter after he lost his job, and his reputation, for stealing at work.[38] Al-Shabaab recruitment inside Kenya was widely covered by the Kenyan press. Nation TV (NTV) and Citizen TV both interviewed several members of non-Somali families that had experienced how religious leaders from specific mosques had succeeded in recruiting non-Somali Kenyan youths.[39] The combination of exposure to international jihadist views, poverty and the presence of Kenyan 'fixers' who took money to transport potential Al-Shabaab recruits into Somalia was highlighted by both stations.[40] An increasing use of Swahili—the major language of Tanzania, Kenya, Uganda, also commonly spoken in parts of Congo, and in Burundi and Rwanda—could also be observed in Al-Shabaab propaganda efforts, some of them clearly targeting an East African audience. Importantly, this trend was also seen in media depicting non-Africans: at times even English videos would have Swahili subtitles.[41] Kenya might also still serve as a place to evacuate wounded Al-Shabaab leaders. In June 2011, for example, several Somali webpages suggested that Bilal El Berjawi, a close aide to Al-Qaeda's Fazul Abdullah, who had suffered head injuries, was smuggled into Kenya for treatment.[42]

Kenya did not only provide recruits—the Pumwani Riyadha Mosque Committee (PRMC), where Ahmed Iman Ali had been a member before he left for Somalia in 2009, was, according to the Monitoring Group, also a regular supplier of funds to the Muslim Youth Centre, which in turn supplies funds to Al-Shabaab inside Kenya. The PRMC entity owned a large section of land in Majengo, including Gikomba market, the largest second-hand clothes market in Kenya, and tax money from this market was sent indirectly to Al-Shabaab as financial support. The allegations in the monitoring report were denied by parts of the Riyadha Mosque administration, while other leaders believed them.[43] It is also highly likely that there were other centers for such financial support, such as several mosques in the Majengo area in Mombasa (not to be confused with Majengo in Nairobi).

The strengthening of ties between Kenyan Islamists and Al-Shabaab seemed to be initiated by the Kenyan radical Islamists themselves; they were the movers, rather than being coerced into action by the Somali Shabaab, and it seemed they had notable influence on Al-Shabaab's propaganda efforts, which from 2009 and onwards increasingly targeted Swahili speakers. The increasing importance of Kenyan Shabaab members also led to an increased emphasis on internationalist ideas. Films, shirts and audio recordings were produced, sometimes inside Kenya. The examples were many; as early as in January 2010, a film commenting on the arrest of the controversial sheikh British-Jamaican Abdullah al-Faisal, arrested by the Kenyan police, was produced by the Muslim Youth Centre's media wing, Hijra Media. It included footage of the deceased Kenyan Al-Qaeda figure Saleh al Saleh Nabhan, and asked for solidarity with Al-Shabaab.[44] The propaganda efforts continued both from Kenya and from Somalia. A separate newspaper of the Kenyan Shabaab, *Gaidi Mtaani*, emerged in 2012 and a YouTube account 'Themzelles', as well as various twitter accounts, were opened.

Gaidi Mtaani employed symbolic language surprisingly familiar to a reader of Kenyan historical narrative. In the second issue it focused on the ironic fact that Kenya now was allied with its colonial oppressors in operations inside Somalia, and claimed that the Kenyan army was poor and inexperienced.[45] According to the magazine, Kenya was 'bought' by its paymasters, the United States, to fight in the latter's 'global struggle against Islam'. Several common arguments are mentioned: first, that Kenyan Muslims see themselves through the eyes of the enslaver, and do not all understand that they are oppressed; second, that Kenyan institutions on their own are severely corrupted; third, that there are clear examples of oppression of Muslims in Kenya, including the arrests of several sheikhs. America is again described as the fount of evil, refusing to support Muslims in their grievances while helping anti-Muslim factions all over the world, and being behind the civil war in Somalia, which crushed the peace created by the Sharia Courts of 2006. In the first issue, the hypothesis that 'Zionists' are behind the Kenyan campaign in Somalia is also discussed, albeit briefly.[46]

The discussion says something about targeted Al-Shabaab propaganda inside Kenya; it is, as in Somalia, attempting to claim that it addresses issues of justice, and that Al-Shabaab in Kenya and Somalia is part of a larger universal struggle against the onslaught of the West, especially the United States and Israel, on Islam. Al-Shabaab's mission thus becomes defensive, and it becomes a tool to protect Islam and combat corruption. Kenyan sources claim that grievances between the coast and central Kenya are still played upon, and indeed one issue of *Gaidi Mtaani* mentions that the United States supported dissidents in the Southern Sudan but not in the Kenyan coastal area.

One of the early speeches of the later leader of the Kenyan Al-Shabaab, Ahmed Iman Ali, followed the same pattern, declaring that Kenyan intervention inside Somalia from October 2011 onwards was a part of a larger global struggle, in which Islam was fighting for its existence, a struggle similarly experienced in Palestine, Bosnia, Iraq, Chechnya, Afghanistan, Pakistan, the Philippines, Yemen and Algeria. It stressed specifically Afghanistan and Iraq, saying the objective of the United States was the extermination of 'millions of Muslims' and Islam, rather than Saddam Hussein and Osama bin Laden. Ali also stressed the administration of justice by the Sharia Courts in Somalia as an example of how peace and justice were established through Islam, and declared that 'Ethiopia was sent by the United States' who in reality were 'Jews', and 'defiled' Somalia.[47] However, perhaps the most worrying part of his speech was the last part, where he stated that 'no one doubts that jihad should now be waged inside Kenya', which was now legally a war zone.[48]

In one sense this comment plays on the worst fears of the Kenyans, a 'blow-back effect' whereby returnees from training in Somalia, or even locally inspired Al-Shabaab activists, conduct attacks inside Kenya. These fears were enhanced by the Kenyan intervention in Somalia in October 2011, and seemingly confirmed by a series of low-tech attacks in Nairobi and Mombasa, although the exact nature of these attacks is hard to evaluate—personal rivalries or even organized crime may have been behind them. The fact remains, however, that one of Kenya's few court judgments on charges of terrorism followed a low-key attack. Elgiva Bwire Oliacha alias Muhamed Seife, an avowed Al-Shabaab member, was involved in two very rudimentary attacks in downtown Nairobi, targeting a bar and a bus stop.[49] The resulting court case was one of the very few instances where the present Kenyan anti-terrorism law was successfully used (a new one is in the process of being made). Several attacks followed this, some on churches, but it was very hard to be sure whether all of them were made by Al-Shabaab. Interestingly, one of the attacks was widely said to involve a British citizen, Samantha Lewthwaite. She was accused by the Kenyan authorities of being one of the terrorists behind a hand grenade attack targeting the Jericho Beer Garden in Mombasa. She is also the widow of one of the bombers of the 7/7 (2005) attack in Britain, Jermaine Lindsay. This case illustrates that the Kenyan Shabaab also has international links.

The Kenyan Al-Shabaab is focusing on a global struggle to protect the *ummah*, and to awaken Kenyan Muslims against their government; it has largely been successful with the former, and unsuccessful with the latter. There are conflicts that can be exploited in the future, such as that between some of the coastal communities and the central highlands, but so far this has, despite allegations to the contrary, not happened. In one sense it is the part of Al-Shabaab that was most prone to terror, and best at transcending borders. Indeed, the Kenyan networks were essential in Al-Shabaab's regional spread.

Tanzania, Uganda, Ethiopia

Tanzania also developed a Shabaab network, organized around the Ansar Muslim Youth Centre (AMYC). The center pre-dates Al-Shabaab and was established as early as 1970. It changed name to its current form in 1988, and became close to the now banned East African chapter of the Al Haramain Saudi Arabian charity; it seemed to drift towards radicalism, and sent young students to study with Rogo in Kenya. The connections between the Al-Shabaab network and Ansar may have started as early as 2005, when the United Nations arms monitoring group claim that AMYC leaders frequented Somalia, but this might have been in support of other factions of the various Sharia Courts of Mogadishu.[50] However, the relationship continued and by 2011 there were as many as seventy-five Tanzanians fighting inside Somalia. Additionally, it was clear by 2012 that Al-Shabaab was explicitly targeting the Tanzanian Muslims in its propaganda; the second issue of *Gaidi*, for example, elaborated how the 1964 revolution in Zanzibar was an example of the oppression and killings of Muslims.[51] In one sense this may have sought to play on the division between mainland Tanzania (Tanganyika) and Zanzibar, where Zanzibar could be viewed as more 'pure Muslim', but that division, serious in Tanzanian politics, has nevertheless been handled peacefully.

Again according to the UN Monitoring Group, a network of recruitment, with its own transport channel, developed as a shared enterprise between Kenyan and Tanzanian Al-Shabaab supporters. This network also involved Ugandans, and was, according to Kenyan police, used to prepare for the 2010 terror attacks in Kampala, when a Tanzanian citizen, Hijar Selemen Nyamandondo, transported suicide vests through Kenya.[52] Indeed the attacks in 2010 seem to indicate the existence of another recruitment network inside Uganda, while a court case in Ethiopia in 2012 seems to indicate the same in that country. However, it should be kept in mind that both Uganda and Ethiopia are said to use torture in interrogation and that some of the allegations might be attempts to tarnish the reputation of opposition forces.[53]

Ugandan police claimed that two Kenyans, Hussein Hassan Agade and Idris Christopher Magondu, were responsible for arranging safe houses. Issa Ahmed Luyima was the ringleader; one of the accused, Mohamood Mugisha, had according to his confession been trained by Al-Shabaab in 2008, while Luyima had joined in 2009.[54] It is quite ironic that, although the macro motivation for the attack (as described in a previous chapter) was to influence the tactical situation in Somalia, the motivation of the members of the attack team seems to have been hatred of United States, combined with the emotional problems of one of the culprits.[55] The operation was a 'successful' regional venture, involving Ugandans, Tanzanians, Kenyans and Somalis. However, the arrests conducted by the Ugandan police after the operation seemed also to target political activists.[56] Little is known about the recruitment networks inside Uganda, the facts being blurred by a lack of on-the-ground reporting and the Ugandan regime's alleged breaches of human rights, but it seems safe to say that recruitment exists, that Swahili Al-Shabaab propaganda also might influence Ugandans, but that it is far less institutionalized than in Kenya.

Ethiopia is in many ways in a similar situation to Uganda; the findings of the police seem to indicate an Al-Shabaab presence, but frequent human rights violations by the police put the results in doubt. Ethiopia saw its own Shabaab court case in which one Kenyan and nine Ethiopians were accused of creating a Shabaab organization inside the country. According to the Ethiopian prosecutor, Hassan Jarsso (alias Abu Miliky Al-Burani), a Kenyan, was recruited by Shabaab from Marsabit in Kenya. He went to Somalia and was trained by Al-Shabaab in the Gaza camp for more than three months. After graduation he first became a fighter and was later selected by Al-Shabaab leadership to organize an underground terror group in Ethiopia. He then moved to Bale in Ethiopia and, apparently recruited from that province, establishing contact with Mohamed Kasim, who recruited the other cell members, using funds from Al-Shabaab in Somalia. Hassan Jarsso in the end confessed, four others denied the charges.[57]

Again it is hard to exactly make out what was going on, as Ethiopia has traditions of politically motivated court cases, targeting opposition groups such as those among the Oromos in Bale.[58] The irony of the court case was that it contributed to religious tension inside Ethiopia, partly a result of the Ethiopian government's desire to maintain heavy handed control of its own population, resulting in large demonstrations in 2012.[59] Indeed, the situation in Uganda and Ethiopia especially, but also in Kenya and Tanzania, illustrates one of the major advantages of Al-Shabaab in the region: the government's emphasis on hard power, including random arrests, rather than soft power, through dialogue including radicals. This is not to say that only soft power is needed, but hard power when applied randomly with little intelligence backing it will arouse suspicion amongst segments of the population, including Muslims, that needed to be reached in order to handle Al-Shabaab. The organization's history in East Africa/ The Horn has been a success story so far, although the exact situation inside Ethiopia and Uganda is hard to assess, and the success has been partly due to the international aspects of Al-Shabaab's ideology.

Al-Shabaab does not always take very good care of its recruits. During the summer of 2011, one source claimed that several foreign fighters of East African origins had been literally dumped: '200–250 East Africans were left at Bakara nobody cares about them and they do not know where to go…', '…. some foreigners and Somalis of Shabaab were left in caves and Shabaab cannot save (them)'.[60] But recruits are at least often provided with a solid network and a sense of belonging to a larger entity, and in some cases international contacts.

Shabaab globally

A field researcher working for the writer checked the nationalities of foreign Al-Shabaab fighters in Mogadishu hospitals after the battles in June 2011, searching for foreigners who had been brought in by Al-Shabaab militias. He found thirty-eight Western and Non-Arab Asians (including Chechens), 123 Africans including people from Kenya, Sudan, Tanzania, Zanzibar and Uganda and two men from South Africa, one American and two Arabs. Among them were some more famous Al-Shabaab fighters, Abu Dauud the American and Sheikh Bilaala al Sudan, and 'Rambo' from Chechnya. The total number was unusually high, since Al-Shabaab seldom leaves wounded soldiers at the hospitals.[61] Although some of the African fighters could have been pushed into service because of poverty, the numbers indicate Al-Shabaab's relative importance for African jihadists, as well as a considerable international presence.

The body count of dead Al-Shabaab fighters conducted by the field researcher indicates the same international diversity, but also how badly the group suffered in 2010–11. Dead foreign fighters were reported to include the head of foreign fighters in Lower Juba, Sh. Hashim (Al-Afgani), killed at Dhoobley, and the deputy commander of Al-Shabaab in the Gedo region, Sheikh Ahmed Abu-Marquuti from the Comoro Islands, killed at Beled Hawa. Several returned Somalis also perished, including Isaak Mohamed Derow from Denmark, Amiir Musa Ibrahim from Finland, Abdiwali Qanyare Farah, Amiir of Bakaara from the United Kingdom, Sh. Abuu Muslim from Bangladesh, Abdullahi Yaya 'Abuu-Mohamed' from Yemen, Abuu Hanaan from Palestine, Abuu Kahsha from Yemen, Amiir Muse Mao Matan from Belgium, Amiir Bashir Abdullahi Abdiwali 'Imbili' from Kenya, and also a Norwegian-Somali, a French-Somali, a Saudi Arabian and a Dutch-Somali lady alleged to have helped Al-Shabaab's front line forces.[62] According to local sources the American attack on 28 May 2011 also killed several foreign fighters. Omar Hammami and Godane were both wounded but not seriously; they escaped by luck as they allegedly exchanged cars with their staff. However, Sheikh Jama Yare, Godane's right hand man, and an Iraqi fighter named Mohamed Iraqi were killed.

The foreign fighters were not always good soldiers, but they helped to enhance a network extending beyond Somalia. Their efforts have already had a significant effect, as illustrated above. They have become a symbol for jihadism in Africa, and at the same time provided a unifying force by which isolated jihadist organizations such as Boko Haram in Nigeria can attach themselves to the larger international jihadist scene. Inside Al-Shabaab, they have acted as glue which actually keeps the organization together, as they can transcend the clan ideologies that plague Somali society. They are not a part of that society, and they could make up as much as 10 per cent of the organization. It might be argued that they present a pan-Islamist element inside Somalia that can create tension with the more nationalist elements within Al-Shabaab, but such a view underestimates the clan tensions within Al-Shabaab, as well as the way in which global and local agendas are fused; the ideological differences are blurred, and many members only have a weak awareness of these differences. It is not a given that all foreign fighters in Somalia share an offensive jihadist ideology; some of them see Somalia as a scene where they defend the Muslim *ummah*.

Does Al-Shabaab have influence outside the region? The answer is clearly yes. Observers in Somalia are said to confirm the presence of Filipino fighters, said by Filipino sources to be members of the Bangsamoro Islamic Freedom Movement, BIFM. There is strong evidence of Al-Shabaab involvement in the training of Jama'atu Ahlis Sunna Lidda'awati Wal-Jihad (People Committed to the Propagation of the Prophet's Teachings and Jihad), more popularly known as Boko Haram. Claims of its involvement in the training of suicide bombers in Nigeria are supported by Al-Shabaab and local observers in Somalia, as well as AMISOM, Boko Haram itself and the Nigerian authorities.[63] It is interesting that Boko Haram seems to mimic Al-Shabaab in several respects, with suicide attacks as well as the use of web forums following the same patterns.[64] Al-Shabaab actually became a frequent threat in Boko Haram propaganda, claiming that there were reserve suicide bombers in training in Somalia.[65] Indeed, the Nigerian police claimed that Mamman Nuur, the alleged ringleader of the attack against the United Nations building in Abuja, as well as Mohammed Abul Barra, the suicide bomber, were graduates from Somalia, Nuur going to Somalia as early as 2009 and returning in 2011. The frequent threats from Boko Haram emphasizing the training in Somalia make this a credible claim, as do eyewitness claims of contact with Nigerian Al-Shabaab fighters inside Somalia.[66]

Boko Haram has also had contacts with Al-Qaeda in the Islamic Maghreb (AQIM), as has Al-Shabaab; AMISOM has found telephone numbers of AQIM members noted by Al-Shabaab commanders in 2011. Indeed, AQIM has been the closest ally of Al-Shabaab. In 2011–2012 AQAP attempted to follow Al-Shabaab's lead in establishing territorial control over a larger area. A large number of Somali fighters, Yemeni sources claimed 300, were committed to this quest, and more seemed to have followed afterwards.[67] Christopher Swift and several other sources claimed that a majority of AQAP fighters were Somalis.[68] Indeed Al-Shabaab's Somali competence can be a very fertile asset in Yemen in order to open up Somali refugee camps for more direct Al-Qaeda recruitment. UDSS sources also reported AQAP ideologues being tasked with streamlining of Al-Shabaab ideology, and playing a key role in Shabaab indoctrination in 2012. Tactically, the AQAP cooperation has historically allowed AQAP to draw reinforcements from Al-Shabaab, which apparently provided sanctuary for AQAP earlier; however, the value for global jihadists in Al-Shabaab does not lie in the willingness of the latter to attack international targets, since it has so far abstained from this, adopting a Somalia-first focus, although its Kenyan branch might change this in the future.

Al-Shabaab's value lies first and foremost in network building; Somalia as a battlefield of jihad allowed militants to build up larger training camps for the first time since Afghanistan, as Al-Shabaab gained control over a part of Somalia larger than Denmark in 2009. And the alumni network has spread around the world. It seems, for example, that institutions in Gothenburg, such as the Bellevue Mosque, hosted radical Al-Shabaab leaders attempting to raise funds and make propaganda for Al-Shabaab's cause outside Somalia, hosting important Al-Shabaab members such as Abdukarim Mumin (at an early stage) and Sheikh Hassan Hussein.[69] The same Bellevue mosque was also frequented by Muhedeen Jelle and Abduhrrahman Hajji, the latter being Denmark's first suicide bomber, while the former was sentenced for attacking the Danish cartoonist Kurt Westegard (who produced the *Gyllandsposten* cartoons of Muhammad) with an axe.[70] Mosques like the Bellevue are of course large entities, and have moderate as well as radical elements, but the mosque and other institutions such as the Islamic Sunni Centre and Troende Unga Fremtidiga Forbilder (TUFF) have hosted radical subgroups that have been very important in the recruitment of Norwegian, Finnish and Swedish Somali jihadists, and were feared by moderate Somali leaders in all three countries. Not all of the members of these networks are Somalis; some others who frequently attended Bellevue planned terrorist attacks later, like Mirsad Bektašević.[71]

There were also some notable examples of Al-Shabaab members playing a role through guidance over the telephone outside Somalia, such as the Holsworthy Barracks plot in Australia in 2009, in which the leaders of the ring behind the attack had frequent contacts with mid-level Al-Shabaab leaders and were inspired by their ideas, but in which even Al-Shabaab did not outright give support to the attack.[72]

The largest contribution Al-Shabaab has made to international jihadism is in its rhetorical world view, depicting Islam as under attack globally and propagandizing very effectively through the internet. The second is, perhaps ironically, that the local dynamics of Al-Shabaab, influenced by clan and ethnicity, allow an opening to convince recruits who join up for other reasons, including recruits from the Somali diaspora, about the Shabaab world view.

9

CONCLUSIONS

Outside observers have tended either to 'localize' or to 'globalize' Hara-kat Al-Shabaab. Both views are erroneous. Al-Shabaab has several dimensions, of which one is global. Al-Shabaab had international connections and was close to Al-Qaeda, or at least its East African group, from its inception. However, it should be remembered that all global messianic ideologies have ingrained weaknesses. The first weakness is practical governance and practical policy making; like the early Soviet Communists, Al-Shabaab discovered that its faith gave it few clues on how to behave when exercising governance, and how power makes an organization more attractive for pure profiteers. Its strength was in many ways the inclination for law and order that its ideology created, highly popular amongst ordinary Somalis. Its main weakness was that it was exposed to the same mechanisms of fragmentation that had made all of the other armed factions so far in the history of the Somali conflict fragment within four years of their creation: clan and poverty. The clan issue cannot easily be escaped by any Somali organization; various clans will try to ally with Al-Shabaab, as local regional recruitment has often meant that the units recruited in a particular location retain clan allegiance. Al-Shabaab fell into all of these traps, and became more clannish over the four years that it exercised local governance in Somalia; it did, however, manage to deal with the issue in a much better way than other organizations, and the ideology kept the leaders together, as did the foreign fighters. Al-Shabaab nevertheless also had problems with governance, where its ideology failed to give exact answers.

This brings forward an important point, first highlighted by Peter Berger in his book *The Sacred Canopy*, which suggested that divine plans encounter problems when facing failures in their predictions.[1] Islamist ideology inspired Al-Shabaab's thirty-three members in 2005, a group so small that it was aloof from wider politics. At this early stage Al-Shabaab did not hold much influence; it did not do much governance either, thus its belief system was not tested through interaction. However, by 2011 things were different; the ideology did not give clear clues as to how problems such as clan and drought should be faced. Al-Shabaab was also exposed to war fatigue: some of its leaders, like Shongola, simply sounded defeatist, claiming, 'I am not dead yet, I am alive, I shall die, at the time Allah decides, not to the delight of the TFG.'[2] Others, such as Omar Hammami, produced speeches that seemed intended to encourage recruits in a difficult time.[3]

There are ideological differences within the top leadership of the organization; a few voices call for international jihad, but even they see that Al-Shabaab's first target must be local, to establish a power base, and that its fight is thus a localized version of a larger defensive jihad. Another ideological stand that remains important for Al-Shabaab, as well as its local followers and sympathizers, is its focus on justice, seeing itself as an alternative to the warlords of Somalia, as well as the corrupt police of the Transitional Federal Government (TFG). The most serious challenge Al-Shabaab would face would come if this image died; thus justice provision becomes important to it. Al-Shabaab's ideological divisions do not merit black and white categorization into 'nice jihadists vs. bad jihadists', but is much more blurred and pragmatic; there are shades of internationalism amongst all top leaders of the organization, but old friendships, differences on pure governance issues and competition for power are all important considerations in explaining the internal dynamics. Predictions about Al-Shabaab's forthcoming collapse, made frequently since 2008, should be treated with caution; its leaders have so far chosen to stay together, tied together by old memories and ideological perceptions. The fact that Al-Shabaab still controls large territories in Southern Somalia, and that the threat of its secret police, the Amniyat, remains potent, means that it should not be counted out of the game yet.

Al-Shabaab has international relevance; it does train its recruits in the messages of Al-Qaeda, it does host Al-Qaeda members, and it does provide one of the few examples in which Al-Qaeda allies have taken territory. There should be no doubt that Al-Shabaab has exported jihadists to other places in the world—the evidence is simply overwhelming in the cases of Kenya and Nigeria, and rather strong in Yemen, Australia and Denmark. Nor should Al-Shabaab's propaganda effort be underestimated, it is professional and conveys extremist views that can motivate youths to become terrorists on their own. The most interesting issue is of course how far Al-Shabaab recruits joining for other reasons, such as clan loyalties, can accept the global views propagated by the organization; the irony is that both nationalism and clanism can be combined with a loose idea of a struggle of a global Islamic *ummah* against attacks especially from the West; the latter is a concept so remote that it can be combined with a more local identity, and can be acted upon even though the local identity dominates. Not all jihadists want to remove the borders in the *ummah*, and at times clan-affiliated leaders can even try, as Hassan Dahir Aweys has done, to demarcate one clan as 'more Islamist' than other clans, and try to show that this is actually the case.

Several of the Al-Shabaab *shura* members have tried to defect from the organization, which indicates that there is a will amongst some members to cooperate with other Somali factions. However, there are several factors that should be kept in mind. First, Al-Shabaab's Amniyat is feared amongst the group's own leaders, and Al-Shabaab has connections even inside AMISOM. Shabaab's assassination strategies have been highly successful also in keeping the organization together. Security arrangements implemented by the Somali government and AMISOM are not trusted, indeed Al-Shabaab has video evidence to show how easily it is able to infiltrate these forces; fear could easily prevent Al-Shabaab leaders from negotiating.[4] Secondly, Al-Shabaab still exists, and holds territories; it is still quite profitable and seemingly advantageous for many Al-Shabaab leaders to stay out of the Somali government, and the anti-terrorist legislation in Western countries might mean that they could be punished by Western authorities even after trying to leave Al-Shabaab. Thirdly, the memories of the early days and the shared ideological links are still there, as are the foreign fighters, perhaps in larger number than in any other non-global jihadist organization, and have acted as a force for peacemaking within the organization and, ironically, as a force for moderation in the phase of Sharia implementation. International issues still hold importance for many ordinary Somalis among others; further problems in the Israel-Palestine conflict, or interventions in Pakistan, will harden Al-Shabaab.

Fourthly, if some Al-Shabaab members join the TFG, its most extreme leaders might be left, and the result could be a more internationally focused organization, a purer terrorist threat; and the TFG would have to change its human rights standards, in order to accommodate defecting Al-Shabaab members. To negotiate with Al-Shabaab is a challenging task, and it should not be believed that the whole of the organization could be included in any negotiated solution, but it might be worth an attempt, and outlying leaders in the organization, such as Hassan Dahir Aweys, might be swayed. Probably not because they are nationalists, but because they are pragmatists. The sad fact remains that these leaders, including Aweys, are of little importance.

Regardless of the results of such negotiations, Al-Shabaab leaves a legacy, it has exported its world views already, and it has contributed to an African momentum for jihad that should be watched closely, and has provided Al-Qaeda with both training grounds, and with experiences in how jihadists can do governance.

NOTES

1. INTRODUCTION

1. Katherine Zimmerman, 'From Somalia to Nigeria,' *The Weekly Standard*, 18 June 2011; United Nations Monitoring Group on Somalia and Eritrea, 'Report of the Monitoring Group on Somalia Pursuant to Security Council Resolution 1853 (2008),' Report S/2011/433, 2011.

2. See for example Anwar Awlaki, 'Speech' (date unknown), http://www.youtube.com/watch?v=abBIhu7Eo6Y&feature=related (accessed 1 June 2011).

3. *Stockholms Tingrett*, 'dom DOM B 7277–10 2010–12–08,' Stockholm, 12 August 2010.

4. Mansoor Moaddel, *Class, Politics, and Ideology in the Iranian Revolution* (New York: Columbia University Press, 1993).

5. See for example P. Norris and R. Inglehart, *Sacred and Secular: Religion and Politics Worldwide* (New York: Cambridge University Press, 2004); Tom Rees, 'Is Personal Insecurity a Cause of Cross-national Differences in the Intensity of Religious Belief?', *Journal of Religion and Society,* 11:1–24, 2009. This does not mean that they claim that terrorism and poverty are linked. One might stipulate a situation where the better off in a society are becoming terrorists inspired by the general religious climate created by poverty as well as human agency.

6. Moaddel *Class, Politics and Ideology;* Stig Jarle Hansen, 'Somalia—Grievance, Religion, Clan, and Profit,' Chapter 8 in S.J. Hansen, A. Mesøy and T. Karadas, *The Borders of Islam: Exploring Samuel Huntington's Faultlines, From Al-Andalus to the Virtual Ummah* (London: Hurst, 2009).

7. Scott Thomas (2005), *The Global Resurgence of Religion and the Transformation of International Relations* (London: Palgrave Macmillan, 2005), 35.

8. Moaddel, *Class, Politics and Ideology.*

9. Robert A. Pape, 'It's the Occupation, Stupid,' *Foreign Policy*, 18 October 2010.

10. Alisha Ryu, 'Suicide bombing increase in Somalia,' VOA, 25 June 2009; Roland Marchal, 'Harakat Al-Shabaab Al Mujahedin,' Report for UK Foreign Office, London, March 2011.

11. Ken Menkhaus, 'A Country in Peril, a Policy Nightmare,' Enough Paper, September 2008; in one sense this is a version of John Esposito's claim that the hatred of the West was caused by under-development and American support for dictators in the region brewed Islamism; John L. Esposito, *Unholy Wars: Terror in the Name of Islam* (New York: Oxford University Press, 2002).

12. Stig Jarle Hansen, 'Internal Developments in Central Somalia,' *Strategic Insights* 30, 2011.

13. Marc Sageman, *Leaderless Jihad: Terror Networks in the Twenty-First Century* (Philadelphia: University of Pennsylvania Press, 2008); Sageman, *Understanding Terror Networks* (Philadelphia: University of Pennsylvania Press, 2004).

14. Reuven Paz, *The Youth are Older: The Iraqization of the Somali Mujahidin Movement*, The Project for the Research of Islamist Movements (PRISM), vol. 6, no. 2, Herzliya, Israel, December 2008.

15. Evan F. Kohlmann, *Shabaab al-Mujahideen: Migration and Jihad in the Horn of Africa*, NEFA Foundation, May 2009.

16. The analysis of Shabaab has suffered from this, and I suspect that the discussion of tribal issues and jihadism in general could have drawn upon such analysis, with cases such as Pakistan and Yemen strongly suggesting a more complex interaction between these two factors.

17. Michael Taarnby and Lars Hallundbaek, *Al-Shabaab: The Internationalization of Militant Islamism in Somalia and the Implications for Radicalisation Processes in Europe* (Copenhagen: Ministry of Justice, 2010).

18. Roland Marchal, 'A Tentative Assessment of the Somali Harakat Al-Shabaab,' *Journal of East African Studies,* 3 (3), 2010; Roland Marchal, 'Harakat Al-Shabaab Al Mujahedin,' Report for the UK Foreign Office, London, March 2011; United Nations Monitoring Group on Somalia and Eritrea, 'Report of the Monitoring Group on Somalia Pursuant to Security Council Resolution 1853 (2008),' Report S/2010/91, 2010.

19. David Shinn, 'Al-Shabaab's Foreign Threat to Somalia,' *Orbis,* 55 (2), 2011.

20. International Crisis Group, 'Counter-Terrorism in Somalia: Losing Hearts and Minds,' *Africa Report,* no. 95, 2002; International Crisis Group, 'Somalia's Islamists,' *Africa Report,* no. 100, 2005.

21. International Crisis Group, 'Somalia's Divided Islamists,' *Africa Briefing,* no. 74, 2010.

22. Michael A. Weinstein, 'Somalia: Al-Shabaab's Split and its Absorption of Hizbul Islam,' Garowe Online, 8 January 2011.

23. Stig Jarle Hansen, 'Shabab, Central Africa's 'Taliban' Grows More Unified,' *Janes Intelligence Review,* 16/11, 2011.

24. See for example Michael Onyego, 'Somali government capitalizes on internal divisions within Al-Shabaab,' VOA, 4 October.

25. 'Shabab's Mixed Messages,' *Jane's Terrorism and Security Monitor,* 27 January 2010.

26. Conversations with Patrick Desplat in Bergen, 13 September 2010.

27. Jim Lobe, 'US Policy Risks Terrorism Blowback in Somalia,' *Mail and Guardian Online*, 5 September 2008, http://www.mg.co.za/article/2008–09–05-us-policy-risks-terrorism-blowback-in-somalia (accessed 19 March 2012).

28. Tedd R. Gurr, *Why Men Rebel* (Princeton, NJ: Princeton University Press, 1970).

29. Robert A. Pape, *Dying to Win: The Strategic Logic of Suicide Terrorism* (New York: Crown Publishing Group/Random House, 2005); Jessica Stern, *The Ultimate Terrorists* (Cambridge, MA: Harvard University Press, 1999); Mark Juergensmeyer, *Terror in the Mind of God* (Berkeley: University of California Press, 2000); Louise Richardson, *What Terrorists Want: Understanding the Terrorist Threat* (London: John Murray, 2006).

30. Olivier Roy, *Globalised Islam: The Search for a New Ummah* (London: Hurst, 2004); Turfyal Choudhury, 'The Role of Muslim Identity Politics in Radicalisation (A Study in Progress)' (London: Department for Communities and Local Government, 2007); Jeff Victoroff, 'The Mind of the Terrorist: A Review and Critique of Psychological Approaches,' *Journal of Conflict Resolution*, vol. 49, no. 1, 2005, 33–42.

31. Frank J. Buijs, Froukje Demant and Atef Hamdy, *Strijders van eigen bodem. Radicale en democratische moslims in Nederland* (Amsterdam: Amsterdam University Press, 2006).

32. Sageman, *Understanding Terror Networks*; Tinka Veldhuis and Jørgen Staun, 'Islamist Radicalisation: A Root Cause Model' (The Hague: Netherlands Institute of International Relations Clingendael, 2009); Edwin Bakker, *Jihadi Terrorists in Europe, their Characteristics and the Circumstances in which they Joined the Jihad: an Exploratory Study*, Clingendael Security Paper (The Hague: Clingendael Institute, 2006).

33. Farad Khosrokhavar, *Suicide Bombers* (London: Pluto Press, 2005).

34. Veldhuis and Staun, 'Islamist Radicalisation' (The Hague: Netherlands Institute of International Relations Clingendael, 2009). Vidino, Raffaello Pantucci and Evan Kohleman (2010) 'Bringing Global Jihad to the Horn of Africa: Al-Shabaab, the Western Fighters, and the Sacralization of the Somali Conflict,' *African Security*, 3, 2010, 230–34.

35. Lorenzo Vidino, Raffaello Pantucci and Evan Kohleman (2010) 'Bringing Global Jihad to the Horn of Africa: Al-Shabaab, the Western Fighters, and the Sacralization of the Somali Conflict,' *African Security*, 3, 2010, 230–34.

36. Ibid.

37. Stevan Weine, John Horgan, Cheryl Robertson, Sana Loue, Amin Mohamed and Sahra Noo, 'Community and Family Approaches to Combating the Radicalization of US Somali Refugee Youth and Young Adults: a Psychosocial Perspective,' *Dynamics of Asymmetric Conflict*, 2 (3), 2010.

38. For example the use of the black flag in the Kismayo campaign in 2006, as an explicit critique of the borders dividing the *ummah*.

39. See for example: 'Al-Shabaab executes two men in Baydhabo for allegedly spying,' *Mareg*, 5 May 2011, http://www.mareeg.com/fidsan.php?sid=19577&tirsan=3 (accessed 30 August 2011); Human Rights Watch, 'Harsh War, Harsh Peace Abuses by al-Shabaab, the Transitional Federal Government, and AMISOM in Somalia,' Report 1–56432–621–7, 2010.

40. See for example Muktar Abu Zubeir (alias Ahmed Godane), '1-Fariin Ku socota Somaliland' http://www.youtube.com/watch?v=DWyUKh6u_jo (accessed 30 Nov. 2010); Zubeir, '2-Fariin Ku socota Somaliland' http://www.youtube.com/watch?v=DWyUKh6u_jo (accessed 30 Nov. 2010); Zubeir, '3-Fariin Ku socota Somaliland,' http://www.youtube.com/watch?v=6Og8xHA_g0w (accessed 30 Nov. 2010).

41. Global Islamic Media Front, 'Interview with Muktar Robow,' *Echo of Jihad*, unknown number.

42. Al Jazeera, 'Al Jazeera interview with Shayk Abu Mansoor part 1 & 2,' 8 March 2009; Reuters, 'Interview: Somali insurgency to intensify-Islamist leader,' 16 December 2007; Al Jazeera, 'Interview with Abdullah Mouhalam Mohamed on increased food production,' 24 March 2010. http://english.aljazeera.net/news/africa/2010/03/2010324103733512123.html (accessed 24 October 2011).

43. Per Gudmunson, 'Jihad—nu också på svenska,' Gudmunson, 3 August 2008 http://gudmundson.blogspot.com/2008/08/jihad-nu-ocks-p-svenska.html (accessed 29 October 2011).

2. SETTING THE STAGE: THE RESURGENCE OF RELIGION IN SOMALIA

1. International Crisis Group, 'Somalia's Islamists,' *Africa Report*, no. 100; see also Abdurahman Moallim Abdullahi, 'The Islamic Movement in Somalia: A Historical Evolution with a Case Study of the Islah Movement (1950–2000),' PhD Thesis, University of Montreal, May 2011 (the best English summary of the Islamic revival in Somalia), 147.

2. Ibid.

3. Ibid.

4. Interview x1, Mogadishu, 5 November 2008.

5. International Crisis Group, 'Somalia's Islamists,' *Africa Report*, no. 100, 6.

6. Ibid.

7. David Shinn, 'Al-Shabaab's Foreign Threat to Somalia,' *Orbis*, 55 (2).

8. See also Clint Watts, Jacob Shapiro and Vahid Brown, 'Al Qaeda's Misadventures in the Horn of Africa,' Report, The Harmony Project.

9. Stig Jarle Hansen, 'Somalia—Grievance, Religion, Clan, and Profit' in S.J. Hansen, A. Mesøy and T. Karadas, *The Borders of Islam: Exploring Samuel Huntingdon's Faultlines, From Al-Andalus to the Virtual Ummah* (London: Hurst, 2009), 129.

10. Ibid.
11. Interview with Ali Mahdi, 2 March 2007.
12. Stig Jarle Hansen, 'Somalia—Grievance, Religion, Clan, and Profit.'
13. Conversation, 21 March 2012.

3. ORIGINS

1. Roland Marchal, 'A Tentative Assessment of the Harakat Al-Shabaab,' *Journal of Eastern Africa Studies*, 3 (3), 2010, 384.
2. Ibid.
3. Abdirahman 'Aynte' Ali, 'The Anatomy of al-Shabaab,' 2010, http://www.scribd. com/doc/34053611/The-Anatomy-of-Al-Shabaab-by-Abdi-Aynte (accessed 24 October).
4. 'The background of Abu Mansoor,' www.kataaib.net (accessed 1 May 2008), now closed. Further details on the AMISOM source will not be given.
5. VOA, 'Taariikhda Al-Shabaab Part 5 Dhageyso,' 2011, http://www.sunatimes. com/view.php?id=1322, (accessed 20 Oct. 2011); VOA, 'Taariikhda Al-Shabaab Part4 Dhageyso,' 2011, http://www.sunatimes.com/view.php?id=1322 (accessed 20 Oct. 2011); VOA, 'Taariikhda Al-Shabaab Part3 Dhageyso,' 2011, http:// www.sunatimes.com/view.php?id=1322 (accessed 20 Oct. 2011); VOA, 'Taariikhda Al-Shabaab Part2 Dhageyso,' 2011, http://www.sunatimes.com/view. php?id=1322 (accessed 20 Oct. 2011); VOA, 'Taariikhda Al-Shabaab Part1 Dhageyso,' 2011, http://www.sunatimes.com/view.php?id=1322 (accessed 20 Oct. 2011); the interviews might be interpreted differently, as Shabaab was consolidated or finalized, depending on one's analysis of the exact Somali wording.
6. For an inquiry into the phenomena see Thomas Hegghammer, 'The Rise of Muslim Foreign Fighters,' *International Security*, 35 (3), 2010.
7. Interview with former Shabaab member (2005–06) in Mogadishu, 19 December 2010.
8. VOA, 'Taariikhda Al-Shabaab Part1 Dhageyso,' (2011), http://www.sunatimes. com/view.php?id=1322 (accessed 20 Oct. 2011).
9. Interview with Rasheed Nur, a Somaliland journalist, by email 2 August 2010.
10. Harakat Al-Shabaab, 'The life of Aden Hashi Ayro part I,' http://www.youtube. com/watch?v=BXRPP_LpKX4&feature=related (accessed 1 August 2010); Harakat Al-Shabaab, 'The life of Aden Hashi Ayro part II' (accessed 1 August 2010); interview with Shabaab member (2005–07) X, Mogadishu, 19 December 2010.
11. Roland Marchal, 'A Tentative Assessment.'
12. Interview with former Shabaab member (2005–06) in Mogadishu, 19 December 2010; the group even tried to get a *fatwa* supporting its efforts from the famous Somali sheikh Mohamed Daoud, but failed. In the end the group rather quoted from Sayyid Qutb.

13. Harakat Al-Shabaab, 'The life of Aden Hashi Ayro part I,' http://www.youtube. com/watch?v=BXRPP_LpKX4&feature=related (accessed 1 August 2010); Harakat Al-Shabaab, 'The life of Aden Hashi Ayro part II' (accessed 1 August 2010); interview with Shabaab member (2005–07) X, Mogadishu 19 December 2010.

14. 'The background of Abu Mansoor,' www.kataaib.net.

15. Ibid.; Al-Shabaab, 'The life of Aden Hashi Ayro part I'; Al-Shabaab, 'The life of Aden Hashi Ayro part II'; interview with Shabaab member (2005–07) X, Mogadishu, 19 December 2010.

16. Harun Khan Amin, 'Report from Somali,' Al-Qaeda document found in Afghanistan, 1996, available from http://www.ctc.usma.edu/aq/pdf/AFGP-2002–600110-Trans-Meta.pdf (accessed 11 November 2010).

17. Ibid.

18. He was said to have trained in the Khalden Camp, the same camp as Saleh Ali Saleh Nabhan.

19. Cedric Barnes and Harun Hassan, 'The Rise and Fall of Mogadishu's Islamic Courts,' *Journal of Eastern African Studies*, 1 (2), 2007, 151–60.

20. Stig Jarle Hansen, 'Civil War Economies, the Hunt for Profit and the Incentives for Peace,' Enemies or Allies Working Paper 1, University of Bath/University of Mogadishu.

21. In an interview with Robow in an obituary of Ayros, Aden Hashi Ayro was said to have travelled to Afghanistan in the 1990s; Al-Shabaab, 'The life of Aden Hashi Ayro part I'; Al-Shabaab, 'The life of Aden Hashi Ayro part II.'

22. David H. Shinn, 'Al Qaeda in East Africa and the Horn,' *The Journal of Conflict Studies*, 27 (1), 2007, is by far the best article on the topic. See also Clint Watts, Jacob Shapiro and Vahid Brown, 'Al Qaeda's Misadventures in the Horn of Africa,' Report, The Harmony Project, 2007.

23. International Crisis Group, 'Counter Terrorism in Somalia, Losing Hearts and Minds?,' 2005; Federal Bureau of Investigation, 'Bombings of the Embassies of the United States of America,' Report, 18 November 1998, Washington.'

24. Ibid.; International Crisis Group, 'Counter Terrorism in Somalia: Losing Hearts and Minds?' *Africa Report*, no. 95.

25. The Kenya attackers were Jihad Muhammed Ali (hereafter referred to as Azzam) and Mohammed Rashed Daoud al-Owhali (hereafter referred to as al-Owhali), flown in from Pakistan in June and August 1998 respectively. The Tanzania attackers were Hamden Khalif Allah Awad (Ahmed the German): Ibid.

26. Julius Kisingo, from Tanzania, might have been an exception; Federal Bureau of Investigation, 'Bombings of the Embassies of the United States of America.'

27. The bomb makers were Muhsin Musa Matwalli Atwah 'Abduhl Rahman,' (Egyptian) and Muhamed Sadiq Odhe (Jordanian), while a minor role was played by Mohamed al-Owhali (Saudi Arabian) and Ghailani (Tanzanian); International Crisis Group, 'Counter Terrorism in Somalia', 2005.

28. Sheik Ahmed Salim Swedan, the man responsible for purchasing and modifying the Tanzania truck, left ten days before the bombing. Mustafa took his family to Mombasa five days before the bombing. The Tanzanian bomb makers Abdul Rahman and Ahmed Khalfan Ghailian left three days before the bombing. At this time Abdul Rahman went to Nairobi and made the final connection on the Kenya bomb which had previously been made by Mohamed Sadiq Odeh, with the help of Mohamed al-Owhali: Ibid.

29. Ibid.; Nelly Lahoud, 'Beware of Imitators: Al-Qa'ida through the Lens of its Confidential Secretary,' The Harmony Program, West Point, USA, 23.

30. In the aftermath of the 1998 attacks, Al-Qaeda managed to withdraw many of its operatives to Afghanistan/Pakistan, preceding the later attacks it coordinated on a global scale: Ibid.

31. Ibid.

32. According to Kenyan police Saleh Ali Nabhan headed the team that attacked the airliner, and Issa Osman Issa (allegedly the one launching the missile) and Mohammad Abdul Malik Abduljabar participated in this group. The exact implementation of the suicide attack is a bit more uncertain, as several individuals allegedly involved in providing safe houses for the attack were all acquitted in court. Two Kenyans, Fumo Mohamed Fumo and Haruni Bamusa, are alleged by the Kenyan police to have driven Nabhan's blue Pajero into the Paradise Hotel, killing fifteen and injuring about eighty; Fumo Mohamed Fumo is claimed to have survived: Ibid.; Stig Jarle Hansen (forthcoming), 'Al Qaeda in East Africa,' unpublished manuscript.

33. International Crisis Group, 'Somalia's Islamists,' *Africa Report*, no. 100; International Crisis Group, 'Counter Terrorism in Somalia,' 15.

34. Nelly Lahoud, 'Beware of Imitators,' 14.

35. International Crisis Group, 'Somalia's Islamists' (2005); International Crisis Group, 'Counter Terrorism in Somalia, Losing Hearts and Minds?' (2005)

36. International Crisis Group, 'Counter Terrorism in Somalia' (2005).

37. Al-Shabaab, 'The life of Aden Hashi Ayro part I'; Al-Shabaab, 'The life of Aden Hashi Ayro part II'; interview x1, x2, Mogadishu.

38. Al Jazeera, 'Interview with Muktar Robow,' 25 February 2009, downloaded from http://forums.islamicawakening.com/f18/aljazeeras-interview-mukhtar-robow-abu-mansour-sahabaab-22323/

39. Interview with former Shabaab member (2005–06) in Mogadishu, 19 December 2010; interview with former Shabaab member, Mogadishu, 19 December 2010; interview x2, Mogadishu, 18 December 2010.

40. International Crisis Group, 'Counter Terrorism in Somalia, Losing Hearts and Minds?,' 2005, 15.

41. Interview x1, Mogadishu, 5 November 2008; Zubeir, Muktar Abu (alias Ahmed Godane), 'Biographical Summary of the Martyred Commander, Allah-willing,

Abu Yusuf al-Nabhani,' 12 October 2009, NEFA foundation, http://www.nefa-foundation.org/miscellaneous/nefa_al-Nabhani1009–2.pdf (accessed 1 August 2010).

42. Arrale had in 1998 travelled to Pakistan, where he studied English Literature at the International Islamic University, and was in 2007 snatched by the United States and escorted to Guantánamo Bay, where he was held for two and a half years without trial, until he was released in 2009: interview with Rasheed Nur, a Somaliland Journalist, per email 2 August 2010.

43. Interview with former Shabaab member (2005–06) in Mogadishu, 19 December 2010.

44. International Crisis Group, 'Somalia's Islamists'; International Crisis Group, 'Counter Terrorism in Somalia, Losing Hearts and Minds?.'

45. Interview with former Shabaab member (2005–06) in Mogadishu.

4. THE FIRST EXPANSIVE PHASE 2005–06: IN THE SHADOW OF THE COURTS

1. Stig Jarle Hansen, 'Den somaliske fredsprosessen,' Commissioned Report for the Norwegian Ministry of Foreign Affairs, 2004, 5.

2. Stig Jarle Hansen, 'Civil War Economies, the Hunt for Profit and the Incentives for Peace,' Enemies or Allies Working Paper 1, University of Bath/University of Mogadishu, 2007, 36; see also Stig Jarle Hansen, 'Warlords, Patrimony, Ethnicism, the Cases of China, Afghanistan and Somalia,' *Peace Research*, 35:2, 2003.

3. Hansen, 'Civil War Economies,' 36.

4. Ibid.

5. Ibid.

6. Ibid., 30.

7. According to one of the founders of the Karar court, the leadership governing that court also included travelling Islamic judges who were transported from area to area, as well as several smaller courts. Nevertheless, although its target was to govern the whole of Mogadishu the council only governed courts of the Abgal clan, and collapsed when the Karar court collapsed.

8. Stig Jarle Hansen, 'Somalia—Grievance, Religion, Clan, and Profit,' Chapter 8 in Hansen, Mesøy and Karadas, *The Borders of Islam: Exploring Samuel Huntington's Faultlines, From Al-Andalus to the Virtual Ummah* (London: Hurst, 2009), 127–38.

9. IRIN News, 'Somalia: Fighting in Mogadishu,' 30 April 1999; Xinhua News, 'Mogadishu Factions Meet to Narrow Gap,' 25 February 1999.

10. Stig Jarle Hansen, 'Somalia—Grievance, Religion, Clan, and Profit.'

11. Ibid.

12. For newspaper and media sources suggesting this see for example Al Jazeera, 'Who are Al-Shabab?,' Al Jazeera, 31 October 2011, http://english.aljazeera.net/

news/africa/2009/08/20098432032479714.html (accessed 31 October 2011); Murithi Muthiga, 'Kenya: Let's talk to the Shabaab, Somalia won't be pacified by military means,' *Daily Nation*, 29 October 2011; Gabe Joselow, 'Is Kenya Battling al-Shabab alone?' VOA, 29 October 2011, http://www.voanews.com/ english/news/africa/Is-Kenya-Battling-al-Shabab-Alone-132640988.html (accessed 31 October 2011).

13. Also known as 'Sheikh Yassin,' Adane was in many ways a typical Mogadishu businessman, deeply religious, with many personal friends in the court system, many of them encountered during visits in Saudi Arabia. Adane also had a need for security for his business, and provided support for various courts. Hansen, 'Somalia—Grievance, Religion, Clan, and Profit'.

14. The two had previously been dividing revenue from El Maan harbor (mainly controlled by Adane), the El Adde harbor, and the Eisly airport: Ibid.

15. The two clashed over something as trivial as the ownership of several cars in the north of Mogadishu in January 2006, as is confirmed by interviews with Adane's former militia: Ibid.

16. Ibid.

17. Ibid.

18. Ibid.

19. Stig Jarle Hansen, 'Sharia Courts Holds Sway in Mogadishu,' *Foreign Report*, 2006, 10.

20. Stig Jarle Hansen, 'Misspent Youth,' *Jane's Intelligence Review*, 20/10 (2008), 7.

21. Utayba, from the Murosade Clan, had been a trader in Bakaraha market; he had been active in al-Iti'sam but had been a frequent guest at the training sessions of Ayro, and in the end joined Shabaab during the conflict with the warlords in early 2006; by mid-2006 he was amongst their most important leaders. Interview with Muqtar Robow 5 March, 2012, conducted by Abdifitah Gelleh.

22. According to some sources Godane also lectured in two Hargeisa mosques, 'Xero Hadhuudh' and the Abu Basher mosque, as well as the Burao 'Barcadle' mosque; interview with Rasheed Nur, a Somaliland journalist, per email 2 August 2010.

23. Ibid.

24. It is important to note that although several analysts accuse Godane of being behind the 2003 Toneli killing, he was acquitted of this attack. See for example staff writer, 'Somaliland "terrorists" get death sentences,' Africa Online, 14 November 2005, http://afrol.com/articles/17243 (accessed 24 February 2005).

25. He has a brother who used to be a senior Somaliland police officer (Awdal, Chief Commissioner 2002–04) but was demoted.

26. Interview x5, Mogadishu, 19 December 2010.

27. Ibid.

28. Interview with NGO leader in Nairobi, 13 August 2011.

29. Roland Marchal, 'A Tentative Assessment of the Somali Harakat Al-Shabaab,' *Journal of East African Studies*, 3 (3), 40.

30. Interview with anonymous member of Hassan Dahir Aweys' staff 2005–06, Mogadishu, 5 September 2006. Interview with former Shabaab member (2005–06) in Mogadishu, 19 December 2010.

31. See http://wikileaks.org/gitmo/pdf/so/dj9so-010027dp.pdf (accessed 24 April 2012).

32. Interview x5, Mogadishu, 19 December 2010.

33. Roland Marchal, 'Harakat Al-Shabaab Al Mujahedin,' Report for the UK Foreign Office, London, March 2011, 16.

34. Interview x11, Mogadishu, 19 December 2010.

35. 'Harakat Al-Shabaab, Mujahidin Youth Movement Eulogizes Commander's "Martyrdom" On 17 December,' 17 December 2008, http://www.biyokulule.com/view_content.php?articleid=1676 (accessed 1 August 2010).

36. Jeffrey Gettleman, 'Demonstrations becomes clashes after Islamists take Somali city,' *New York Times* 26 September 2006.

37. Interview given to Risk Intelligence, 1 April 2010.

38. Interview x13, Mogadishu 20 April 2009.

39. Osama Bin Laden, 'Messages,' July 2006, audiotape.

40. Stig Jarle Hansen, 'Misspent Youth,' 7; see also Abu Mansoor Al-Amriki (The American Mujahid In Somalia), 'A Message To The Mujahideen in Particular & the Muslims in General,' posted to jihadist website 7 February 2008, http://prisonerofjoy.blogspot.com/2008/02/abu-mansoor-al-amriki-american-mujahid.html (accessed 1 November 2011).

41. It should be noted that Godane also worked on emigration issues and might have been involved: Ibid.

42. Staff writer, 'Abu Huriyyah Amir Abdul Muhaimin,' *Milat Ibrahim*, 11 December 2008; Jeanne Meserve and Mike M. Ahlers, 'Seattle case raises questions about war on terror,' CNN online, 18 December 2006.

43. Andrea Elliott, 'The terrorist next door,' *New York Times*, 27 January 2010.

44. United States District Court, Southern District of Texas, The United States against Daniel Joseph Maldonado, 13 February 2007.

45. Daniel Joseph Maldonado, 'My imprisonment in Kenya and America,' http://old.cageprisoners.com/articles.php?id=21648 (accessed 21 December 2010).

46. On return to the US, he pleaded guilty to training with a terrorist organization and was sentenced to ten years in prison; his statements are important sources on the Shabaab dynamics of 2006. Echoing statements have come from Shabaab defectors active in 2006.

47. UPI 'Danes say men plotted to cut throats,' 31 Jan. 2011, http://www.upi.com/Top_News/World-News/2011/01/31/Danes-say-men-plotted-to-cut-throats/UPI-12011296508387/ (accessed 21 October 2011).

48. KLISI Newscast, 'San Diego Jewish boy, Jehad Mostafa, suspected in plot to finance Al-Shabaab in Somalia,' KLISI Newscast; available on http://www.

youtube.com/watch?v=uI_1n9gNUQw&feature=related (accessed 23 October 2011).

49. Daniel Joseph Maldonado, 'My imprisonment in Kenya and America,' 2006, http://old.cageprisoners.com/articles.php?id=21648, accessed 21 December 2010.

50. Gregory D. Johnsen, 'Tracking Yemen's 23 Escaped Jihadi Operatives—Part 1,' *Terrorism Monitor*, 5 (18), 2007.

51. Gregory D. Johnsen, 'Tracking Yemen's 23 Escaped Jihadi Operatives—Part 2,' *Terrorism Monitor*, 5 (19), 2007.

52. Interview x12, Mogadishu, 3 April 2009.

53. Stig Jarle Hansen, 'Revenge or Reward? The Case of Somalia's Suicide Bombers,' *Journal of Terrorism Research*, 1 (1), 2010.

54. Ibid.

55. Alisha Ryu, 'Former members of radical Somali group give details of their group,' VOA Mogadishu, 6 January 2007.

56. In Ryu's interview several hundred other outstanding students were flown to Eritrea and given an additional two months of advance training in explosives and guerrilla war tactics. Abdi says he and the others were given detailed instructions on how to make roadside bombs, car bombs, and suicide vests, using explosives material cannibalized from various weapon systems.

57. Cedric Barnes and Harun Hassan, 'The Rise and Fall of Mogadishu's Islamic Courts,' *Journal of Eastern African Studies*, 1 (2), 2007, 151–60.

58. BBC, '"Al-Qaeda" arrest in East Africa,' 7 June 2007, http://news.bbc.co.uk/2/hi/6729015.stm (accessed 24 October 2011).

5. PHOENIX FROM THE ASHES: INSURGENCY 2007–08

1. Interview x13, Mogadishu, 20 April 2009.

2. Omar Hammami, 'The story of an American Jihadi Part 1,' 2011, http://www.scribd.com/doc/93732117/The-Story-of-an-American-Jihaadi (accessed 20 May 2012).

3. Human Rights Watch, 'Shell-shocked Civilians under Siege in Mogadishu,' *Human Rights Watch Report*, 10 (12), 2007.

4. Ibid.

5. This illustrates the confusion even amongst Shabaab, and shows how the Shabaab leaders still saw themselves as parts of the Sharia Court movement. Ayr for example released an audio message about this time, announcing that he was safe and calling people to continue fighting, but also appealing for resistance against Ethiopia.

6. Conversations with *Aftenposten* journalist Jørgen Lohne, 5 February 2007.

7. Cecilia Hull and Emma Svensson, 'African Union Mission in Somalia (AMISOM), Exemplifying African Union Peacekeeping Challenges,' *FOI-R-2596—SE*, 2008, 26.

8. Hammami, 'The Story of an American Jihadi, Part 1,' 92.

9. Ibid., 94.

10. Ibid., 99.

11. This group had originally been trained by Ayro, when they were known as the Al-Irshad Islamic Court, and he considered them as Shabaab, but they had given their *bay'ah* to Sheikh Abdulqadir.

12. Jihad Unspun, 'YIM press statement,' 2007, http://old.kavkazcenter.com/eng/content/2007/09/07/8823.shtml, http://old.kavkazcenter.com/eng/content/2007/10/04/8933.shtml (accessed 13 September 2009). For example, the organization took responsibility for the murder of Shakir Shafee on 5 September 2007, and that of Abd Wersha on 3 October the same year. On 10 October General Ahmad Jalo was assassinated. Assassinations became a common Shabaab strategy; Human Rights Watch, 'So Much to Fear,' Human Rights Watch Report 1–56432–415-X, 2008, 90.

13. Telephone interview with a friend of the family, 1 August 2011.

14. Ibid.

15. Human Rights Watch, 'So Much to Fear,' 90.

16. Ibid.

17. Interview x2, Mogadishu, 18 December 2010.

18. Indaadde's men managed to hide thirty-five technicals all around Lower Shabelle.

19. Stig Jarle Hansen, 'Misspent Youth,' (2008), 7; see also Abu Mansoor Al-Amriki (The American Mujahid In Somalia), 'A Message,' 2008.

20. Ibid.

21. Hammami, 'The Story of an American Jihadi, Part 1,' 102.

22. Stig Jarle Hansen, 'Report to the Norwegian Ministry of Foreign Affairs,' Report 5, 2007; the count was based on Shabaab's numbers compared and checked with the UNDSS numbers for these years.

23. Interview x2, Mogadishu, 18 December 2010.

24. Telephone interview with human rights activist in Baidoa, 15 May 2009.

25. Staff writer, 'One killed as Somali Islamists bring in Afghan-trained commander,' Garowe Online, 7 October 2007, http://www.garoweonline.com/artman2/publish/Somalia_27/One_killed_as_Somali_Islamists_bring_in_Afghan-trained_commander.shtml (accessed 24 October 2011).

26. International Crisis Group, 'Somalia: To Move Beyond the Failed State,' *Africa Report*, no. 147, 23 Dec. 2008.

27. Ibid.

28. Harakat Al-Shabaab, 'The Will of Abu Ayyub al-Muhajir,' released 1 March 2008, http://www.myhesbah.com/v/showthread.php?t=170168 (accessed 1 November 2009).

29. Evan F. Kohlmann, 'Shabaab al-Mujahideen: Migration and Jihad in the Horn of Africa,' Nefa Foundation Report, May 2009, 45.

30. Global Islamic Media Front (GIMF), 'An Interview With the Commander Abi Mansoor (Mukhtaar Ali Robo), the Spokesman of the Youth Islamic Movement in Somalia,' *Sada al-Jihad* issue 25, May 2008.
31. Harakat Al-Shabaab, 'March Forth,' distributed in Mogadishu September 2009.
32. Harakat Al-Shabaab, 'The Will of Abu Ayyub al-Muhajir.'
33. Telephone interview with Muktar Robow, conducted in cooperation with Shwashank Bengali, 1 December 2008.
34. For the threat to Denmark, see Harakat Al-Shabaab, 'The Will of the Martyr Abdul Aziz Saad, May Allah Accept Him,' http://www.alhesbah.net/v/showthread.php?t=197107, 30 October 2008 (accessed 1 November 2009).
35. Global Islamic Media Front, 'An Interview With the Commander Abi Mansoor.'
36. Ibid.
37. Harakat Al-Shabaab, 'Ambush at Bardale,' http://www.alfaloja.info/vb/showthread.php?t=54142, 2009 (accessed 5 May 2009).
38. Stig Jarle Hansen, 'Revenge or Reward? The Case of Somalia's Suicide Bombers,' *Journal of Terrorism Research*, 1 (1), 2010.
39. Ibid.
40. Ibid.
41. Ibid.
42. Staff writer, 'Joining the fight in Somalia,' *New York Times*, 12 June 2009.
43. The known members of the second wave were Mustafa Ali, Muhamed Hassan 'Misky,' Mohamoud Hassan 'snake,' Troy Kastigar, Abdikadir Ali Abdi, Abdisalan Ali, Jamal Sheik Bana and Barhan Hassan. The average age was nineteen. Mahemoud Hassan was involved in gang related violence: *New York Times*, 'Joining the fight in Somalia,' 12 June 2009.
44. Kamal Hassan had once worked as a waiter at his family's restaurant near the Towers, and he was on the resource committee at the mosque. Several friends said in interviews that he had defected from Shabaab and returned to Minneapolis. See BBC News, 'Minnesota man admits Somalia terror plot,' 19 July 2011, http://www.bbc.co.uk/news/world-us-canada-14195832 (last accessed 7 February 2013).
45. Stevan Weine, John Horgan, Cheryl Robertson, Sana Loue, Amin Mohamed and Sahra Noo, 'Community and Family Approaches to Combating the Radicalization of US Somali Refugee Youth and Young Adults: a Psychosocial Perspective,' *Dynamics of Asymmetric Conflict*, 2 (3), 2010.
46. United Nations Monitoring Group on Somalia and Eritrea, Report of the Monitoring Group on Somalia Pursuant to Security Council Resolution 1853 (2008),' Report S/2010/91, 2010.
47. Michael Taarnby and Lars Hallundbaek, *Al-Shabaab: The Internationalization of Militant Islamism in Somalia and the Implications for Radicalisation Processes in Europe*, Report for the Danish Ministry of Justice, 45.

48. Telephone interview with local person in Kismayo, x14 (Date will not be given).
49. Ibid.
50. The three most powerful commanders in Merka were the Deputy Chief of Police Nuriye Ali Farah, the Governor Mohamed Mahmoud Elmi, and Commander Arifli Ghani; the two first were killed in the Shabaab attack.
51. Stig Jarle Hansen, 'Report to the Norwegian Ministry of Foreign Affairs,' Report 6.
52. Ibid.
53. Mohamed Husein Gaas, 'A New Hope? Former Rebel Takes Over as Somali President,' *Jane's Intelligence Review*, March 2009, 24–9.
54. Ibid.
55. Ibid.

6. THE GOLDEN AGE OF AL-SHABAAB (2009–10)

1. See for example Anwar Awlaki, 'Speech,' (unknown date), http://www.youtube.com/watch?v=abBIhu7Eo6Y&feature=related (accessed 1 June 2011).
2. Mohamed Husein Gaas, 'A New Hope? Former Rebel Takes Over as Somali President,' *Jane's Intelligence Review*, March 2009, 24–9.
3. Interview with former Shabaab member (2005–06) in Mogadishu. 19 December 2010.
4. Anonymous, 'Regarding the conquest of Kismayo,' Report sent to Risk Intelligence, 2010.
5. From 2008 to early 2009, Qalid was an instructor in different Al-Shabaab camps in Lower Shabelle, Middle Jubba, and Bay. He also got more training himself, and started teaching more advanced courses like urban and guerrilla warfare. He was made a commander of a company-sized unit that was part of the offensive in June 2009, but in the end was killed in Karan, in an attack on a police station: Ibid.
6. Ibid.
7. Ibid.; see also Garowe Online, 'Somalia: Yemen-born 'foreign fighter' killed in Mogadishu,' 6 December 2010, http://www.garoweonline.com/artman2/publish/Somalia_27/Somalia_Yemen-born_foreign_fighter_killed_in_Mogadishu.shtml (accessed 1 November 2011).
8. David Shinn, 'Al-Shabaab's Foreign Threat to Somalia,' *Orbis*, 55 (2), 2011, 209.
9. Interview with Rahanwhein elders, Nairobi, 11 December 2010.
10. Interview x13, Nairobi, November 2008.; interview x15, Mogadishu, 20 April 2009.
11. Staff writer, 'Fresh fighting starts in Central Somalia Hawiye heartlands,' *Terror Free Somalia*, 13 January 2009, http://terrorfreesomalia.blogspot.com/2009/01/death-shabaab.html (accessed 6 November 2011).

12. Interview with Sheik Mhyedin, 19 April 2009.

13. Interview with refugee x20, and businessman x21 in Nairobi, 3 December 2010.

14. Roland Marchal, 'Harakat Al-Shabaab Al Mujahedin,' Report for the UK Foreign Office, London, March 2011.

15. Dalje, 'Ethiopians Leave, Somali Insurgents Take Baidoa,' 26 January 2009, http://dalje.com/en-world/ethiopians-leave-somali-insurgents-take-baidoa/228262 (accessed 1 November 2011); Reuters, 'Somali insurgents take Baidoa after Ethiopians leave,' 27 January 2009, http://archive.tuscolatoday.com/?p=54990 (accessed 1 November 2011).

16. Marchal, 'Harakat Al-Shabaab Al Mujahedin.'

17. Mohamed Haji Abdow Nurow, who had mental problems, murdered his mother; immediately Al-Shabaab arrested him, and after three days he was shot before a public gathering: telephone interview with human rights activist in Baidoa, 15 May 2009.

18. Interview with Rahanwhein elders, Nairobi, 11 December 2010; telephone interview with human rights activist in Baidoa, 15 May 2009.

19. International Crisis Group, 'Somalia's divided Islamists,' *Africa Briefing*, no. 74 (2010).

20. Ibid.

21. See for example Gerard Prunier, 'Somalia: beyond the quagmire,' *open democracy net, http://www.opendemocracy.net/article/somalia-beyond-the-quagmire* (accessed 11 April 2011); the Anole group was of course never a part of Shabaab.

22. Stig Jarle Hansen, 'Somalia Report to the Norwegian Ministry of Foreign Affairs,' Report, 5, 11.

23. Telephone interview with human rights activist in Baidoa, 1 February 2009.

24. Ibid.

25. Interview x12, Mogadishu, 3 April 2009; interview x13, Mogadishu 20 April 2009.

26. Marchal, 'Harakat Al-Shabaab Al Mujahedin.'

27. Stig Jarle Hansen, 'Faction Fluctuation—The Shifting Allegiances within Hizbul Islam,' *Jane's Intelligence Review*, 6/11, 2010, 45.

28. Ibid.

29. Shabelle Media Network, 'Calm returns to Mogadishu,' 23 May 2009.

30. Shabelle Media Network, 'Fresh fighting starts in Mogadishu,' 14 June 2009.

31. United Nations High Commissioner for Refugees, 'UNHCR Briefing Sheet,' February Report 2010–11.

32. Ibid.

33. Interview with Muktar Robow by telephone, conducted in cooperation with Shwashank Bengali, 1 December 2008; interview x13, Mogadishu 20 April 2009.

34. Interview with refugee from Kismayo, Nairobi, September 2009, conducted by Michael Scheldrup.

35. Interview with NGO leader in Nairobi, 13 August 2011.

36. Interview with refugee x2 from Kismayo, Nairobi, September 2009, conducted by anonymous field researcher and Michael Scheldrup.

37. Interview x1, conducted by Michael Scheldrup in Nairobi, 13 August 2010.

38. Interview with refugee x3 from Kismayo, Nairobi, September 2009, conducted by anonymous field researcher and Michael Scheldrup.

39. Ibid.

40. Ibid.

41. The *wilaya* court was headed first by Sheik Hassan Enow, then by Sheik Husein, while the district court was headed by Sheikh Abdulaahi.

42. Interview with refugee x6 from Kismayo, Nairobi, 5 September 2009, conducted by anonymous field researcher and Michael Scheldrup.

43. Ibid.

44. Interview with refugee x3 from Kismayo, Nairobi, 5 September 2009, conducted by anonymous field researcher and Michael Scheldrup.

45. The Qadi of the local (not the regional) court of Kismayo was Mohamed Awil, a young, well-educated sheikh from the Absame clan, who had studied the Sharia and religion with Sheikh Hassan Turki. As an orphan who lost his both parents in southern Somalia during the civil war, Mohamed, together with many other youngsters, was raised under the tutelage of Sheikh Hassan Turki in Ras Kamboni, who was at the time leader of Al-Ittihad al-Islamiya in lower Juba.

46. See for example Harakat Al-Shabaab, 'Graduation Ceremony at the Abdullah Azzam Training Center for Islamic Propagation in the Islamic Province of Banadir (Mogadishu),' Global Islamic Media Front, 2 May 2010, http://theunjustmedia.com/Islamic%20Perspectives/May10/Graduation%20Ceremony%20 at%20the%20Abdullah%20Azzam%20Training%20Center%20for%20 Islamic%20Propagation%20in%20the%20Islamic%20Province%20of%20Banadir%20(Mogadishu).htm (accessed 1 November 2011).

47. Interview with refugee x3 from Kismayo, Nairobi 7 September 2009, conducted by anonymous field researcher and Michael Scheldrup.

48. Ibid.

49. Interview with NGO leader in Nairobi, 13 August 2011.

50. At times it was referred to as the *fatwa* council.

51. Interview with NGO leader in Nairobi, 13 August 2011.

52. Ibid.

53. Ibid.

54. Stig Jarle Hansen, 'The Enemy's Enemy—Eritrea's involvement in Somalia,' *Janes Intelligence Review*, vol. 21/10, 2009, 13.

55. Other camps in the area include the Abdi dhoore camp, 60 km of northeast of Kismayo. b. Beerhaani (Beerxaani), 60 km north of Kismayo. c. Bantaa, about 55 km north of Buale, in Middle Juba.

56. Interview x2, Mogadishu, 18 December 2010; Interview x11, Mogadishu, 19 December 2010. Interview x1, x2, Oslo, 5 June 2011.

57. Ibid.

58. ABC News, 'Somalia's Al-Shabaab recruits Holy warriors with US$400 Bonus,' 18 April 2010.

59. See for example Harakat Al-Shabaab, 'Eulogy for Abu Umar al-Baghdadi and Abu Hamza al-Muhajer by the Shabaab al-Mujahedeen in Somalia,' http://www. archive.org/details/Song-of-Terror-faaluja (accessed 3 June 2010); Sudarsan Raghavan 'Foreign fighters gain influence in Somalia's Islamist Al-Shabaab militia,' *Washington Post*, 8 June 2010.

60. Ibid.

61. Rana Safdaralik Khan, 'A Somali leader of Al Qaida calls on Obama to convert to Islam,' *Allvoices* 28 December 2010, http://www.allvoices.com/contributed-news/7739879-a-somali-leader-of-al-qaida-calls-on-obama-to-convert-to-islam (accessed 10 November 2011).

62. Sarah Childress, 'Somalia's Al-Shabaab to ally with Al Qaeda,' *Wall Street Journal*, 2 February 2010.

63. AFP, 'Somalia's Shabaab declare that it would send fighters to support Al Qaeda,' 1 January 2010.

64. Conversation with Iqbal Jazbay, former foreign policy coordinator of the African National Congress of South Africa, 3 August 2011.

65. Peter Orengo and Cyrus Ombati, 'Two held in Mombasa over Nairobi explosion,' *The Standard*, 22 December 2010: the whole incident could have been an accident.

66. United Nations Monitoring Group on Somalia and Eritrea, 'Report of the Monitoring Group on Somalia Pursuant to Security Council Resolution 1853 (2008),' *Report* S/2010/91, 2010.

67. Al Jazeera, 'Three charged in Ugandan bombing,' 31 July 2010.

68. Tim Pipard, 'Al-Shabab's agenda in the wake of the Kampala suicide attacks,' CTC Sentinel, 2 July 2010.

69. Interview x1, x2 in Oslo, 5 June 2011.

70. *Göteborgs Tingsrätt*, 'Dom,' B 7277–10, 2010; UPI 'Swedish court frees Somali terror suspects,' 2 March 2010.

71. Nina Larson, 'Danish attack plot suspect in previous arrests,' AFP, 31 December 2010.

72. Fatuma Noor, 'My encounter with Somali-American Jihadists in Nairobi,' *Nairobi Star*, 27 June 2011.

73. Interview x1, Mogadishu (by telephone), 1 September 2011.

74. *Göteborgs Tingsrätt*, 'Dom,' B 7277–10, 2010; UPI, 'Swedish court frees Somali terror suspects.'

75. Justin Fishel, 'FOXWIRE: Navy Seals kill wanted terrorist in Somali raid,' Fox News, 14 September 2009, http://www.foxnews.com/story/0,2933,550100,00. html (accessed 10 November 2011).

76. There were signs that AMISOM was virtually undefeatable for Shabaab, as on 21 May 2010, when an attack against Villa Somalia (the presidential palace) was defeated by AMISOM armor.

77. This in turn led the Shabaab to raid bases inside Kenya and Ethiopia, as on 27 May 2010.

78. NGO Security Programme, 'AS issued an Arabic statement announcing the foundation of a news channel called Al Kata'ib to 'take the jihad to the propaganda front,' Daily Security Report, 27 July 2010.

79. Radio Mogadishu, 'Interview with Mohamed Jama Mohamud, Mohamed Farah, Mohamed Ibrahim, Hassan Mohamed Saciid, Ahmed Mohamed' aired in December 2010.

80. Ibid.

81. The whole offensive carried a symbolic meaning; 28 August 2010 was the anniversary of the Battle of Badr (625 CE) in which Muslim forces led by the Prophet achieved what is considered to be one of the most significant victories over their Quraishi enemies, and 30 August was the date of the conquest of Mecca (630 CE).

82. At least two of the attackers were suicide bombers and blew themselves up after firing on people in the hotel: NGO Security Programme, 'Advisory regarding current Al-Shabaab offensive in Mogadishu,' Mogadishu Advisory, 24 August 2010.

83. Staff writer, 'Violence kills 43 in the Somali capital,' Press TV, 27 August 2010.

84. NGO Security Programme, 'A contingent of AMISOM forces are trapped in Jubba Hotel in Shangani district of Mogadishu following takeover of the all the adjacent areas surrounding the Hotel, Daily Security Report, 7 September 2010.

85. NGO Security Programme, 'Some TFG military soldiers withdrew from key positions in Abdul Aziz and Hodan districts protesting delay of salary arrears payment,' Daily Security Report, 7 September 2010.

86. NGO Security Programme, 'Head of Hawiye Council of Elders told media that AS failed in its Ramadan offensive,' Daily Security Report, 13 September 2010.

7. THE ERA OF TROUBLES (2010–)

1. Michael A. Weinstein (2011), 'Somalia: Al-Shabaab's Split and its Absorption of Hizbul Islam,' Garowe Online, 8 January 2011, http://www.garoweonline.com/artman2/publish/Somalia_27/Somalia_Al-Shabaab_s_Split_and_its_Absorption_of_Hizbul_Islam_Intelligence_Brief.shtml

2. Interview with Shabaab leader by telephone, 1 August 2011.

3. Ibid.

4. Garowe Online, 'Somalia: Secret meeting between Aweys, Abu-Mansoor over new insurgent group,' 6 October 2010, http://www.garoweonline.com/artman2/

publish/Somalia_27/Somalia_Secrets_meeting_between_Aweys_Abu-Man-soor_over_new_insurgent_group.shtml (accessed 6 October 2010).

5. Garowe Online, 'Somalia: Abu-Mansoor denies dispute with Godane,' 9 Octo-ber. 2010, http://www.garoweonline.com/artman2/publish/Somalia_27/Abu-Mansoor_denies_dispute_with_Godane.shtml (accessed 9 October 2010).

6. Garowe Online, 'Somalia: Al-Shabaab to avenge Sheikh Muktar Abu-Yazid,' 21 October 2010, http://www.garoweonline.com/artman2/publish/Somalia_27/Somalia_Al-Shabaab_to_avenge_Sheikh_Muktar_Abu-Yazid.shtml (accessed 20 October 2010).

7. Ibid.

8. See for example NGO Security Programme, 'AS leaders from Bakool region met to discuss the current differences that has emerged between Muktar Robow aka Abu Mansoor and Ahmed Godane aka Abu Zubayr,' Daily Security Report, 3 October 2010.

9. *Sunna Times*, 'The rift within AS deepens as mediation efforts by some of the ranks failed due to tough preconditions set by Sheikh Muktar Robow,' 4 Octo-ber 2010, http://www.sunatimes.com/view.php?id=485O2/AS in crisis/20101005. 2338 (accessed 5 October 2010).

10. Ibid.

11. Ibid.

12. Roland Marchal, 'Harakat Al-Shabaab Al Mujahedin,' Report for the UK For-eign Office, London, March 2011.

13. Media monitor, '13 December 2010 Somalia round up,' *Somalia Report*, http://www.somaliareport.com/index.php/post/30/13_Dec_2010_Somalia_News_Roundup (accessed 24 October 2011).

14. Interview with NGO leader in Nairobi, 13 August 2011.

15. Interview x3, Mogadishu (by telephone), 1 September 2011; interview with Shabaab sub-commander, 9 September 2011.

16. Interview x3, Mogadishu (by telephone), 1 September 2011.

17. Marchal (2011), 'Harakat Al-Shabaab'.

18. Ibid.

19. NGO Security Programme (2011), 'South-Central Offensive,' *NSP Weekly Secu-rity Report*, Week, 5–12 March 2011.

20. Interview x1, Nairobi, 10 November 2011; Interview x2 Nairobi, 11 November.

21. Ibid.

22. Interview with anonymous private contractor, Mogadishu, 19 December 2010.

23. Radio Mogadishu, 'Interview with 6 Shabaab defectors,' 2010.

24. Stig Jarle Hansen, 'Faction Fluctuation—The Shifting Allegiances within Hiz-bul Islam,' *Janes Intelligence Review*, 6/11, 2010.

25. Ibid.

26. Ibid.

27. NGO Security Programme, 'End of Hizbul Islamiya,' NSP Weekly Security Report, 23 December 2010.
28. Interview with NGO leader in Nairobi, 13 August 2011.
29. NGO Security Programme, 'AS Extends Area of Control, Toro-Torow village, Awdhegle district, Lower Shabelle region,' Daily Security Report, 14 December 2010; NGO Security Programme, 'End of Hizbul Islamiya,' NSP Weekly Security Report, 23 December 2010.
30. Harakat Al-Shabaab, 'حفل ختم عنوان فرحة المسلمين بتوحد المجاهدين الإثنين,' http://alqimmah.net/showthread.php?t=22643 (accessed 1 June 2011).
31. NGO Security Programme, 'Ahmed Godane a.k.a Sheikh Mukhtar Abu Zubeyr welcomed unification of AS and HI and announced intention of AS to double number of attacks against TFG/AMISOM,' Daily Security Report, 31 December 2010.
32. NGO Security Programme, 'End of Hizbul Islam.'
33. AFP, 'Somali Islamists tell pirates to destroy Ukrainian arms ship,' 2 October 2008.
34. J.E. London, 'Somalia's Muslim jihad at sea,' *Washington Times*, 22 April 2009, available at http://www.washingtontimes.com/news/2009/apr/22/somalias-muslimjihad-at-sea/ (accessed 26 August 2009).
35. Roger Middleton, 'Piracy in Somalia: Threatening Global Trade, Feeding Local Wars,' Chatham House Briefing Paper, AFP BP 08/02. The Chatham House report cites only one explicit source to support its allegations that there is a link between piracy and Shabaab, a source that failed to fully corroborate its assertion.
36. Martin Plaut, 'Pirates working with Islamists,' BBC News, 19 November 2008.
37. Stig Jarle Hansen, 'Pirates of the greater Gulf of Aden, myths, misconceptions and remedies,' NIBR Report 2009, 29.
38. Stig Jarle Hansen, 'The Attack on Haradhere. The background and implications for the maritime sector,' *Marisk Special Analysis*, 21 May 2010.
39. Its forces were relatively weak, between 60 and 140.
40. Stig Jarle Hansen, 'The Dynamics of Somali Piracy,' *Journal of Conflict and Terrorism Studies*, vol. 35, no. 7–8, July 2012, 523–530.
41. There were notable exceptions to this; as some pirates had close relatives in Shabaab controlled areas, they were persuaded to pay tax, and some of the major syndicate leaders also tried later to bribe Shabaab to let them go back to Haradhere. Stig Jarle Hansen, 'The Pirates of Haradhere,' Specially commissioned report for Risk Intelligence, 2011, 2.
42. Ibid.
43. It was reported that Gacmo Dhere (or Dulyadeyn), a former chief commander under Hassan Turki, was one of seven top Shabaab officials killed in the fighting. It has also been reported that Hassan Jimbiley, a senior Shabaab officer and former First Deputy Governor of the Lower Shabelle region, died in the fighting for Dhoobley. The report of Dulyadeyn's killing turned out to be incorrect.

44. The Gedo anti-Shabaab offensive only had limited success and the coalition even lost a town, Buhsar, not because of Shabaab attacks but because of coalition infighting. The only victory scored against Shabaab was, quite ironically, by the forces Aden Madobe of Ras Kamboni (a breakaway from Hisbul Islam), which managed to dislodge Shabaab from Hawina on 22 and 23 May.

45. Shiham Muhamud, 'Afmadow's Al-Shabaab leader wounded,' *Sunna Times*, 8 July 2011.

46. Ioannis Gatsiounis, 'Somali terror group curtailed,' *Washington Times*, 10 July 2011.

47. See Christopher Anzalon, 'IN PICTURES: Somalia's Harakat al-Shabaab Release More Photographs of Last Week's Conference Eulogizing Usama bin Laden,' Tales from the Occident, 2011, http://occident.blogspot.com/2011/05/somalias-harakat-al-shabab-release-more.html (accessed 24 October 2011).

48. Ibid.

49. Harakat Al-Shabaab, 'حركة الشباب المجاهدين القيادة العامة بيان في رثاء الشيخ الإمام أسامة بن لادن رحمه الله ___ فاز الشهيد ورب الكعبة ___ نحسبه والله حسيبه,' http://alqimmah.net/showthread.php?t=22643 (accessed 1 June 2011); All Africa, 'Al-Shabaab says that it will cooperate with Al Qaedas new leader,' 17 June 2011, http://allafrica.com/stories/201106171119.html, quoting Shabelle Media Network.

50. AFP, 'US drone wounds top Islamists in Somalia,' 29 June 2011.

51. Marchal, 'Harakat Al-Shabaab'.

52. Interview with Shabaab leader by telephone, 1 August 2011.

53. United Nations Monitoring Group on Somalia and Eritrea, 'Report of the Monitoring Group on Somalia Pursuant to Security Council Resolution 1853 (2008),' Report S/2011/43, 2011, 183.

54. BBC News, 'UN declares Somalia famine in Bakool and Lower Shabelle,' BBC, 20 July 2011; Xan Rice, 'Somalia famine relief effort hit harder by food aid delays than by rebels,' *The Guardian*, 4 August 2011.

55. Interview with NGO leader in Nairobi, 13 August 2011.

56. AFP, 'Qaeda-linked Shabaab ban WFP in Somalia,' 1 March 2010.

57. Interview with Muktar Robow, 11 September 2011 (conducted with the help of anonymous Somali project assistant).

58. BBC News, 'Ethiopian troops capture Beledweyne from Somalia militants,' 31 December 2011, http://www.bbc.co.uk/news/world-africa-16372453 (accessed 1 August 2012).

59. BBC News, 'Somalia al-Shabab militant base of Baidoa captured,' 22 February 2012, http://www.bbc.co.uk/news/world-africa-17127353 (accessed 1 August 2012).

60. Guled, Abdi, 'Somali, Ethiopian troops seize town, fighters flee,' *Boston Globe*, 22 March 2012, http://www.boston.com/news/world/africa/articles/2012/03/22/somali_ethiopian_troops_seize_town_fighters_flee (accessed 1 August 2012).

61. Interview with TFG civil servant, Nairobi, 23 July 2012.

62. BBC News, 'Fresh Somalia fighting forces thousands to flee,' 15 February 2012, http://www.bbc.co.uk/news/world-africa-17048223 (accessed 1 August 2012).

63. Ken Menkhaus, 'Presentation' at the Wilton Park Conference 18–24 March 2012.

64. Conversation with Member of Parliament and NCA 'Ali' on 17 July 2012, Mogadishu; conversations with Ali Madahay Nuur, president of Hirran and Middle Shabelle state, 19 July 2012, Mogadishu.

65. Landinfo, 'Hawiye klanen douduble,' report published 8 May2012.

8. LOSE SOME, WIN SOME

1. Gérard Prunier, 'Somalia: Civil War, intervention and withdrawal 1990–1995,' July 1995, 6, WRITENET Country Papers, UK, http://www.asylumlaw.org/docs/somalia/country_conditions/Prunier.pdf (accessed 1 August 2012).

2. Interview with anonymous Warsangeli elder, Garowe, 6 July 2012.

3. The Monitoring Group on Somalia and Eritrea, 'Report of the Monitoring Group on Somalia and Eritrea,' Nairobi, 16 June 2012, 50.

4. Robert Pelton, Sucaad Miire and Mohamed Nuxhurkey, 'Atoms militia declares allegiance to Shabaab,' *Somalia Report*, 25 February 2012, http://www.somali-areport.com/index.php/topic/23 (accessed 1 June 2012).

5. Interview with local intellectual and former coast guard officer, Garowe, 8 July 2012.

6. Monitoring Group on Somalia and Eritrea, 2011, 19–20.

7. Ibid., 20.

8. Somalia Online, 'Atom denies Al-Shabaab links: militia leader says Puntland conflict is over natural resources,' 18 May 2011, http://www.somaliaonline.com/community/showthread.php/56861-Mohamed-Said-Atam-denies-Al-Shabaab-Links.

9. JD, 'Galgala militias disagree with Shabaab,' *Somalia Report*, 29 February 2012.

10. *Somalia Report*, 'What is the Galgalla Conflict,' 12 April 2012, http://somaliare-port.com/index.php/writer/198/Assia_Shidane (accessed 1 August 2012).

11. Ibid.; Kilwe was born in 1981 in Dahar of Halaane, and was a Warsangeli Dubais and a graduate from the same university as Atom: the East African University. He was accused by the Somaliland police of theft in 2003, but was acquitted, and was again accused of terrorism in 2006, when allegedly he was also questioned by the Americans.

12. Ibid.

13. See for example Aish Ali Awas, 'Foreign fighters for Al-Qaeda in the Arabian Peninsula,' *Yemeni Times*, 5 July 2012.

14. On 12 April 2012, Shabaab-affiliated media carried a speech given by Muumin following his arrival in eastern Sanaag, effectively declaring jihad against Puntland, and denouncing the Faroole administration as an 'apostate' authority.

15. One of the exceptions being the controversies surrounding Khalid Balala and his Islamic Party of Kenya in the early 1990s; see Arye Oded (1996), 'Islamic Extremism in Kenya, the Rise and Fall of Sheik Khalid Balala,' *Journal of Religion in Africa* XXVI, 4.

16. Shashank Bengali and Jonathan S. Landay, 'U.S. allies in Africa may have engaged in secret prisoner renditions,' McClatchy Newspapers, 14 March 2007.

17. Xan Rice, 'Kenyan constitution signed into law,' *The Guardian*, 27 August 2010; see also National Council for Law Reporting with the Authority of the Attorney General (2010), 'The Constitution of Kenya,' http://www.kenyaembassy.com/pdfs/The%20Constitution%20of%20Kenya.pdf (accessed 1 August 2012).

18. Based on an estimate of 6,000 Shabaab members in total.

19. Matthew Rosenberg, 'Al Qaeda skimming charity money,' CBS News, 11 February 2009, http://www.cbsnews.com/2100–224_162–621621.html (accessed 2 August 2012).

20. Clint Watts, Jacob Shapiro and Vahid Brown, 'Al Qaeda's (mis)adventures in the Horn of Africa,' Combating Terrorism Center Report, 2 July 2007.

21. Ibid.

22. Stig Jarle Hansen, 'Why support the Harakat Al-Shabaab,' report submitted to DFID, 25 August 2012.

23. Rogo was released on bail after the arrest in 2003 and was fully acquitted on 29 June 2005. The Kenyan police tried to link Rogo to other case, the Mulado case of 20 December 2010, where a grenade explosion occurred at the Kampala coach terminal; during a routine inspection, a passenger, Albert Olando, dropped a bag containing a hand grenade that exploded, and the police designated Olando a Shabaab member. However, the evidence was too weak for conviction, though Rogo's name had been found in Olando's notes; Rogo was again released. In 2012, Rogo was arrested and charged with possession of firearms and explosives, and given police bail; then he was shot dead on 28 August 2012.

24. Interview with Richard Ndambuki, Nairobi, 23 July 2012.

25. Africanseer, 'Police seize videos used to promote terror,' 2011, http://news.africanseer.com/countries/kenya/104615-police_seize_videos_used_to_promote_terror.html (accessed 24 October 2011); Rogo also has his own blog http://aboudrogo.blogspot.com/2011/05/sheikh-aboud-rogo-sheikh-aboud-rogo-is.html

26. NTV, 'Rahim Khan and Samir Hashim deny charges,' 2011, http://www.youtube.com/watch?v=eYWzCnlJz5A (accessed 1 August 2012).

27. Abu Nusbah, 'Kenya's African Crusade—the Youth of Somalia will Remain Standing & Victorious,' *Minbar Ansar-ul-Deen* (English translation); http://minbaransardeen.com/2011/11/02/kenyas-african-crusade-the-youth-of-somalia-will-remain-standing-victorious/ (accessed 1 August 2012).

28. See for example Harakat Al-Shabaab, 'Operation Linda Uislamo,' *Gaidi Mtaani*,

no. 1, 4 April 2012, http://azelin.files.wordpress.com/2012/04/gaidi-mtaani-issue-1.pdf (accessed 23 June 2012).

29. *The Star,* 'Yemeni suspect reveals Somali Islamist recruitment and training in Kenya,' 17 September 2011.

30. Ibid.

31. NTV, 'Imams protest over activist's death,' Youtube, 2012, http://www.youtube.com/watch?v=4qDcHXmpJPA&feature=relmfu (accessed 1 August 2012); see also NTV, 'Pressure mounts on govt. to act fast over Khan's murder,' Youtube, 2012, http://www.youtube.com/watch?v=wAa9O8eE6ec&feature=relmfu (accessed 1 August 2012)

32. Harakat Al-Shabaab, 'The long road to Kismayo,' *Gaidi Mtaani,* no. 2, 1 July 2012, http://azelin.files.wordpress.com/2012/06/gaidi-mtaaniissue-2.pdf (accessed 23 June 2012).

33. United Nations Monitoring Group on Somalia and Eritrea (2011), 'Report of the Monitoring Group on Somalia Pursuant to Security Council Resolution 1853 (2011),' Report S/2011/433, 141.

34. Ibid., 142.

35. On 7 March 2011, Kenyan security officials issued an alert against nine MYC members suspected to have trained in Somalia, including Juma Ayub Otit Were 'Taxi Driver'; Abass Mohamed Mwai, a combatant fighting in Somalia alongside Shabaab; Sylvester Opiyo Osodo alias 'Musa,' and Abdulrahman Mutua Daud.

36. Angira Zaddox, 'Army remains on the alert on Somali border,' *Daily Nation,* 13 March 2011.

37. Standard Media Group, 'Nakumatt enhances security following terror alert,' 8 March 2011 http://www.standardmedia.co.ke/?articleID=2000030739&pageNo=2 (accessed 7 August).

38. *Toronto Star,* 'Kenya braces for attacks as Somalia's war continues,' 13 July 2012.

39. See Citizen TV, 'Kenyan youths recruited by Shabaab,' Youtube, 2011, http://www.youtube.com/watch?v=O6vmesX2iss (accessed 26 August 2011); NTV (2011), 'The enemy within,' Youtube, http://www.youtube.com/watch?v=-_wnKSU-Hwc (accessed 26 August 2011).

40. The NTV programme also showed how the Shabaab was able to buy arms and get recruits through the Kenyan town of Isiolo, also suggesting that several Kenyan soldiers acted as instructors for the Shabaab inside Kenya; however, that programme might have been exposed to swindlers in the army trying to take advantage of potential Al-Shabaab recruits, or even a provocation operation by Kenyan intelligence.

41. See Harakat Al-Shabaab, 'British Al Shabab Fighter In Somalia,' http://www.liveleak.com/view?i=190_1292810498 (accessed 24 October 2011).

42. *PuntlandTalk,* 'High alert on terror after Al-Shabaab member Bilal El Berjawi wounded, now in Kenya,' http://puntlandtalk.net/node/1687 (accessed 24 October 2011).

NOTES

43. Maxwell Masawa, 'Riyadha Mosque splits over Al-Shabaab link,' *The Star*, 8 August 2011, http://www.the-star.co.ke/national/national/35067-riadha-mosque-split-over-al-shabaab-link (accessed 7 August 2012).

44. United Nations Monitoring Group on Somalia and Eritrea, 'Report of the Monitoring Group on Somalia and Eritrea,' Nairobi, 16 June 2011, 50.

45. Harakat Al-Shabaab, 'The long road to Kismayo,' *Gaidi Mtaani*.

46. Harakat Al-Shabaab, 'Operation Linda Uislamo,' *Gaidi Mtaani*.

47. Ahmed Iman Ali, 'Lecture by Ahmad Imam Ali,' Al Kataib Media, http://www.metacafe.com/watch/7950113/al_kataib_media_lecture_by_ahmad_iman_ali_h/ (accessed 8 August 2012).

48. Ibid.

49. Jo Adentunji and agencies, 'Deadly explosion hits Nairobi bus stop,' *The Guardian*, 24 October 2011; Tom Odula, 'Kenyan Grenade Supsect—I am a Shabaab member,' Associated Press, 26 October 2012, http://news.yahoo.com/kenya-grenade-suspect-im-al-shabab-member-132633695.html?_esi=1 (accessed 1 August 2012)

50. United Nations Monitoring Group on Somalia and Eritrea, 'Report of the Monitoring Group on Somalia and Eritrea,' Nairobi, 16 June 2011, 111.

51. Harakat Al-Shabaab, 'The long road to Kismayo,' *Gaidi Mtaani*.

52. United Nations Monitoring Group on Somalia and Eritrea (2011), 'Report of the Monitoring Group on Somalia Pursuant to Security Council Resolution 1853 (2011),' Report S/2011/433, 141.

53. Human Rights Watch, 'Uganda: Torture, Extortion, Killings by Police Unit,' HRW News, http://www.hrw.org/news/2011/03/23/uganda-torture-extortion-killings-police-unit (accessed 8 August); Human Rights Watch, 'Ethiopia: Submission to the UN Committee against Torture,' submitted in September 2010 for the 2–3 November 2010 session.

54. Global Jihad, 'Kampala blasts: 4 main suspects,' http://www.globaljihad.net/view_page.asp?id=2073 (accessed 8 August 2012); AFP, 'Kampala bomb suspect rages against the US,' http://www.google.com/hostednews/afp/article/ALeqM5gALjCfhatQbqJBxn-5HqwejhvSaw (accessed 8 August 2012).

55. AFP, 'Kampala bomb suspect rages against the US,' http://www.google.com/hostednews/afp/article/ALeqM5gALjCfhatQbqJBxn-5HqwejhvSaw (accessed 8 August 2012).

56. Human Rights Watch, 'Uganda: Kenyan Rights Defender to Be Tried for Kampala Bombings,' HRW News, 1 December 2010, http://www.hrw.org/news/2010/11/30/uganda-kenyan-rights-defender-be-tried-kampala-bombings (accessed 8 August 2012).

57. Ismael, 'Ethiopia brings terrorism charges against alleged Al Qaeda members,' *Ethio-somali*, 21 May 2012, http://www.ethiosomali.com/index.php?option=com_content&view=article&id=1836:ethiopia-brings-terrorism-charges-

against-alleged-al-qaeda-members&catid=1:latest-news&Itemid=50 (accessed 8 August 2012)

58. See for example Ben Rawlence, 'Why are all Ethiopian eyes on Brussels,' *De Morgan*, 19 July 2012.

59. Peter Heinlein, 'Ethiopian government, Muslims clash about ideology,' VOA, 21 May 2012.

60. Interview x1, Mogadishu (by telephone), 1 September 2011.

61. Ibid.

62. Ibid.; interview x5, Nairobi, 11 November 2011.

63. *The Nigerian Voice*, 'Boko Haram import militias from Somalia, vows fiercer attacks,' 16 June 2011; Reuters, 'Nigeria says Boko Haram, al Qaeda-link behind UN attack,' 31 August 2011; All Africa, 'Al-Shabaab says that it will cooperate with Al Qaeda's new leader.'

64. See Shannon Connel, 'To be or not to be: Is Boko Haram a Foreign Terrorist Organization?' *Global Security Studies*, 3 (3), 2012, 89.

65. Ibid.; Mike Pflanz, 'Al-Qaeda-linked suicide bomber targets Nigeria police station,' *The Daily Telegraph*, 16 June 2011.

66. Peter Pham, 'Boko Haram's Evolving Threat,' *Africa Security Brief*, 20 April 2012; the writer was aware of Nigerians in Somalia in 2010.

67. Aish Ali Awas, 'Foreign fighters for Al Qaeda in the Arab Peninsula,' *Yemeni Times*, 5 July 2012.

68. Christopher Swift, 'Arc of Convergence: AQAP, Ansar al-Shari'a and the Struggle for Yemen,' CTC Sentinel, 5 (6), 2012.

69. Magnus Sandelin, 'Jihad,' Reporto, Stockholm, 121; Amund Aune Nilsen, 'Somalisk terrorleder ble radikalisert I sverge,' *Nrk Nyheter*, 5 August 2012.

70. Ibid.

71. Magnus Sandelin, 'Jihad,' 44.

72. Andrew Zammit, 'The Holsworthy Barracks Plot: A Case Study of an Al-Shabab Support Network in Australia,' CTC Sentinel, 5 (6), 2012.

9. CONCLUSIONS

1. Peter L. Berger, *The Sacred Canopy: Elements of a Sociological Theory of Religion* (New York: Anchor Press, 1990), 87.

2. Fuad Khalif 'Shongola', '"I am not dead yet, I am alive, I shall die, at the time Allah decides, not to the delight of the TFG,"' audio recording released through www.Somaliwarmonitor.worldpress.com (accessed 12 November 2011)

3. Omar Hammami 'Abu Mansoor Al-Amriki, 'Lessons learned,' Al-Kataa'ib (Shabaab media wing), www.Somaliwarmonitor.worldpress.com (accessed 12 November 2011).

4. Harakat Al-Shabaab, 'AMISOM and the Inevitable End,' Al-Kataa'ib, www.Somaliwarmonitor.worldpress.com (accessed 12 November 2011).

BIBLIOGRAPHY

ABC News, 'Somalia's Al-Shabaab recruits Holy warriors with $400 Bonus,' 18 April 2010.)

Abdullahi, Abdurahman Moallim, 'The Islamic Movement in Somalia: A Historical Evolution with a Case Study of the Islah Movement (1950–2000),' PhD Thesis, University of Montreal, May 2011 (the best English summary of the Islamic revival in Somalia).

Adentunji, Jo and agencies, 'Deadly explosion hits Nairobi bus stop,' *Guardian* 24 October 2011.

Africanseer, 'Police seize videos used to promote terror,' 2011, http:// news.africanseer.com/countries/kenya/104615-police_seize_videos_used_to_promote_terror.html (accessed 24 October 2011).

AFP, 'Somali Islamists tell pirates to destroy Ukrainian arms ship,' 2 October 2008.

——— 'Somalia's Shabaab declare that it would send fighters to support Al Qaeda,' 1 January 2010.

——— 'Qaeda-linked Shabaab ban WFP in Somalia,' 1 March 2010.

——— 'Kampala bomb suspect rages against the US,' 12 August 2010, http:// www.google.com/hostednews/afp/article/ALeqM5gALjCfhatQbqJBxn-5HqwejhvSaw (accessed 8 August 2012).

——— 'US drone wounds top Islamists in Somalia,' 29 June 2011.

Africa Online, 'Somaliland "terrorists" get death sentences,' 14 November 2005, http://afrol.com/articles/17243 (accessed 24 February 2005).

Al-Amriki, Abu Mansoor, '(The American Mujahid In Somalia)—A Message To The Mujahideen in Particular & the Muslims In General,' posted to jihadist website, 7 February 2008, http://prisonerofjoy.blogspot.com/2008/02/abu-mansoor-al-amriki-american-mujahid.html (accessed 1 November 2011).

Al Jazeera, 'Aljazeera interview with Shayk Abu Mansoor part 1 & 2,' 8 March 2009.

——— Interview with Muktar Robow,' 25 February 2009, downloaded from http://forums.islamicawakening.com/f18/aljazeeras-interview-mukhtar-robow-abu-mansour-sahabaab-22323/ (accessed 11 November 2010).

——— 'Shabab credit for Somali food boom,' 24 March 2010, http://english.aljazeera.net/news/africa/2010/03/2010324103733512123.html (accessed 24 October 2011).

——— 'Three charged in Ugandan bombing,' 31 July 2010.

——— 'Who are Al-Shabab?' Al Jazeera 31 October 2011, http://english.aljazeera.net/news/africa/2009/08/20098432032479714.html (accessed 31 October 2011).

All Africa, 'Al-Shabaab says that it will cooperate with Al Qaeda's new leader,' 17 June 2011, http://allafrica.com/stories/201106171119.html quoting Shabelle Media Network.

Al Libi, Abu Yahya, 'To the Army of Distress in Somalia,' As-Sahab Media Foundation, 25 March 2007 (dated February 2007).

Al-Qaeda (various writers): 'Five letters to the Africa corps,' AFGP-2002–600053, retrieved from the Harmony project. http://www.ctc.usma.edu/aq/aq_600053–1.asp.

Ali, Abdirahman 'Aynte', 'The Anatomy of al-Shabaab,' 2010, http://www.scribd.com/doc/34053611/The-Anatomy-of-Al-Shabaab-by-Abdi-Aynte (accessed 24 October).

Amin, Harun Khan, 'Report from Somalia,' Al Qaeda document found in Afghanistan, 1996, available from http://www.ctc.usma.edu/aq/pdf/AFGP-2002–600110-Trans-Meta.pdf (accessed 11 November 2010).

Anonymous, 'Regarding the conquest of Kismayo,' Report sent to Risk Intelligence, 2010.

Anzalon, Christopher, 'In Pictures: Somalia's Harakat al-Shabaab Release More Photographs of Last Week's Conference Eulogizing Usama bin Laden,' Tales from the Occident, 2011, http://occident.blogspot.com/2011/05/somalias-harakat-al-shabab-release-more.html (accessed 24 October 2011).

Awas, Aish Ali, 'Foreign fighters for Al-Qaeda in the Arabian Peninsula,' *Yemeni Times*, 5 July 2012.

Aweys, Hassan Dahir, 'Press conference,' *Wamo News* 7 November 2011, http://waamonews.com/?p=13744 (accessed 14 November 2011).

Awlaki, Anwar, 'Speech,' http://www.youtube.com/watch?v=abBIhu7Eo6Y&feature=related (accessed 1 June 2011).

Bakker, Edwin, *Jihadi Terrorists in Europe, their Characteristics and the Circumstances in which they Joined the Jihad: an Exploratory Study*, Clingendael Security Paper (The Hague: Clingendael Institute, 2006).

Barnes, Cedric and Harun Hassan, 'The Rise and Fall of Mogadishu's Islamic Courts,' *Journal of Eastern African Studies*, 1 (2), 2007, 151–60.

BBC News, '"Al-Qaeda" arrest in East Africa,' 7 June 2007, http://news.bbc.co.uk/2/hi/6729015.stm (accessed 24 October 2011).

——— 'Minnesota man admits Somalia terror plot,' 19 July 2011.

——— 'UN declares Somalia famine in Bakool and Lower Shabelle,' 20 July 2011.

——— 'Ethiopian troops capture Beledweyne from Somalia militants,' 31 December 2011, http://www.bbc.co.uk/news/world-africa-16372453 (accessed 1 August 2012).

——— 'Fresh Somalia fighting forces thousands to flee,' 15 February 2012, http://www.bbc.co.uk/news/world-africa-17048223 (accessed 1 August 2012).

——— 'Somalia al-Shabab militant base of Baidoa captured,' 22 February 2012, http://www.bbc.co.uk/news/world-africa-17127353 (accessed 1 August 2012).

Bengali, Shashank and Jonathan S. Landay, 'U.S. allies in Africa may have engaged in secret prisoner renditions,' McClatchy Newspapers, 14 March 2007.

Berger, Peter L, *The Sacred Canopy: Elements of a Sociological Theory of Religion* (New York: Anchor Press, 1990).

Bin Laden, Osama, 'Messages,' July 2006, audiotape.

Byman, Daniel, 'Denying Terrorist Safe Havens: Homeland Security Efforts to Counter Threats from Pakistan, Yemen and Somalia,' Testimony before the Subcommittee on Oversight, Investigations and Management of the House Committee on Homeland Security, Washington, 3 June 2011.

Childress, Sarah, 'Somalia's Al-Shabaab to ally with Al Qaeda,' *The Wall Street Journal*, 2 February 2010.

Citizen TV, 'Kenyan youths recruited by Shabaab,' 2011, http://www.youtube.com/watch?v=O6vmesX2iss (accessed 26 August 2011).

Clottey, Peter, 'Kenya official denies financing Al-Shabaab,' VOA, 3 August 2011.

Connel, Shannon, 'To Be Or Not To Be: Is Boko Haram a Foreign Terrorist Organization?' *Global Security Studies*, 3 (3), 2012.

Dalje, 'Ethiopians leave, Somali insurgents take Baidoa,' 26 January 2009, http://dalje.com/en-world/ethiopians-leave-somali-insurgents-takebaidoa/228262 (accessed 1 November 2011).

Dalmar, 'Somalia: Puntland's Anti-piracy Forces—Smokescreen for Hunting Oil & Minerals Unlawfully,' Somali UK, 2011, http://wwww.somaliuk.com/Forums/index.php?topic=7331.0;wap2 (accessed 12 November 2011).

Dixon, Robyn, 'Nigeria militant group Boko Haram's attacks attract speculation,' *LA Times*, 13 September 2011.

Elliott, Andrea, 'A call to jihad, answered in America,' *New York Times*, 11 July 2009.

——— 'The terrorist next door,' *New York Times*, 27 January 2010.

Esposito, John L., *Unholy Wars: Terror in the Name of Islam* (New York: Oxford University Press, 2002).

Federal Bureau of Investigation, 'Bombings of the Embassies of the United States of America,' Report, 18 November 1998, Washington.

Fishel, Justin, 'FOXWIRE: Navy Seals kill wanted terrorist in Somali raid,' Fox News, 2009, http://www.foxnews.com/story/0,2933,550100,00.html (accessed 10 November 2011).

Gaas, Muhamed Hussein, 'A New Hope? Former Rebel Takes Over as Somali President,' *Jane's Intelligence Review*, March 2009.

Garowe Online, 'One killed as Somali Islamists bring in Afghan-trained commander,' 7 October 2007, http://www.garoweonline.com/artman2/publish/Somalia_27/One_killed_as_Somali_Islamists_bring_in_Afghantrained_commander.shtml (accessed 24 October 2011).

———— 'Somalia: Secret meeting between Aweys, Abu-Mansoor over new insurgent group,' 6 October 2010, http://www.garoweonline.com/artman2/publish/Somalia_27/Somalia_Secrets_meeting_between_Aweys_Abu-Mansoor_over_new_insurgent_group.shtml (accessed 6 October 2010).

———— 'Somalia: Abu-Mansoor denies dispute with Godane,' 9 October 2010, http://www.garoweonline.com/artman2/publish/Somalia_27/Abu Mansoor_denies_dispute_with_Godane.shtml (accessed 6 October 2010).

———— 'Somalia: Al-Shabaab to avenge Sheikh Muktar Abu-Yazid,' 20 October 2010, http://www.garoweonline.com/artman2/publish/Somalia_27/Somalia_Al-Shabaab_to_avenge_Sheikh_Muktar_Abu-Yazid.shtml (accessed 21 October 2010).

———— 'Somalia: Yemen-born 'foreign fighter' killed in Mogadishu,' 6 December 2010, http://www.garoweonline.com/artman2/publish/Somalia_27/Somalia_Yemen-born_foreign_fighter_killed_in_Mogadishu.shtml (accessed 1 November 2011).

Gatsiounis, Ioannis, 'Somali terror group curtailed,' *Washington Times*, 10 July 2011.

Gettelman, Jeffrey, 'Demonstrations becomes clashes after Islamists take Somali city,' *New York Times*, 26 September 2006.

Global Islamic Media Front (GIMF), 'An Interview With the Commander Abi Mansoor (Mukhtaar Ali Robow), the Spokesman of the Youth Islamic Movement in Somalia,' *Sada al-Jihad*, Issue 25, May 2008.

Göteborgs Tingsrätt, 'Dom,' B 7277–10, 2010.

Gudmunson, Per, 'Jihad—nu också på svenska,' *Gudmunson*, 3 August 2008, http://gudmundson.blogspot.com/2008/08/jihad-nu-ocks-p-svenska.html (accessed 29 October 2011).

Guled, Abdi, 'Somali, Ethiopian troops seize town, fighters flee,' *Boston Globe*, 22 March 2012, http://www.boston.com/news/world/africa/articles/2012/03/22/somali_ethiopian_troops_seizetown_fighters_flee. (accessed 1 August 2012).

Hammami, Omar 'Abu Mansoor Al-Amriki', 'Lessons learned,' Al-Kataa'ib [Al-Shabaab media wing), 2011, www.Somaliwarmonitor.worldpress.com (accessed 12 November 2011).

Hansen, Stig Jarle (forthcoming): 'Al Qaeda in East Africa,' unpublished manuscript.

———— 'Warlords, Patrimony, Ethnicism, the Cases of China, Afghanistan and Somalia,' *Peace Research*, 35:2, 2003.

———— 'Den somaliske fredsprosessen,' Commissioned Report for the Norwegian Ministry of
Foreign Affairs, 2004.

———— 'Sharia courts hold sway in Mogadishu,' *Jane's Foreign Report*, 10, 2006.

———— 'Report to the Norwegian Ministry of Foreign Affairs,' Report 5, 2007.

———— 'Civil War Economies, the Hunt for Profit and the Incentives for Peace,' Enemies or Allies Working Paper 1, University of Bath/University of Mogadishu, 2007.

———— 'Misspent Youth,' *Jane's Intelligence Review*, 20/10, 7, 2008.

———— 'Report to the Norwegian Ministry of Foreign Affairs,' Report 6, 2008.

———— 'The Enemies Enemy—Eritrea's Involvement in Somalia,' *Jane's Intelligence Review*, 21/10, 2009.

———— 'Pirates of the Greater Gulf of Aden, Myths, Misconceptions and Remedies,' NIBR Report 29, 2009.

———— 'Somalia—Grievance, Religion, Clan, and Profit,' Chapter 8 in Hansen, Mesøy and Karadas, *The Borders of Islam: Exploring Samuel Huntington's Faultlines, From Al-Andalus to the Virtual Ummah* (London: Hurst, 2009), 127–38.

———— 'Revenge or Reward? The Case of Somalia's Suicide Bombers,' *Journal of Terrorism Research*, 1 (1), 2010.

———— 'The Attack on Haradhere. The Background and Implications for the Maritime Sector,' *Marisk Special Analysis*, 21 May 2010.

———— 'Faction Fluctuation—The Shifting Allegiances within Hizbul Islam,' *Jane's Intelligence Review*, 6/11, 2010.

———— 'The Pirates of Haradhere,' specially commissioned report for Risk Intelligence, 2011.

———— 'Shabab, Central Africa's 'Taliban' Grows More Unified,' *Jane's Intelligence Review*, 16/11, 2011.

———— 'The Dynamics of Somali Piracy,' *Journal of Conflict and Terrorism Studies*, August 2012.

———— 'Why support the Harakat Al-Shabaab,' report submitted to DFID, 25 August 2012.

Hansen, Stig Jarle and Atle Mesøy, 'The Muslim Brotherhood in the Wider Horn of Africa,' *NIBR Report*, 33, 11, 2009.

Hansen, Stig, Atle Mesøy and Karadas, *The Borders of Islam: Exploring Samuel Huntington's Faultlines, From Al-Andalus to the Virtual Ummah* (London: Hurst, 2009).

Harakat Al-Shabaab, 'The Life of Aden Hashi Ayro part I,' http://www.you-tube.com/watch?v=BXRPP_LpKX4&feature=related (accessed 1 August 2010).

—— 'The life of Aden Hashi Ayro part II' (accessed 1 August 2010).

—— 'Mujahidin Youth Movement Eulogizes Commander's 'Martyrdom' On 17 December,' 17 December 2008, http://www.biyokulule.com/view_content.php?articleid=1676 (accessed 1 August 2010).

—— 'The Will of Abu Ayyub al-Muhajir,' released 1 March 2008, http://www.myhesbah.com/v/showthread.php?t=170168 (accessed 1 November 2009).

—— 'March forth,' distributed in Mogadishu September 2009.

—— 'The Will of the Martyr Abdul Aziz Saad, May Allah Accept Him,' http://www.alhesbah.net/v/showthread.php?t=197107, 30 October 2008 (accessed 1 November 2009).

—— 'Ambush at Bardale,' http://www.alfaloja.info/vb/showthread.php?t=54142 (accessed 5 May 2009).

—— 'Eulogy for Abu Umar al-Baghdadi and Abu Hamza al-Muhajer by the Shabaab al-Mujahedeen in Somalia,' http://www.archive.org/details/Song-of-Terror-faaluja (accessed 3 June 2010).

—— 'Graduation Ceremony at the Abdullah Azzam Training Center for Islamic Propagation in the Islamic Province of Banadir (Mogadishu),' Global Islamic Media Front, 2 May 2010, http://theunjustmedia.com/Islamic%20Perspectives/May10/Graduation%20Ceremony%20at%20the%20Abdullah%20Azzam%20Training%20Center%20for%20Islamic%20Propagation%20in%20the%20Islamic%20Province%20of%20Banadir%20(Mogadishu).htm (accessed 1 November 2011).

—— 'حفل خت عنوان فرحة المسلمين بتوحد المجاهدين الإثنين' http://alqimmah.net/showthread.php?t=22643 (accessed 1 June 2011).

—— 'British Al shabab Fighter In Somalia,' http://www.liveleak.com/view?i=190_1292810498 (accessed 24 October 2011).

—— 'حركة الشباب المجاهدين القيادة العامة بيان في رثاء الشيخ الإمام أسامة بن لادن رحمه الله __فاز الشهيد ورب الكعبة. نحسبه والله حسيبه http://alqimmah.net/showthread.php?t=22643 (accessed 1 June 2011).

—— : 'حركة الشباب المجاهدين القيادة العامة بيان في رثاء الشيخ الإمام أسامة بن لادن رحمه الله __فاز الشهيد ورب الكعبة. نحسبه والله حسيبه http://alqimmah.net/showthread.php?t=22643 (accessed 1 June 2011).

—— 'Operation Linda Uislamo,' Gaidi Mtaani number 1, 4 April 2012, http://azelin.files.wordpress.com/2012/04/gaidi-mtaani-issue-1.pdf (accessed 23 June 2012).

——— 'The Long Road to Kismayo,' *Gaidi Mtaani* no. 2, 10 July 2012.

Hegghammer, Thomas, 'The Rise of Muslim Foreign Fighters,' *International Security*, 35 (3), 2010.

Heinlein, Peter, 'Ethiopian Government, Muslims clash about ideology,' VOA, 21 May 2012.

Hull, Cecilia and Emma Svensson, 'African Union Mission in Somalia (AMISOM), Exemplifying African Union Peacekeeping Challenges,' FOI-R-259-SE, 26, 2008.

Human Rights Watch, 'Shell-shocked: Civilians under Siege in Mogadishu,' *Human Rights Watch Report*, 10 (12), 2007.

——— 'So Much to Fear,' *Human Rights Watch Report* 1–56432–415-X, 90, 2008.

——— 'Harsh War, Harsh Peace. Abuses by al-Shabaab, the Transitional Federal Government, and AMISOM in Somalia,' *Human Rights Watch Report* 1–56432–621–7, 2010.

——— 'Uganda: Kenyan Rights Defender to Be Tried for Kampala Bombings, *Human Rights News*, 1 December 2010, http://www.hrw.org/news/2010/11/30/ uganda-kenyan-rights-defender-be-tried-kampala-bombings (accessed 8 August 2012).

——— 'Uganda: Torture, Extortion, Killings by Police Unit,' *HRW News*, 2011, http://www.hrw.org/news/2011/03/23/uganda-torture-extortion-killings-police-unit (accessed 8 August 2011).

International Crisis Group, 'Counter-Terrorism in Somalia: Losing Hearts and Minds,' *Africa Report*, no. 95, 2002.

——— 'Counter Terrorism in Somalia, Losing Hearts and Minds?,' *Africa Report*, no. 95, 2005.

——— 'Somalia's Islamists,' *Africa Report*, no. 100, 2005.

——— 'Somalia: To Move Beyond the Failed State,' *Africa Report*, no. 147, 23 December 2008.

——— 'Somalia's Divided Islamists,' *Africa Briefing*, no. 74, 2010.

Ismael, 'Ethiopia brings terrorism charges against alleged Al Qaeda members,' *Ethio-somali* 21 May 2012, http://www.ethiosomali.com/index.php?option= com_content&view=article&id=1836:ethiopia-brings-terrorism-charges-against-alleged-al-qaeda-members&catid=1:latest-news&Itemid=50 (accessed 8 August 2012).

IRIN News, 'Somalia: fighting in Mogadishu,' 30 April 1999.

Jane's (2010): Shabab's Mixed Messages,' *Jane's Terrorism and Security Monitor*, 27 January.

JD (2012): 'Galgala militias disagree with Shabaab,' *Somalia Report*, 29 February 2012.

Jihad Unspun, 'YIM press statement,' 2007, http://old.kavkazcenter.com/eng/ content/2007/09/07/8823.shtml (accessed 13 September 2009).

Johnsen, Gregory D., 'Tracking Yemen's 23 Escaped Jihadi Operatives—Part 1,' *Terrorism Monitor*, 5 (18), 2007.

—— 'Tracking Yemen's 23 Escaped Jihadi Operatives—Part 2,' *Terrorism Monitor*, 5 (19), 2007.

Joselow, Gabe, 'Is Kenya battling al-Shabab alone?' VOA, 29 October 2011, http://www.voanews.com/english/news/africa/Is-Kenya-Battling-al-Shabab-Alone-132640988.html (accessed 31 October 2011).

Juergensmeyer, Mark, *Terror in the Mind of God: The Global Rise of Religious Violence* (Berkeley: University of California Press, 2000).

Kataaib, 'The background of Abu Mansoor,' www.kataaib.net (accessed 1 May 2008) (now closed).

Khalif, Fuad 'Shongola', 'I am not dead yet, I am alive, I shall die, at the time Allah decides., not to the delight of the TFG,' audio recording released through www.Somaliwarmonitor.worldpress.com in 2011 (accessed 12 November 2011).

Khan, Rana Safdaralik, 'A Somali Leader of Al Qaida Calls on Obama to Convert to Islam,' Allvoices 28 December 2010, http://www.allvoices.com/contributed-news/7739879-a-somali-leader-of-al-qaida-calls-on-obama-to-convert-to-islam (accessed 10 November 2011).

Kitimo, Antonio and Amina Kibrigde, 'Five arrested over links to Al-Shabaab,' *Daily Nation*, 9 May 2011.

Kjærgaard, Jan, Hans Chr. Blem and Jan Søgaard, 'Fem anholdt for trusler mod Pia Kjærsgaard,' *Extrabladet*, 18 February 2010, http://ekstrabladet.dk/112/article1301621.ece (accessed 10 November 2011).

KLISI Newscast, 'San Diego Jewish Boy, Jehad Mostafa, Suspected in Plot to Finance Al-Shabaab in Somalia,' KLISI Newscast 2010; available on http://www.youtube.com/watch?v=uI_1n9gNUQw&feature=related (accessed 23 October 2011).

Kohlmann, Evan F., 'Shabaab al-Mujahideen: Migration and Jihad in the Horn of Africa,' *Nefa Foundation Report*, May 2009, 45.

Landinfo, 'Hawiye klanen douduble,' Report published 8 May 2012.

Larson, Nina, 'Danish attack plot suspect in previous arrests,' AFP, 31 December 2010.

Lobe, Jim, 'US Policy Risks Terrorism Blowback in Somalia,' *Mail and Guardian*, 5 September 2008, http://www.mg.co.za/article/2008–09–05-us-policy-risks-terrorism-blowback-in-somalia (accessed 19 March 2012).

London, J.E., 'Somalia's Muslim jihad at sea,' *Washington Times*, 22 April 2009, available at http://www.washingtontimes.com/news/2009/apr/22/somalias-muslimjihad-at-sea/ (accessed 26 August 2009).

Maldonado, Daniel Joseph, 'My imprisonment in Kenya and America,' 2006, http://old.cageprisoners.com/articles.php?id=21648 (accessed 21 December 2010).

Marchal, Roland, 'A Tentative Assessment of the Somali Harakat Al-Shabaab,' *Journal of East African Studies*, 3 (3), 2010.

——— 'Harakat Al-Shabaab Al Mujahedin,' Report for the UK Foreign Office, London, March 2011.

Mareeg, 'Al-Shabaab executes two men in Baydhabo for allegedly spying,' 5 May 2011, http://www.mareeg.com/fidsan.php?sid=19577&tirsan=3 (accessed 30 August 2011).

Masawa, Maxwell, 'Riyadha Mosque splits over Al-Shabaab link,' *The Star*, 8 August 2011, http://www.the-star.co.ke/national/national/35067-riadha-mosque-split-over-al-shabaab-link (accessed 7 August 2012).

Media Monitor, '13 December Somalia round up,' *Somalia Report*, 2011, http://www.somaliareport.com/index.php/post/30/13_Dec_2010_Somalia_News_Roundup (accessed 24 October 2011).

Menkhaus, 'Somalia: A Country in Peril, a Policy Nightmare,' *Enough Paper*, 3 September 2008.

——— Presentation at the Wilton Park conference, 18–24 March 2012.

Middleton, Roger, 'Piracy in Somalia: Threatening Global Trade, Feeding Local Wars,' Chatham House Briefing Paper AFP BP 08/02, 2008.

Millat-e-Ibrahim, 'Abu Huriyyah Amir Abdul Muhaimin,' 11 December 2008.

Moaddel, *Class, Politics, and Ideology in the Iranian Revolution* (New York: Columbia University Press, 1993).

Muhamud, Shiham, 'Afmadow's Al-Shabaab leader wounded,' *Sunna Times*, 8 July 2011.

Muthiga, 'Kenya: let's talk to the Shabaab, Somalia won't be pacified by military means,' *Daily Nation*, 29 October 2011.

National Council for Law Reporting with the Authority of the Attorney General, 'The Constitution of Kenya,' 2010, http://www.kenyaembassy.com/pdfs/The%20Constitution%20of%20Kenya.pdf (accessed 1 August 2012).

New York Times, 'Joining the fight in Somalia,' 12 July 2009.

NGO Security Programme, 'AS issued an Arabic statement announcing the foundation of a news channel called Al Kata'ib to "take the jihad to the propaganda front".' Daily Security Report, 27 July 2010.

——— 'Advisory regarding current Al-Shabaab offensive in Mogadishu,' *Mogadishu Advisory*, 24 August 2010.

——— 'A contingent of AMISOM forces are trapped in Jubba Hotel in Shangani district of Mogadishu following takeover of the all the adjacent areas surrounding the Hotel,' Daily Security Report, 7 September 2010.

——— 'Some TFG military soldiers withdrew from key positions in Abdul Aziz and Hodan districts protesting delay of salary arrears payment,' Daily Security Report, 7 September 2010.

——— 'Head of Hawiye Council of Elders told media that AS failed in its Ramadan offensive,' Daily Security Report, 13 September 2010.

——— 'AS leaders from Bakool region met to discuss the current differences that has emerged between Muktar Robow aka Abu Mansoor and Ahmed Godane aka Abu Zubayr,' *Daily Security Report*, 3 October 2010.

——— 'AS Extends Area of Control, Toro-Torow village, Awdhegle district, Lower Shabelle region,' *Daily Security Report*, 14 December 2010.

——— 'End of Hizbul Islamiya,' *NSP Weekly Security Report*, 23 December 2010.

——— 'Ahmed Godane a.k.a Sheikh Mukhtar Abu Zubeyr welcomed unification of AS and HI and announced intention of AS to double number of attacks against TFG/AMISOM,' *Daily Security Report*, 31 December 2010.

——— 'South-Central Offensive,' *NSP Weekly Security Report* Week 5–12 March 2011.

The Nigerian Voice, 'Boko Haram import militias from Somalia, vows fiercer attacks,' 16 June 2011.

Nilsen, Amund Aune, 'Somalisk terrorleder ble radikalisert I sverge,' *Nrk Nyheter*, 5 August 2012.

Noor, Fatuma, 'My encounter with Somali-American Jihadists in Nairobi,' *Nairobi Star* 27 June 2011.

Norris, P. and R. Inglehart, *Sacred and Secular: Religion and Politics Worldwide* (New York: Cambridge University Press, 2004).

NTV, 'Rahim Khan and Samir Hashim deny charges,' Youtube, 2010, http://www.youtube.com/watch?v=eYWzCnlJz5A (accessed 1 August 2012).

——— (2011): 'The enemy within, episode 1,' Youtube, 2011, http://www.youtube.com/watch?v=-_wnKSU-Hwc (accessed 26 August 2011).

——— 'Balala denies Al-Shabaab links,' Youtube, 2011, http://www.youtube.com/watch?v=7Pi4CZYXX40 (accessed 24 October 2011).

——— (2012a): 'Imams protest over activist's death,' Youtube, 2012, http://www.youtube.com/watch?v=4qDcHXmpJPA&feature=relmfu (accessed 1 August 2012).

——— (2012b): 'Pressure mounts on govt. to act fast over Khan's murder,' Youtube, 2012, http://www.youtube.com/watch?v=wAa9O8eE6ec&feature=rel mfu (accessed 1 August 2012).

Nusbah, Abu, *'Kenya's African Crusade—the Youth of Somalia will Remain Standing & Victorious,' Minbar Ansar-ul-Deen* (English translation), 2011, http://minbaransardeen.com/2011/11/02/kenyas-african-crusade-the-youth-of-somalia-will-remain-standing-victorious/ (accessed 1 August 2012).

Oded, Arye, 'Islamic Extremism in Kenya, the Rise and Fall of Sheik Khalid Balala,' *Journal of Religion in Africa* XXVI, 1996, 4.

Odula, Tom, 'Kenyan Grenade Supsect—I am a Shabaab member,' Associated Press, 26 October 2012, http://news.yahoo.com/kenya-grenade-suspect-im-al-shabab-member-132633695.html?_esi=1 (accessed 1 August 2012).

BIBLIOGRAPHY

Onyego, Michael: 'Somali government capitalizes on internal divisions within Al-Shabaab,' VOA, 4 October 2010.

Orengo, Peter and Cyrus Ombati, 'Two held in Mombasa over Nairobi explosion,' *The Standard*, 22 December 2010.

Pape, Robert A., *Dying to Win: The Strategic Logic of Suicide Terrorism* (New York: Crown Publishing Group/Random House, 2005).

——— 'It's the Occupation, Stupid,' *Foreign Policy*, 18 October 2010.

Paz, Reuven, 'The Youth are Older: The Iraqization of the Somali Mujahidin Movement,' The Project for the Research of Islamist Movements (PRISM), vol. 6, no. 2, Herzliya, Israel, December 2008.

Pelton, Robert, Sucaad Miire and Mohamed Nuxhurkey, 'Atoms militia declares allegiance to Shabaab,' *Somalia Report*, 25 February 2012, http://www.somaliareport.com/index.php/topic/23 (Accessed 1 June 2012).

Pflanz, Mike, 'Al-Qaeda-linked suicide bomber targets Nigeria police station,' *The Daily Telegraph*, 16 June 2011.

Pham, Peter, 'Boko Haram's Evolving Threat,' *Africa Security Brief*, 20 April 2012.

Pippard, Tim, 'Al-Shabab's Agenda in the Wake of the Kampala Suicide Attacks,' CTC Sentinel, 2 July 2010.

Plaut, Martin, 'Pirates working with Islamists,' BBC News, 19 November 2008.

Press TV, 'Violence kills 43 in the Somali capital,' 27 August 2010.

Prunier, Gérard, 'Somalia: Civil War, intervention and withdrawal 1990–1995 (July 1995)' (PDF), *WRITENET Country Papers, UK*. http://www.asylumlaw.org/docs/somalia/country_conditions/Prunier.pdf. (acessed 1 august 2012).

——— 'Somalia: beyond the quagmire,' Open Democracy, 2009, http://www.opendemocracy.net/article/somalia-beyond-the-quagmire (accessed 11 April 2011).

PuntlandTalk, 'High alert on terror after Al-Shabaab member Bilal El Berjawi wounded, now in Kenya,' http://puntlandtalk.net/node/1687 (accessed 24 October 2011).

Radio Mogadishu, 'Interview with Mohamed Jama Mohamud, Mohamed Farah, Mohamed Ibrahim, Hassan Mohamed Saciid, Ahmed Mohamed,' aired in December 2010.

——— 'Interview with 6 Shabaab defectors,' unknown date, 2010.

Raghavan, Sudarsan, 'Foreign fighters gain influence in Somalia's Islamist Al-Shabaab militia,' *Washington Post*, 8 June 2010.

Rawlence, Ben, 'Why are all Ethiopian eyes on Brussels,' *De Morgan*, 19 July 2012.

Rees, Tom, 'Is Personal Insecurity a Cause of Cross-national Differences in the Intensity of Religious Belief?' *Journal of Religion and Society*, 11:1–24, 2009.

Reuters, 'Interview: Somali insurgency to intensify—Islamist leader,' 16 December 2007.

——— 'Somali insurgents take Baidoa after Ethiopians leave,' 27 January 2009, http://archive.tuscolatoday.com/?p=54990 (accessed 1 November 2011).

—— 'Nigeria says Boko Haram, al Qaeda-link behind UN attack,' 31 August 2011.

Rice, Xan, 'Kenyan constitution signed into law,' *The Guardian*, 27 August 2010.

—— 'Somalia famine relief effort hit harder by food aid delays than by rebels,' *The Guardian*, 4 August, 2011.

Richardson, Louise, *What Terrorists Want: Understanding the Terrorist Threat* (London: John Murray, 2006).

Rosenberg, Matthew, 'Al Qaeda skimming charity money,' *CBS News*, 11 February 2009, http://www.cbsnews.com/2100–224_162–621621.html (accessed 2 August 2012).

Roy, Olivier, *Globalised Islam: The Search for a New Ummah* (London: Hurst, 2004).

Ryu, Alisha, 'Former members of radical Somali group give details of their group,' VOA Mogadishu, 6 January 2007.

—— 'Suicide bombing increase in Somalia,' VOA 25 June 2009.

Sageman, Marc, *Leaderless Jihad: Terror Networks in the Twenty-First Century* (Philadelphia: University of Pennsylvania Press, 2008).

—— *Understanding Terror Networks* (Philadelphia: University of Pennsylvania Press, 2004).

Sandelin, Magnus, 'Jihad,' Reporto, Stockholm, 2012.

Scott, M. Thomas, *The Global Resurgence of Religion and the Transformation of International Relations* (London: Palgrave Macmillan, 2005).

Shabelle Media Network, 'Calm returns to Mogadishu,' 23 May 2009.

—— 'Fresh fighting starts in Mogadishu,' 14 June 2009.

Shinn, David H., 'Al Qaeda in East Africa and the Horn,' *The Journal of Conflict Studies*, 27 (1), 2007.

—— 'Al-Shabaab's Foreign Threat to Somalia,' *Orbis*, 55 (2), 2011.

Somalia Online, 'Atom denies Al-Shabaab links: militia leader says Puntland conflict is over natural resources' (18 May 2011). Available from http://www.somaliaonline.com/community/showthread.php/56861-Mohamed-Said-Atam-denies-Al-Shabaab-Links.

Somalia Report, 'What is the Galgalla Conflict,' 12 April http:// somaliareport.com/index.php/writer/198/Assia_Shidane (accessed 1 August 2012).

The Star, 'Shabaab recruits train in Mombasa,' 17 September 2011, http://www.the-star.co.ke/national/national/40754-Shabaab-recruits-trainin-mombasa (accessed 24 October 2011).

Stern, Jessica, *The Ultimate Terrorists* (Cambridge, MA: Harvard University Press, 1999).

Stokholms tingrett, 'dom DOM B 7277–10 2010–12–08,' Stockholm, 12 August 2010.

Suna Times, 'The rift within AS deepens as mediation efforts by some of the ranks failed due to tough preconditions set by Sheikh Muktar Robow,' 4 October

2010, http://www.sunatimes.com/view.php?id=485O2/AS in crisis/20101005. 2338 (accessed 5 October 2010).

Swift, Christopher, 'Arc of Convergence: AQAP, Ansar al-Shari'a and the Struggle for Yemen,' CTC Sentinel, 5 (6), 2012.

Taarnby, Michael and Lars Hallundbaek, 'Al-Shabaab, The Internationalization of Militant Islamism in Somalia and the Implications for Radicalisation Processes in Europe,' Report for the Danish Ministry of Justice, 2010.

Terror Free Somalia, 'Fresh fighting starts in Central Somalia Hawiye heartlands,' 13 January 2009, http://terrorfreesomalia.blogspot.com/2009/01/death-shabaab.html (accessed 6 November 2011).

Toronto Star, 'Kenya braces for attacks as Somalia's war continues,' 13 July 2012.

United Nations Arms Monitoring Group, 'Report of the Monitoring Group on Somalia Pursuant to Security Council Resolution 1853 (2008),' Report S/2010/91, 2010.

United Nations Monitoring Group on Somalia and Eritrea, 'Report of the Monitoring Group on Somalia Pursuant to Security Council Resolution 1853 (2008),' Report S/2011/43, 2011.

———— 'Report of the Monitoring Group on Somalia and Eritrea,' Nairobi, 16 June 2012 (numbers not given on the copy).

United Nations High Commissioner for Refugees, 'UNHCR Briefing Sheet,' February Report, 2010, 1.

United States Attorney's Office, Minneapolis, 'Terror charges unsealed in Minnesota against eight defendants,' 23 November 2009.

United States District Court, Southern District of Texas, 'The United States against Daniel Joseph Maldonado,' 13 February 2007.

UPI, 'Danes say men plotted to cut throats,' 31 January 2011, http://www.upi.com/Top_News/World-News/2011/01/31/Danes-say-men-plotted-to-cut-throats/UPI-12011296508387/ (accessed 21 October 2011).

———— 'Swedish court frees Somali terror suspects,' 2 March 2011.

Veldhuis, Tinka and Jørgen Staun, *Islamist Radicalisation: A Root Cause Model* (The Hague: Netherlands Institute of International Relations Clingendael, 2009).

Victoroff, Jeff, 'The Mind of the Terrorist. A Review and Critique of Psychological Approaches,' *Journal of Conflict Resolution*, vol. 49, no. 1, 2005, 33–42.

Vidino, Lorenzo Raffaello Pantucci and Evan Kohleman, 'Bringing Global Jihad to the Horn of Africa: Al-Shabaab, the Western Fighters, and the Sacralization of the Somali Conflict,' *African Security* 3, 2010, 230–34.

VOA, 'taariikhda Al-Shabaab Part5 Dhageyso,' VOA, http://www.sunatimes.com/view.php?id=1322 (accessed 20 October 2011).

———— 'Taariikhda Al-Shabaab Part4 Dhageyso,' VOA, http://www.sunatimes.com/view.php?id=1322 (accessed 20 October 2011).

——— 'Taariikhda Al-Shabaab Part3 Dhageyso,' http://www.sunatimes.com/view.php?id=1322 (accessed 20 October 2011).

——— 'Taariikhda Al-Shabaab Part2 Dhageyso,' http://www.sunatimes.com/view.php?id=1322 (accessed 20 October 2011).

——— 'Taariikhda Al-Shabaab Part1 Dhageyso,' http://www.sunatimes.com/view.php?id=1322 (accessed 20 October 2011).

Watts, Clint, Jacob Shapiro and Vahid Brown, 'Al Qaedas Misadventures in the Horn of Africa,' *Report*, The Harmony Project, 2007.

Weine, Stevan, John Horgan, Cheryl Robertson, Sana Loue, Amin Mohamed and Sahra Noo, 'Community and Family Approaches to Combating the Radicalization of US Somali Refugee Youth and Young Adults: a Psychosocial Perspective,' *Dynamics of Asymmetric Conflict*, 2 (3), 2010.

Weinstein, Michael A., Somalia: Al-Shabaab's Split and its Absorption of Hizbul Islam,' Garowe Online, 8 January 2011.

Xinhua News, 'Mogadishu factions meet to narrow gap,' 25 February 1999.

Zaddox, Angira, 'Army remains on the alert on Somali border,' *Daily Nation*, 13 March 2011.

Zammit, Andrew, 'The Holsworthy Barracks Plot: A Case Study of an Al-Shabab Support Network in Australia,' CTC Sentinel, 5 (6), 2012.

Zimmerman, Katherine, 'From Somalia to Nigeria,' *The Weekly Standard*, 18 June 2011.

Zubeir, Muktar Abu (aka Ahmed Godane), 'Biographical summary of the martyred commander, Allah-willing, Abu Yusuf al-Nabhani,' 12 October 2009, retrieved from NEFA foundation, http://www.nefafoundation.org/miscellaneous/nefa_al-Nabhani1009–2.pdf (accessed 1 August 2010).

——— '1-Fariin Ku socota Somaliland' http://www.youtube.com/watch?v=DWyUKh6u_jo (accessed 30 November 2010).

——— '2-Fariin Ku socota Somaliland,' http://www.youtube.com/watch?v=DWyUKh6u_jo (accessed 30 November 2010).

——— '3-Fariin Ku socota Somaliland,' http://www.youtube.com/watch?v=6Og8xHA_g0w (accessed 30 November 2010).

Interviews/conversations conducted by the writer

The role of the respondent is given where possible, but sources are often anonymized for their own safety; the identity of the respondent can be revealed only after approval from the respondent him/herself. The number after the 'x' indicates the number in the order in which persons were interviewed by the writer when they visited a particular city in Somalia or Oslo in a particular year.

Interview with anonymous member of Hassan Dahir Aweys staff 2005–2006, Mogadishu, 5 September 2006.

BIBLIOGRAPHY

Conversations with *Aftenposten* journalist Jørgen Lohne, 5 February 2007.

Interview x1, Mogadishu, 5 November 2008.

Interview x13, Nairobi, November 2008.

Interview with Muktar Robow by telephone, conducted in cooperation with Shwashank Bengali, 1 December 2008.

Interview x12, Mogadishu, 3 April 2009.

Interview with Sheikh Mhyedin, 19 April 2009.

Interview x13, Mogadishu, 20 April 2009.

Interview x15, Mogadishu, 20 April 2009.

Interview with human rights activist in Baidoa by telephone, 1 February 2009.

Interview with human rights activist in Baidoa by telephone, 15 May 2009.

Interview with Rasheed Nur, a Somaliland journalist, by email, 2 August 2010.

Conversations with Patrick Desplat in Bergen, 13 September 2010.

Interview with Rahanwhein elders, Nairobi, 11 December 2010.

Interview with anonymous private contractor in Mogadishu, 19 December 2010,.

Interview with former Shabaab member (2005–06) in Mogadishu, 19 December 2010.

Interview with former Shabaab member in Mogadishu, 19 December 2010.

Interview x2, Mogadishu, 18 December 2010.

Interview x11, Mogadishu, 19 December 2010.Interview with refugee x20 and businessman x21 in Nairobi, 3 December 2010.

Interview x1, x2 in Oslo, 5June 2011.

Interview by telephone with a friend of the family, 1 August 2011.

Conversation with Iqbal Jazbay, former foreign policy coordinator of the African National Congress of South Africa, 3 August 2011.

Interview with Shabaab leader by telephone, 1 August 2011.

Interview with NGO leader in Nairobi, 13 August 2011.

Interview x1 by telephone, Mogadishu, 1 September 2011.

Interview x3 by telephone, Mogadishu, 1 September 2011.

Interview with Muktar Robow, 11 September 2011, conducted with the help of anonymous Somali project assistant.

Interview with Shabaab sub-commander, 9 September 2011.

Interview by telephone with local person in Kismayo, x14 (date will not be given).

Interview x4, Nairobi, 10 November 2011.

Interview x5, Nairobi, 11 November 2011.

Interview with anonymous Warsangeli elder, 6 July 2012, Garowe.

Interview with local intellectual and former coast guard officer, 8 July 2012, Garowe.

Conversation with Member of Parliament and NCA, 'Ali,' 17 July 2012, Mogadishu.

Conversations with Ali Madahay Nuur, president of Hirran and Middle Shabelle state, 19 July 2012, Mogadishu.

BIBLIOGRAPHY

Interview with Richard Ndambuki, 23 July 2012, Nairobi.
Interview with TFG civil servant, 23 July 2012, Nairobi.

Interviews conducted by Michael Scheldrup

Interview with refugee from Kismayo, Nairobi (unknown date), September 2009. Conducted by Michael Scheldrup.
Interview with refugee x2 from Kismayo, Nairobi (unknown date), September 2009. Conducted by anonymous field researcher and Michael Scheldrup.
Interview x1 conducted by Michael Scheldrup in Nairobi, 13 August 2010.
Interview with refugee x3 from Kismayo, Nairobi, 5 September 2009, conducted by anonymous field researcher and Michael Scheldrup.
Interview with refugee x4 from Kismayo, Nairobi (unknown date), September 2009, conducted by anonymous field researcher and Michael Scheldrup.
Interview with refugee x6 from Kismayo, Nairobi, 5 September 2009, conducted by anonymous field researcher and Michael Scheldrup.

INDEX